A CENTURY OF
WELSH
MURDERS AND
EXECUTIONS

A CENTURY OF
WELSH
MURDERS AND
EXECUTIONS

JOHN J. EDDLESTON

SUTTON PUBLISHING

First published in the United Kingdom in 2008 by
Sutton Publishing, an imprint of The History Press Limited
Cirencester Road · Chalford · Stroud · Gloucestershire · GL6 8PE

British Library Cataloguing in Publication Data
A catalogue record for this book is available from the British
Library.

ISBN 978 0 7509 4961 3

Typesetting and origination by
The History Press Limited.
Printed and bound in England by Ashford Colour Press Ltd, Gosport, Hampshire.

CONTENTS

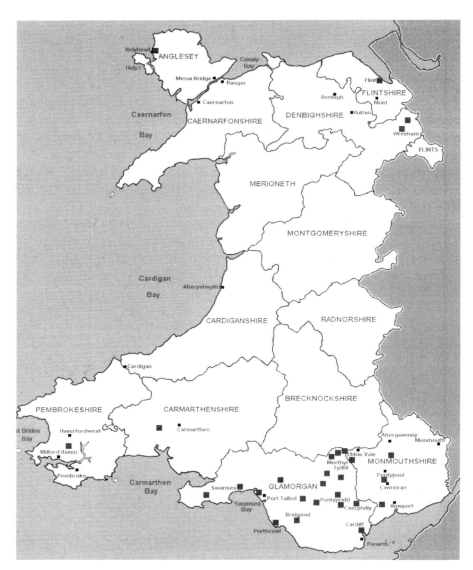

The locations of Welsh murders which ended in execution in the twentieth century.

ACKNOWLEDGEMENTS

I would like to thank a number of people for their assistance in preparing this volume. First I would like to say thank you to Yvonne Eddleston for all the help she gave in researching the stories.

I would also like to say thank you to Nick Kelland of Rhondda Cynon Taff, and Phil Baker of wales-pictures.com for granting permission to use some of their images. Also to the Public Record Office for the two photographs on pages 26 and 54.

Finally, I wish to thank Matilda Pearce of Sutton Publishing for all the help and encouragement she has given.

Unless otherwise stated, the pictures are all from the author's private collection. All permissions have been obtained.

1

CHANGING STORIES

William Augustus Lacey was a native of Kingston, Jamaica. A well travelled man, he had spent time in America before arriving in Liverpool. From there he moved on to Merthyr where he worked in a local colliery and first met Augustus O'Connor. The two men became friends before Lacey moved on again, this time to Pontypridd. Later, Lacey returned to America where he remained until the SS *Flintshire* brought him, and his old friend O'Connor, back to Britain.

Mary O'Connor (née Joseph) and her family lived at 38 Hoo Street, Port Tennant. Mary and her children had been staying with her parents while her husband was at sea, but they now moved to lodgings at 16 Maritime Terrace and Lacey moved into the same address. There was, however, another daughter living at home, 19-year-old Pauline, who had already given birth to a child, which had died at 5 months old.

Pauline was now free of her previous relationship and, through her sister and brother-in-law, met Lacey, who was ten years her senior. There was an instant attraction between them. When it became plain that her parents did not approve, Pauline ignored them and, on Easter Tuesday, 1900, she married William at Swansea Registry Office. Soon afterwards, the newlyweds moved to Pontypridd where Lacey had found work for himself as a labourer at the Tymawr Colliery.

By all accounts, Pauline Lacey was a beautiful woman and this caused her husband to be very jealous. Even when the couple were courting, he had gone so far as to tell Mary O'Connor that he was worried about someone else paying her attention and added, 'If I don't have her, I'll have the rope for her.'

Largely because of Lacey's jealousy, there were constant rows between husband and wife. Lacey and Pauline had first gone to live together at Maritime Terrace, a house owned by William and Georgina Webb. After two months though, the constant quarrelling between them caused Georgina to give Lacey notice to quit and as a consequence, the Laceys took two rooms, one upstairs and one down, at 21 Barry Terrace, where they moved on 22 June.

The Lacey's new landlady, Catherine Vaughan, was a witness to many arguments between the couple. These rows seemed to reach a pitch on Wednesday, 4 July when a letter arrived for Pauline from her parents. Delivered at 5 p.m., the letter made it clear that there was a place for her at her parents' home.

Lacey worked on the nightshift at the colliery, but had last been to work on 3 July, no doubt thinking that his wife might be seeing other men while he was out. By 5 July, this led to yet another argument, Pauline accusing him of being lazy. It was 11 p.m. that night by the time the Laceys went to bed but even then the argument continued. Catherine Vaughan had retired earlier, but through the partition wall she could hear them shouting. It was only when Catherine knocked on the wall and asked them to be quiet that things calmed down.

The next morning, Friday, 6 July, Lacey and Pauline came downstairs at 9.30 a.m. and immediately the quarrel started afresh. As they ate breakfast, Pauline again referred to Lacey missing work. After half an hour of this, Catherine Vaughan had had enough and went to a neighbour's house for some peace and quiet, leaving Pauline alone in the house with her husband.

It was sometime between 10.45 a.m. and 11 a.m. when Catherine heard shouting coming from her house, and another neighbour, Mrs Clee, came to tell her that something terrible was happening. Returning home, Catherine opened the front door, fully expecting to find yet another argument in full swing, but instead she found something worse. Pauline Lacey lay on her back in a pool of blood, her clothing open at her breast. Of Lacey himself, there was no sign, so Catherine closed the door behind her and returned to her neighbour's house.

Emily McKenny lived at 11 Barry Terrace and, after hearing from Catherine what had happened, returned with her to no. 21. Together, the two ladies made a more careful examination of the scene and saw that Pauline's throat had been cut. On the floor, near Pauline's body, lay a closed razor, the black handle of which was covered in blood.

William Lacey, meanwhile, had walked to the police station where he found PC David Evans, and announced, 'I have come to give myself up for killing my wife.' Evans cautioned Lacey and then put him into the cells while he went to Barry Terrace to check the story for himself. Having seen Pauline's body, Evans returned to the station where he charged Lacey with murder. In reply, Lacey said, 'She told me yesterday morning that she will not live with me no more.' He went on to say that Pauline had suggested she might be happier with the man who had been the father of her baby and intimated that when he came home from work, she would be gone. Pauline had also claimed that Lacey had been intimate with her sister, Mary Ann O'Connor. Lacey continued, 'I loves [sic] my wife to the ground she walks. Before any man would have the benefit of her I would rather see her lying in the ground, likewise myself. I did it like a man and gave myself up.'

On 7 July, the inquest on Pauline Lacey opened at Pontypridd before Mr Edmund Bernard Reece. The first witness was Mary Ann O'Connor, who, after giving evidence of identification, outlined the history of the relationship between Lacey and her sister. Finally, Mary denied that there had ever been anything improper between her and the prisoner.

Catherine Vaughan told the court of the constant arguments between Pauline and Lacey and said that Pauline had complained to her more than once that her husband had struck her. Catherine's final testimony was that on 3 July, she had seen a fight between Lacey and his brother-in-law, Augustus O'Connor, during which Lacey had pulled out a razor. According to Catherine, this altercation had taken place because Lacey claimed he had seen O'Connor kissing Pauline.

PC Evans told the court of Lacey's appearance at the police station, when blood had been observed on his hands and singlet. A statement Lacey had made was then read out. It began:

On Friday morning I rose from my bed. My wife was lying in bed awake. I says to her 'I'll go down and get you a cup of tea.' I went down. I went to Mrs Vaughan's kitchen and drew some tea. I went back to my room and poured out to her a cup full and likewise myself. Before I took it to her I first had mine. She come down before I took it up to her. I says to her 'Sit down, here's a cup of tea for you.' She said she would not drink a cup of tea that I had made.

The statement went on to say that Pauline told Lacey that her heart was full owing to what she had heard about him and her sister. Lacey denied again that there was any truth in it and suggested that they should go away to the Rhondda. Pauline replied that she didn't want to go and would rather he killed her.

At this, Lacey had fallen to his knees and begged her to stay with him, but Pauline had lain down on the floor and asked him to kill her. He told her he couldn't do such a terrible thing, and had reached out to hold her. Pauline stood up at this point, and only then did Lacey notice that she had his razor in her waistband. Before he could do anything, Pauline opened it out and cut her own throat. Unable to kill herself, she begged him to finish her off. Finally, Lacey took the razor from his wife and did as she had asked, before walking to the police station and giving himself up.

After medical evidence had been given, the final witness to take the stand was Mary Clee who lived at 20 Barry Terrace, the house next door to the Laceys. She stated that at 11 a.m. on 6 July, she had been standing at her front door when she heard screams coming from no. 21. Going to the front door, she heard Pauline shout, 'Oh Lacey, don't!' and afraid that Lacey was beating his wife, ran to fetch her mother. The two ladies went to the door of no. 21 together, but everything was now quiet. After a few minutes, Lacey came out of the house and walked a few yards down the street, buttoning up his coat. He then broke into a run, towards the town centre. Looking through the window of 21 Barry Terrace, Mary Clee saw Pauline lying in a pool of blood – her mother then went to fetch Mrs Vaughan.

Having heard all this evidence, the jury had little trouble in returning a verdict of wilful murder against Lacey. Later that same day, he made his first appearance at the police court when the proceedings were adjourned until 11 July. On that date, Lacey gave evidence on his own behalf, repeating his story of finishing Pauline off when she had first cut her own throat, but he now elaborated upon the story.

According to this new version of events, Lacey claimed that when Pauline brought the razor out of her waistband, she had lashed out at him with it and cut his breast. At this point, Lacey opened his shirt and showed the courtroom a cut on his chest. He then shouted, 'No! I am not guilty. It never came across my mind to do it. She asked me to do it and I did it. Oh I loved my wife. I love her now and I love the ground where she is.'

Despite this impassioned outburst, Lacey was committed for trial at the next assizes. On the same day, 11 July, Pauline Lacey was laid to rest at Swansea, her body being taken by the 6.27 a.m. train from Pontypridd.

Lacey faced his trial at Swansea on 2 August 1900, before Mr Justice Grantham. The case for the prosecution lay in the hands of Mr S.T. Evans and Mr R.E. Vaughan Williams, while Lacey was defended by Mr W. Bowen Rowlands and Mr A.C. Thomas.

In addition to the witnesses already referred to, the prosecution called Lacey's former landlady, Georgina Webb. She said that she had never heard Lacey threaten his wife but on one occasion had seen him strike her. Pauline, though, had not been afraid to retaliate and had lashed out with a fish kettle. At this, Lacey had smacked Pauline's face, took his razor from a drawer and put it into his pocket before walking out of the house, saying that he was going to drown himself.

Emily McKenny again told the court of viewing the body after the attack, but also spoke of an event on 2 July when Pauline and Lacey had come to her house and stayed for supper. While they were there, Pauline had called her husband lazy and talked about going back to live with her parents. This annoyed

Lacey, who said he would do for her if she did and drew his finger across his throat to emphasise the point.

Medical testimony was given by Dr Howard Davies, who had attended 21 Barry Terrace at 11 a.m. on 6 July. He told the court that when he arrived at the house, Pauline was lying on her back in the front room, her head towards the window. Her throat was cut from ear to ear, which had severed her windpipe and all the large blood vessels on both sides of her neck. The wound in the throat showed more than one cut and there were other superficial cuts on the left cheek, lower jaw and chest. There were also cuts to Pauline's left little finger and the back of her right wrist, which might have been defence wounds. Dr Davies was unable to say if any of these wounds might have been inflicted by Pauline herself but stated that the number of superficial injuries might have indicated a scuffle of some kind, though it was impossible to say who might have been holding the razor at the time.

At 2 p.m., the court adjourned and Lacey's barrister consulted with him to see if he wished to give evidence on his own behalf. Lacey said he wished to do so and gave his testimony after the court had reconvened. Lacey told much the same story as before, telling the court that the man he had considered his friend, Augustus O'Connor, had sought to cause trouble between himself and Pauline by telling her that her husband was involved with her sister. Pauline had believed Augustus and had become depressed and suicidal. At this point in the proceedings, Lacey retracted his earlier statements and denied any part in the death of his wife. He had not finished her off and had only said this at the police station and before the magistrates because he was excited and did not know what he was saying. Pauline had taken her own life and he was not involved in any way.

The jury had now heard two different versions of events from Lacey about what had taken place inside 21 Barry Terrace. After a short deliberation, they decided that this was not a case of suicide and that Lacey had deliberately killed his wife. The death sentence was passed and Lacey was returned to Cardiff Prison.

Less than three weeks later, despite strenuous efforts to obtain a reprieve, Lacey was hanged at Cardiff by James and William Billington. A crowd of several thousand gathered outside the jail to wait for the hoisting of the black flag, which marked the first Welsh execution of the century.

2

A SPLIT IN THE FAMILY

Jeremiah Callaghan, 1902

Jeremiah Callaghan, an Irishman known to his friends as 'Jerry Canteen', had been Hannah Shea's lover for a number of years and they had four children as a result. Callaghan, though, led a somewhat precarious life, seldom working and therefore unable to provide a stable family home. As a result, he lived in a lodging house at Tredegar while Hannah, together their son and three daughters, stayed at a workhouse or wherever else they could find a bed.

In October 1902, 38-year-old Hannah and the children were living at the Bedwellty Union workhouse in Tredegar. They still met up with Callaghan on a regular basis, but this enforced separation led Callaghan to brooding on his situation and slowly he managed to convince himself that the reason Hannah did not seem too perturbed by the situation was that she had found herself another man.

On Saturday, 4 October, Hannah and her family, together with a number of friends, left the Union workhouse to walk into Tredegar to see Callaghan, who had taken work there as a stonemason's labourer. Once the group arrived in the town, Hannah sent her 14-year-old son, also named Jeremiah, to see Mr Phillips, the relieving officer for the district, to ask him for a note which would allow them to return to the workhouse that night. Jeremiah did as he was asked and, having obtained the note, started to walk back towards the railway station where he had left Hannah. Passing down Commercial Road, Jeremiah Shea called in at Mr Morgan's yard at the top of North Lane where his father was working, and told him that the family had arrived in town.

Callaghan asked Jeremiah where Hannah was. The boy said he was just going off to look for her whereupon his father told him to wait until he had finished work and picked up his pay, when they would go and look for her together. In due course, Callaghan left the stone yard and started to search for Hannah in the various public houses around the town.

One of his first ports of call was the Red Lion. There, Callaghan found Mrs Price and Mary Clifford, two of Hannah's fellow workhouse inmates who had walked into town with her, but Hannah was nowhere to be seen. Seeing Callaghan there, Mary Clifford told him that Hannah had gone along Commercial Road with Mrs Prothero, another member of the group. Mary added that Hannah had gone to get a note so they could return to the workhouse. This immediately raised Callaghan's suspicions, for his son had just told him that he had done the exact same thing.

Walking back along Commercial Road, Callaghan and Jeremiah came to the Miners Inn where they finally found Hannah, Mrs Prothero and her son outside. Not surprisingly, Callaghan immediately accused Hannah of drinking and when she denied it, he grabbed hold of her and threw her to the ground. Hannah climbed to her feet and, with her son following, walked up Church Street where she found a policeman and complained to him that she had just been assaulted. Callaghan walked away, leaving Hannah and Jeremiah to return to the Miners Inn.

Some time later, Hannah, Jeremiah and Mrs Prothero walked on to the Circle, where Callaghan happened to be. On seeing Hannah approach, he asked them all to go and have a drink with him. At first they refused but soon changed their minds and together they went to the Black Prince, where they drank two or three quarts of beer, all of which Callaghan paid for.

After finishing their drinks, the group left together and began to walk back towards the railway station. Callaghan, who was by now quite drunk, fell down by the market but managed to pull himself up and carry on to the station. When they arrived, Callaghan asked, 'We are here by now aren't we?', apparently not even sure where he was. Told that they were on the right road, they carried on walking towards the workhouse.

Along the way, Callaghan, who was by now staggering, fell down for a second time and had to grasp Hannah's wrist to pull himself up. They continued along the road until they finally reached the narrow path which led up to the workhouse. Jeremiah Shea and two of his sisters were slightly ahead of Hannah and Callaghan, who were walking along together with the third sister about 6yds behind. At this point Hannah saw Jane Hannam, a friend of hers who worked at the Union, and the two ladies exchanged the time of day, Jane asking Hannah if she was heading back to the workhouse. Even as Hannah answered 'Aye', Jane saw Callaghan turn around and something shiny glinted in his right hand as he withdrew it from his pocket.

With a cry of 'I'll give you "aye" you bugger', Callaghan pushed Hannah against a brick wall, drawing something across her throat as he did so. Hannah managed to push Callaghan away and then ran down the hill as young Jeremiah threw stones at his father to distract him. Callaghan turned and moved menacingly towards Jeremiah and his sisters, who all scarpered. They managed to lose Callaghan, but by the time Jeremiah returned to where he had last seen his mother, Hannah was lying on the path at the bottom of the hill with a rapidly growing crowd gathering around her.

Sarah Jane Morris lived at 67 Whitworth Terrace, Tredegar, and worked as a cleaner at the workhouse. She had left work at 6.20 p.m. on 4 October and was standing talking to her boyfriend, John Williams, on the path to the workhouse, when she heard a terrible scream. Running down the hill towards the place from which the scream had emanated, Sarah passed Jeremiah Shea who was on his way up the hill, running away from his father. A short distance further down, Sarah passed Callaghan who, by now, was leaning against a wall for support. Further still down the hill, Sarah saw Hannah running and finally falling. She ran to where the stricken woman lay and supported her. Sarah could not help but notice the deep wound in Hannah's throat.

It was at this point that William John Pritchard, a collier from Tredegar, came upon the scene, having heard the scream himself. He took the apron that Sarah Morris was wearing and wrapped it around Hannah's throat in an attempt to staunch the bleeding. As he did so, Amy Lucy Pearl, a trained nurse, also arrived at the scene on her way back from a trip into the town. She gave instructions to Mr Pritchard as to what he should do, while she fetched her first-aid kit. Seeing that Hannah was in good hands, Amy then ran up to the workhouse, where she saw Callaghan in the yard. She told William Thomas, the master, what had happened down the hill and then went back to where Hannah lay. Nothing could be done for the poor woman though, and within minutes, Hannah Shea had breathed her last. Her body was carried back up to the workhouse and laid out in the mortuary there.

Mr Thomas, the workhouse master, hearing that Hannah was dead, summoned Callaghan into his office and told him to sit down. Callaghan sat on the sofa and asked to see his children. 'Not just now,' William Thomas replied, at which Callaghan calmly took his pipe from his coat pocket and lit up. As he did so, Mr Thomas noticed that Callaghan's hands were heavily stained with blood, a fact to which he appeared to be totally oblivious. Having given instructions that Callaghan was to be detained, Mr Thomas then followed his prisoner out into the yard where Callaghan began dancing and capering about.

By the next day, Sunday, 5 October, Callaghan had sobered up and expressed complete surprise that he should be facing a charge of murder. He claimed to have no memory of Hannah Shea's death. Taken into custody, Callaghan made his first appearance at a special hearing of the Tredegar police court on Monday, 6 October, where only evidence of arrest was given.

On Monday, 13 October, Callaghan was again up before the magistrates when a further remand was ordered, until 21 October. On that date, Mr R.H. Spencer detailed the case for the Director of Public Prosecutions while Callaghan was represented by Mr Sydney Jenkins. All the witnesses were heard and the prisoner was committed to the next assizes.

The Town Clock in the Circle, Tredegar, where Jeremiah Callaghan met up with his common-law wife on the day he cut her throat. (Reflective Images)

So it was that 42-year-old Jeremiah Callaghan appeared before Mr John Forbes QC, the recorder of Hull, at Monmouth on 22 November 1902. The case for the prosecution was led by Mr J.R.V. Marchant, who was assisted by Mr St John G. Micklethwait. Callaghan was defended by Mr Harold Hardy.

The first witness was Elizabeth Prothero, who testified that when the party had left the Black Prince, Callaghan had been quite intoxicated, but she would not describe him as drunk. Earlier that day, Elizabeth had witnessed the argument between Callaghan and Hannah, when he had first found her outside the Miners Inn. Once the altercation was over, the couple seemed to be on good terms again.

Frank Shea of 10 Iron Street, Tredegar, was the father of the dead woman. He stated that although Hannah had been single, her association with Callaghan had led to the birth of six children, four of whom were still alive. Shea said that he had seen Callaghan drunk many times and when he was in that state, he often threatened Hannah and knocked her about. On more than one occasion, Shea had heard Callaghan say that he '...would be hanged for her', the last time being on 4 October, the day Hannah died.

Jeremiah Shea told the court what he had seen on 4 October and added that Callaghan had fallen over several times on the walk back to the workhouse. Once he had even been carrying Bridget, one of his daughters, when he fell, but the child had fortunately not been hurt.

Jane Hannam told of meeting Hannah as she was returning to the workhouse. When she asked Hannah if she was going back to the Union, even before she had replied 'Aye', Callaghan had said, 'This will be your last home here.' He pulled out a knife and pulled Hannah from side to side in order to draw the knife across her throat.

Sarah Jane Morris told the court that she had been talking to her boyfriend, John Williams, when the attack upon Hannah Shea took place. As she and John ran past Callaghan to see what help they could offer the stricken woman, they heard Callaghan shout, 'Where's them children?' When Sarah caught up with Hannah, the poor woman was holding the left side of her neck and as Sarah helped to support her, John Williams ran to fetch help. This testimony was confirmed by Mr Williams, an engine driver of 49 Whitworth Terrace, who added that when he passed Callaghan, he was picking some paper up from the floor and wiping blood from his hands with it. He came upon the scene and saw Hannah being tended to by Amy Pearl. Williams then went to the police station and reported the matter to Superintendent Allen.

In addition to saying what she had seen on 4 October, Amy Pearl also stated that on 5 October, she had stripped Hannah's body at the workhouse. On the back of Hannah's left hand, a scrap of paper was stuck to the flesh with dried blood. Upon closer examination, Amy found that it was part of the relieving officer's admission order.

Dr Isaac Crawford had been called to the scene of the attack at around 6.35 p.m. When he arrived, Hannah was still alive and he saw a deep incised wound on the left side of her neck. The jugular vein had been severed and, despite his ministrations, Hannah died at 6.45 p.m. The next day, Dr Crawford performed the post-mortem. The wound he had observed had been inflicted with great force and in addition to the jugular, two other main arteries had been cut.

Dr Crawford had also attended the workhouse and seen Callaghan there. The prisoner was certainly under the influence of drink but he could speak and there was nothing to suggest that he was suffering from delirium tremens at the time, although he did add that the symptoms could disappear quite quickly.

The final prosecution witness was Superintendent Francis Allen. Having been informed of the incident by John Williams, he proceeded to the scene, arriving there at 6.35 p.m., just before Hannah died. Leaving the woman in the hands of Dr Crawford, Allen went up to the workhouse where he saw Callaghan in the yard, with several other men, walking around and smoking a pipe. Callaghan was taken back inside, cautioned and then charged with murder. The prisoner was searched and Superintendent Allen found a knife in Callaghan's left waistcoat pocket. It was wet with blood. The search also revealed a small Irish whiskey bottle, which was empty, and 6s in cash. The backs of both of Callaghan's hands were covered with blood. The next day, Allen made a careful search of the pathway and found the other portion of the admission ticket which Hannah had with her when she was attacked.

Callaghan's defence claimed that the attack had taken place during an outburst of insanity, brought on by delirium tremens. Mr Hardy claimed in his closing speech that where the intention to commit a crime was essential to a case, then whether a man is drunk or not was of the utmost importance.

The jury were out for thirty-five minutes and while they were considering their verdict, Callaghan appeared to be oblivious to the seriousness of his situation, engaging his solicitor in casual conversation while he waited. When the verdict came in, Callaghan was found guilty as charged. After the sentence had been passed, Mr Forbes added, 'I don't wish by any words of mine to aggravate the painful situation in which you stand, but from the circumstances under which you committed the murder, I can hold out to you no hope of reprieve.'

On 10 December, Forbes' words were confirmed when the Home Office informed Callaghan's solicitor that the Home Secretary had found no grounds for recommending a reprieve to His Majesty. Two days later, on Friday, 12 December 1902, Jeremiah Callaghan was hanged at Usk Prison by William and John Billington.

It was a dull morning, with a bitterly cold east wind blowing. Daylight was only just breaking as Callaghan, who had spent a restless night, took his position on the trapdoor. He kissed the crucifix the priest held to his lips and cried out, 'Holy mother pray for me. Jesus help me', before the lever was pulled and his body plunged into the pit.

3

COUSINS

William Hughes, 1903

William Hughes, a native of Denbigh, had been an agricultural labourer before joining the army, serving in India, first with the 22nd Regiment and latterly with the Royal Welsh Fusiliers. After a tour of duty totalling ten years and nine months, Hughes was demobbed in 1890. Two years later he married Jane Hannah Williams, his first cousin, and, for a time at least, they lived happily enough together at various addresses in Wrexham.

After five years, however, Hughes left his wife and moved to Birkenhead. Jane followed him there and they managed to patch things up, during which time she gave birth to a child, which died soon afterwards. She was so distressed by this that she spent several months in Chester Asylum. The couple continued living together when Jane was released, and by December 1901, they had three living children; two boys and a girl.

But tragedy struck the family again when, later that same month, the middle child, a girl who was by then aged 8, died. Soon afterwards, Hughes walked out of the family home, leaving Jane to look after the two remaining children alone. As a result, Jane was forced to apply to the parish for relief, and an allowance of 4s per week was granted to her on 31 December 1901. This did not help, though, and the children, boys aged 10 and 6 respectively, were forced to go with their mother into the workhouse.

Hughes was arrested for deserting his family, and was brought before the Board of Guardians on 7 August 1902. He received three months' imprisonment, which he served at Shrewsbury. On his release, on Thursday, 6 November, he returned to live with his mother, sister and her husband, at Ruabon.

By this time, Jane and her sons had left the workhouse, but the children returned to the dreadful establishment in the same month that their father was sent to prison. Jane had now taken employment as a housekeeper for a gentleman named Thomas Maddocks who lived at Old Rhosrobin. One reason why Jane might have left her sons behind was that Mr Maddocks, a widower, already had five children of his own. The sleeping arrangements at the house were that Jane and the children shared one room while Maddocks had another. Hughes, though, found it easy to convince himself that there was more to this arrangement than had been made public, and came to believe that his wife was cohabiting with Maddocks.

On the day of his release from prison, Jane saw Hughes outside her sister Sarah's house and she asked him what he intended to do about his sons. Hughes said he knew they were in the workhouse and that they could stay there. Jane replied that she would get Hughes 'another six months'. He made no comment, but reported the matter to the police. Later that same day, Hughes went to visit his two children but as he returned home, he encountered Jane again and she sarcastically remarked, 'Have you been looking for your children?' Once again Hughes reported this to the police, and that night went to stay with his brother-in-law, Robert Williams.

On the morning of Friday, 7 November, Hughes went to the house where Jane was staying and asked her for some of his clothes which she had taken with her. Jane told her husband that her brother-in-law had worn them out. Hughes then asked for his watch, but she refused to hand it over. He did, however, manage to retrieve a small silver teapot which had belonged to the daughter he had lost.

Hughes returned to the house occupied by his mother and sister. At 1 a.m. on Monday, 10 November, he rose, collected his brother-in-law's shotgun and two cartridges, told his mother he was going out, and left. Just ninety minutes later, at around 2.30 a.m., Hughes was at Thomas Maddocks' house.

Maddocks' eldest child, an 11-year-old boy also named Thomas, slept in the same room as Jane. When a knock came at the front door in the small hours, Jane assumed it must be the boy's father having come home from his work at the Wrexham and Acton colliery. She told Thomas junior to open the door. Surprised at having been told by Thomas that Mr Hughes was downstairs waiting to see her, Jane pulled a skirt over her nightdress and went down to talk to him.

Hughes demanded to know where Maddocks was. Told that he was still at work, William realised that he would be thwarted in his intention to kill both his unfaithful wife and her lover, so he levelled the shotgun at Jane and fired both barrels into her at close range. In fact, the barrel was so close that her clothing caught fire and her flesh was slightly charred. Jane, though, knew none of this – she was dead before her body hit the floor.

At 3.25 a.m., Constable Thomas Pryce Rees was on his beat in the High Street. There he was approached by Hughes, who confessed that he had shot his wife and wished to give himself up. Rees arrested Hughes and escorted him to the police station. Later that same morning, Hughes was charged with murder.

Events moved quickly, and at noon, Hughes made his first appearance before the magistrates. When his name was called, the 42-year-old prisoner stepped smartly forward and listened intently as details of his arrest were given by PC Rees. At the time, Hughes was still carrying the shotgun in his left hand.

Details of the circumstances of Jane acting as housekeeper for Mr Maddocks were then given, during which Hughes interrupted by shouting, 'Living tally with him for twelve months!' When told he would be charged with murder, Hughes then shouted, 'It is a pity he was not there too. It would have been the same for the two of them!' The proceedings were then adjourned for one week.

The police court hearing re-opened on Monday, 17 November, but since the inquest was due to take place the following day, Hughes was again remanded for one week. The next day, 18 November, the inquest heard all the evidence. As expected, a verdict of murder was returned and less than one week later, on 24 November, Hughes was sent by the magistrates to face his trial.

The assizes opened at Ruthin on 27 January 1903, but Hughes' case was only heard on 29 January, before Mr Justice Bruce. The prosecution was led by Mr D.A.V. Colt-Williams who was assisted by Mr Trevor F. Lloyd, while Hughes was defended by Mr E. Jones Griffiths MP, and Mr E. Owen Roberts. The first act of the judge was to ensure that all the jurors could speak English. One stated that he knew only a little English and could not understand long words, whereupon he was removed and replaced by another man.

One of the early witnesses was Edward Williams, the relieving officer of the number three district of the Wrexham Union. He stated that relief had been granted to Jane Hughes from the period 31 December 1901 to 23 July 1902, when her money had been stopped because it had been suggested that her behaviour was improper. Mr Williams also said that it had been the Union who had instructed him to take legal proceedings against Hughes for deserting his family.

Miriam Williams was one of Jane's sisters and lived at 28 James Street, Wrexham. She told the court that she had seen Jane at their mother's house on the morning of 6 November, the day that Hughes was to be released from prison. The house was opposite Sarah Hart's and was in the street, between the two houses where Hughes and Jane first saw each other that day. That same afternoon, Miriam and Jane went out together and met Hughes near Cobden Mill. It was then that Jane asked him what he was going to do about his children and he made the remark about them staying in the workhouse.

As Thomas Maddocks entered the witness box, Hughes nudged one his guards and pointed at him. Maddocks told the court that his wife had died three years before. They had had five children, three of whom still lived with him at home. According to Maddocks, Jane had become his housekeeper on 12 August but he had seen nothing of her husband until Hughes appeared at his house at 4.45 a.m. on 7 November, asking to see his wife. Hughes had finally left, taking with him the silver teapot which had belonged to his daughter.

Turning to the time of the attack upon Jane, Maddocks said that he went to work at between 5.30 p.m. and 6 p.m. on 9 November, returning home for something to eat at 9.30 p.m. Some thirty minutes later he returned to work where he stayed until 6 a.m. on 10 November. Maddocks was also able to show that it had been pure chance that saved his life: all that week he had been on the day shift, but was asked to go into work this one night for a special job.

Robert Jones was Hughes' brother-in-law, and it had been his house where Hughes was staying when he had left in the small hours of 10 November. The gun used to kill Jane belonged to Robert and was kept in a drawer in the kitchen. There were only two cartridges in the house but they were not kept in the same drawer as the gun. It was not until later on the morning of 10 November that his wife noticed that the gun and the cartridges had been taken.

Thomas Maddocks junior said that he was asleep when Jane told him to get up to answer the front door. Upon opening the door, Thomas saw Hughes, who asked after his father. Thomas told him he was still at work, whereupon Hughes asked after Mrs Hughes and was told that she was upstairs in bed. Without waiting to be asked, Hughes walked into the house and called up for his wife. When she got downstairs she said to her husband, 'Now, what are you going to do?' and sent Thomas back to bed. Thomas heard no reply except for two loud noises; then the front door was banged shut and all fell quiet.

PC Harvey had gone to the house where the shooting took place at about 4.30 a.m. on 10 November. The front door was closed but unlocked and upon entering, Harvey found Jane lying at the foot of the staircase. She was on her right side with her knees drawn up and her head resting against the wall. There were no signs of a struggle having taken place.

Dr Drinkwater, who had performed the post-mortem, was unable to attend the court due to an accident a few days before in which he had been thrown from a horse-drawn gig, so his deposition was read out. Dr Drinkwater described a circular incised wound, the size of a florin, on Jane's right breast. The charge had passed downwards through the body. Two ribs had been shattered and fragments of bone from them had been blown into the body. The shot had also penetrated the right lung, the right side of the heart and one kidney. There was a second wound, lower than the first and on the left side. This proved to be an exit wound, from which part of the intestines and stomach protruded.

The defence did not dispute that it had been Hughes who had taken the life of his wife, but sought to show that his sanity was in doubt. Their first witness was Dr W.W. Herbert, the medical officer at Denbigh Asylum, who had made an examination of Hughes on 24 December. He had found Hughes in general good health but also discovered that he was suffering from heart disease. Dr Herbert also observed three scars on Hughes' head, which the prisoner claimed had come from a fall when he was a boy, and another at the back of his head from a blow which he had received from his brother-in-law.

Of the crime itself, Hughes told Dr Herbert that he remembered nothing after he had had the gun in his hand, adding that there had been a loud buzzing in his head. He went on, 'I was not drunk, but I felt I had to do it, and I would have shot anyone who tried to stop me on the road, and I am glad God did not send anyone. All I remember thinking of was that I only had two cartridges, one for each, and I must be careful of them. When my wife came down I could not make her out or see clearly; there was a mist over my eyes. I never thought of consequences.' Dr Herbert had since examined Hughes for a second time and his conclusion was that Hughes was a man of a nervous instability which predisposed him to insanity as a result of malaria, syphilis and alcoholism.

Dr Cox was the medical superintendent at Denbigh Asylum. He had interviewed Hughes on three occasions and had concluded that on the morning of the crime, Hughes was not responsible for his actions as he was suffering from a disordered mind.

Having heard all the evidence, the jury retired at 4.28 p.m. Just nine and a half minutes later, the jury returned to court and confirmed that Hughes was guilty as charged.

Nineteen days later, at 8 a.m. on Tuesday, 17 February 1903, William Hughes walked firmly to the gallows at Ruthin Prison with a photograph of himself and his family during happier times. As he approached the scaffold, he kicked off his unlaced boots, saying that he had come into the world barefoot and would leave it the same way. He was then hanged by William and John Billington. It was the only execution at Ruthin in this century.

4

THE INTRUDER

Eric Lange, 1904

At 11.45 p.m. on Saturday, 10 September 1904, Mary Jones retired to her bed at the Bridgend Hotel, Pentre, near Ystrad in the Rhondda Valley. Mary was the wife of the pub's landlord, John Emlyn Jones, but he stayed downstairs, clearing up the public bars. It was not until 2 a.m. on the Sunday morning that a weary Mr Jones finally climbed into bed beside his wife and their baby.

The bedroom which Mr and Mrs Jones shared had a window overlooking the yard at the rear, and as John Jones retired, the room was still reasonably well lit. The gas lamp was on, though turned down, and a night-light burned on the dressing table. So, when a noise disturbed Mary at 3.30 a.m. she was able to see the room clearly and could not help but notice that a man's face was peering at her through the brass frame at the foot of the bed.

Mary Jones jumped up in bed, calling for her husband. Before John could come to the aid of his wife though, the intruder was upon her and struck her very hard with a heavy object. The blow landed on the left side of Mary's head, and blood immediately flowed from a deep wound on her temple. Even as Mary reeled from this onslaught, she could see the man had raised his hand to strike a second time but she managed to move to one side and the object crashed into her arm, injuring only her elbow.

By this time, John Emlyn Jones had leapt out of bed and, as he moved around the foot of the bed to grapple with the intruder, the stranger moved towards him and met him halfway. A fierce struggle began, with the stranger raining blows onto John with an object which Mary could now see was wrapped in brown paper. While the two men fought, Mary, still bleeding badly from her wounds, moved across the bed to shield the baby.

It soon became clear that John Jones was getting the worst of the tussle, for the intruder first pinned him to the bed and then dragged him to the far wall where he slammed him against the plaster and began to throttle him. Bravely, Mary went to her husband's aid and managed to pull the man by the arm. At the same time, she somehow managed to open the bedroom door and the two men tumbled out onto the landing.

There were various members of staff living on the premises and one of these was John Henry Carpenter, the cellarman. He was a fit, strong young man and Mary shouted 'Jack! Jack!' up to the attic where he slept. Carpenter, by now woken by the racket, shouted back that he was coming and Mary cried back, 'Come down quick, there is someone here murdering us!'

Even before Carpenter could pull on his trousers, the struggle was over. As Mary turned to face the stairs, she saw that the intruder had fled, leaving John Jones clutching the banister for support. Mary heard a thud which sounded like someone falling downstairs, but she was more concerned about her husband and threw her arm around his waist and guided him back to their bedroom. It was clear that he was badly injured, for even before he reached the bed, John Jones collapsed.

As Mary tried her best to lift him, John Carpenter came into the room, a revolver in his hand. Mary asked him to hurry down to the bar and bring up a tot of brandy, but it seemed to have no effect. The stricken man was lifted onto his bed and then Mary went to the room occupied by Katie Richards, her niece, and asked her to run for the doctor. In the event, both Katie and Carpenter went to fetch Dr Thomas, who only lived 300yds away, after Katie had first called down to a man passing the pub and asked him to bring the police.

It was 3.45 a.m. when Dr William Evans Thomas arrived at the Bridgend Hotel, only to find that his patient was already dead. Just five minutes later, Inspector John Williams arrived and, after speaking to Dr Thomas, he made an inspection of the premises.

The intruder had affected his entrance by climbing up a ladder placed in the backyard against the pub wall, which reached up to the window of a lavatory facing the river and the railway. This window was 13ft from the ground and had a faulty catch, which meant that it was easy to remove one of the frames. Downstairs, the cash register in the bar was partly open but Mary Jones confirmed that there was rarely any cash kept in the till overnight. The intruder had apparently discovered this for himself and then decided to see if he could find anything of value upstairs. He had tried to be quiet, for a pair of men's brown shoes were found at the foot of the stairs. Mary Jones confirmed that these had not belonged to her husband and when John Carpenter, the only other man living on the premises, said that they were not his either, it seemed reasonable to assume that they had belonged to the killer of John Jones. The man, whoever he was, had run off without collecting his shoes.

Inspector Williams now examined the bedroom where the attack had started. Inside, on the floor to the left side of the bed, Inspector Williams found an old rasp wrapped in brown paper and tied tightly with cord. This was the weapon described by Mrs Jones and since the paper bore a number of spots of blood, it was obviously the cosh used to attack her and her husband.

Examining the dead man, the inspector noted that there were eight cuts on his left hand and a wound on his forearm, just over an inch long. These were defence wounds. The stab wound which had led to John Jones' death was also an inch long, in his left breast. But of course, it would be for the post-mortem to determine if this was the case, and if that stab had been inflicted with the rasp found at the scene.

One other clue was discovered. Near the cosh lay a man's cap with a label inside reading 'A. Barrett & Co., Hatters and Hosiers, Cleveland Terrace, Middlesborough.' Once again, Mary Jones and John Carpenter confirmed that this cap did not belong to anyone in the pub, indicating that it belonged to the killer who might well have connections with the north-east of England.

The killer would certainly be a conspicuous individual and easy enough to spot. Almost certainly bloodstained and possibly sporting bruises and scratches from his fight with John Jones, he was without a cap and wore no shoes. These details were quickly passed to all police stations in the area, and it was this report which led PC David John Woods, who was based at Pontypridd, to go to Rhondda Road, where the railway line from Pentre ran. Since the railway line ran at the back of the premises, it was possible that the killer had made good his escape by walking along the line.

PC Woods took up his position at 4.30 a.m. and it was a full hour later that he saw someone walking along the line, coming from the direction of Pentre. As the man drew level, Woods jumped out and

The Bridgend Hotel, where Eric Lange murdered the landlord, John Jones. It is possible that the young man standing in the doorway (underneath the name of the hotel) is John Henry Carpenter, the cellarman. (Rhondda Cynon Taf/Aberdare Library)

identified himself. Shining his lantern upon the man, Woods saw that there was a patch of what looked like blood on the man's right cheek. His trousers were torn at the knee and blood seeped through from a wound on his leg. The man wore no cap and, even more significantly, no boots. He was asked where he had walked from and replied, 'Pentre.' Satisfied that this was the man he was looking for, Woods told him that he would have to accompany him to the police station.

Another officer, PC Williams, arrived and together the two policemen took the prisoner to the station at Pontypridd, where the man identified himself as 30-year-old Eric Lange, a Russian seaman born at Riga.

Told that a man was being held in custody, Inspector Williams travelled to Pontypridd, taking with him the shoes and cap found at the Bridgend Hotel. Williams began by saying to Lange, 'Here's your boots, put them on.' Lange did as he had been asked and it was noted that the shoes fitted perfectly. The same thing happened with the cap and, after being cautioned, Lange was escorted to Ton Pentre police station where he was examined by Dr Thomas. He reported that there were two wounds on Lange's left knee. There were several patches of blood on Lange's coat and his stockings were very dirty and worn through from walking along the railway line. Later that same day, an identity parade was organised and Lange was picked out from among five men by Mrs Jones. Told that he would be charged with murder, Lange made a number of statements which were taken down by Inspector Williams.

Lange began by saying, 'Yes, I went in there for money but could not find any in the bars. I went upstairs and entered the bedroom which was lit up. My mate said, "You go in, the money is in the bags." I went in and when I was looking for the money she waked [*sic*] up and shouted. I then hit her with the bar and he woked [*sic*] up too and caught hold of me.

Ystrad Road, Pentre, at the time of John Jones' murder. (Reflective Images)

'I struck him several times, flat with the bar. We had a struggle and both of them tried to stop me. I lost the bar and rushed out the same way as I came in, over the ladder, head first. My mate Harry must have been behind as I heard somebody coming after me. I don't remember taking the knife out, only to open the window when I went in and I only hit him with that thing in the paper.'

Lange told police that he was a ship's fireman on board the SS *Patria* which was lying in Cardiff Docks. The ship had docked the previous Friday, 9 September, with a cargo of timber. Later that same morning though, Lange admitted he had lied about this and said that he had actually arrived in the area a week or so ago, from Liverpool.

Matters then moved very quickly. The inquest on the dead man opened at the Pentre police station before Mr Rees Jenkin Rhys on 12 September when evidence of identification was given. Matters were adjourned until the following day when a verdict of wilful murder was returned. The police court hearing also opened on 12 September, at Ystrad, during which, Superintendent Coles gave evidence of arrest. He related that when Lange had been searched at the police station, two knives had been found on him and also two handkerchiefs, both of which bore bloodstains. After this evidence had been heard, the proceedings were adjourned until 21 September, when Lange was finally sent for trial on two charges: burglary and murder.

The assizes opened at Cardiff two months later and Eric Lange faced his trial before Mr Justice Bray on 28 November 1904. The prosecution was led by Mr W.D. Benson who was assisted by Mr Ivor Bowen, while Lange was defended by Mr Morgan Morgan.

Mary Jones was a crucial witness for the prosecution and she again detailed the attack on the morning of Sunday, 11 September. After the assailant had made good his escape, she had helped

John Carpenter to carry John to his bed. He was still alive but seemed to be in great pain and was crying out for fresh air.

John Henry Carpenter, the cellarman at the Bridgend Hotel, testified that after closing time on the Saturday, he had examined the premises with Mr Jones to ensure that everything was secure. He had retired to his attic room at 2.30 a.m. only to be woken an hour later by Mrs Jones calling for help. Carpenter had pulled on his trousers, collected his revolver and gone downstairs. He found Mrs Jones, with her nightdress heavily bloodstained, suffering from some injury to her head. Later, after taking some brandy up to Mr Jones, he and Miss Richards went for the doctor.

Katie Richards slept in the room next door but one to Mr and Mrs Jones. She had heard some of the commotion outside and when her aunt shouted for help, she was on her way out of the room when she met her aunt coming in. Seeing the blood on Mrs Jones' nightdress, Katie threw open her bedroom window and shouted to a man who was passing that he should run for the police.

Of even more interest though was Katie Richards' story that she had seen Eric Lange in the public bar a week before the attack had taken place. On the morning of the attack, Katie had not seen the intruder but when she gave her evidence at the inquest and the police court, she had recognised the prisoner as a man she had seen in the bar some days before.

In fact, other witnesses showed that there had been an even earlier link between Eric Lange and the Bridgend Hotel, though at that time, Lange had been using a different name.

Florence Morgan had been a barmaid at the hotel for the past five years and she reported that in the summer of 1901, a foreigner had come to work there. He had performed his duties well and there were no complaints over his work. After a few weeks he had left and when she asked him why he had handed in his notice, he had replied, 'I don't care for the place.'

Florence attended the police court on the morning of 12 September and as soon as she saw Lange, she knew she had seen him somewhere before. Now she realised that he was the same man who had worked at the hotel in 1901. To prove this, she described a number of tattoos which the worker had sported, including a red and blue star on the back of his left hand, the initials E.L. close to his left thumb and a blue dot on the third finger of his left hand. There were also the initials L.O. on his left forearm and an anchor on the back of his right hand, near the thumb. All of these marks had been found on Eric Lange. Finally, Florence handed an old diary to Inspector Williams which showed that the foreigner who worked at the hotel in 1901 was then calling himself Eugene Lorenz.

Inspector Williams now gave evidence on what he had found in the diary which referred to a time when the landlord of the hotel had been Mr Gould. An entry for Friday, 19 July 1901 read, 'Eugene Lorenz commenced today at 12s per week.' The next entry referring to the new worker was dated Saturday, 27 July and read, 'Eugene Lorenz paid two days, 3s 5d at 12s per week. One week kept in hand.' Further entries relating to his pay were dated 3 August and 10 August, with the final entry being on Saturday, 24 August which read, 'Eugene Lorenz leaving, £1 4s 0d.'

Further confirmation was given by Walter Burbridge, a drayman who lived at 8 Station Street, Treherbert. In 1901, he too worked at the hotel and recalled a foreigner coming to work there in July. The two men slept in the same room so Burbridge was also able to detail the tattoos, and when shown Lange's photograph by the police, Burbridge had no hesitation in saying that he knew the man as Eugene Lorenz.

The cap found at the scene of the crime had borne a label showing that it was purchased in Middlesborough. Evidence was now called to show that Lange had links with that area. PC Woods, the arresting officer, stated that when the prisoner had been searched at the police station, a watch had been found on him which was engraved 'Lingwood & Son. Middlesborough'. Further links were confirmed by Mr J.E. Sammert who lived in Victoria Villas, Grove Hill, Middlesborough, who said that he had known Lange, as Eugene Lorenz, for more than five years. He knew that Lange had been born in Riga and had once served in the German Navy. He had arrived in Middlesborough some five years ago, marrying an Irish girl, Bridget Annie Gallagher on 1 May 1901.

Details of the wounds suffered by John Jones were given by Dr Thomas, who had performed the post-mortem. There was a superficial wound on the right forearm and an abrasion on the right thumb. A deeper wound ran from the ring finger on the left hand to the outer side of the fingers and was probably a defence wound. On the chest, $1\frac{1}{2}$ins below the level of the nipples and close to the breastbone, was a single stab wound 1in long and some $2\frac{1}{2}$ins deep. This wound had injured the heart sac and cut into the right ventricle and was the direct cause of death. The rasp found at the scene could have been used to cause the abrasions on the head but had certainly not been used to stab the victim.

The only defence witness was the prisoner's wife, Bridget Lorenz, who testified that they had three children. Her husband had lived with her in Middlesborough until 10 September when he had been paid off his employment. This had worried him and seemed to make him strange in his mind. He became very concerned about money and left home saying that he was going to look for work.

Throughout the trial, as various witnesses gave their evidence, Lange moaned loudly in the box. As Dr Thomas spoke of the injuries, Lange was heard repeatedly intoning the word, 'Oyeh!' This behaviour, together with the testimony of his wife, might have led the jury to believe that there was some kind of mental imbalance, which might have accounted for Lange's actions. For that reason, one of the final witnesses was Dr Egerton Beggs, the medical officer at Cardiff Prison. He stated that he had examined Lange a number of times since his reception at the jail, and there had been no signs of any form of insanity.

Having listened to all of the evidence, the jury took just twenty-seven minutes to decide that there had been no accomplice named Harry, and that Lange had entered the Bridgend Hotel alone and killed John Jones in order to escape. The prisoner was then sentenced to death.

In the weeks that followed, Bridget Lorenz visited her husband as many times as she could. All of these visits took place with a heavy iron grill keeping them apart and towards the end of Lange's stay in the condemned cell, Bridget wrote to the governor and asked that their last meeting might take place without the grill. Permission was granted and this last tearful encounter took place on 20 December when Bridget brought her three children to say goodbye to their father.

At 8 a.m. on the morning of Wednesday, 21 December 1904, Eric Lange, alias Eugene Lorenz, was hanged at Cardiff by William Billington and John Ellis as a crowd estimated at 600 strong waited outside the prison gates.

5

THE BABY FARMER

Rhoda Willis (Leslie James), 1907

David Evans, a boot and shoe repairer, lived at 55 George Street, Pontypool and had first opened his business in May 1906. Five months later, on 26 October, Evans' wife left him, selling most of his furniture in the process. He was forced to carry on and try to maintain the house by himself. He found this task increasingly difficult and it was with some relief that he noticed, in January 1907, an advertisement in the *Evening Express* from a woman seeking a position as a housekeeper.

Evans replied to the advertisement, and after a number of letters had passed between them, he agreed to employ Leslie James for the sum of 2s per week plus board and lodging. On Monday, 28 January 1907, 43-year-old Mrs James moved into the house at George Street and commenced her duties.

Some two or three weeks later, Mrs James received a letter from an address in Abertillery. This letter distressed her and when David Evans inquired what was the matter, she informed him that a few weeks before she had come to his house, she had been delivered of a child which, unable to keep, she had given to a Mrs Carruthers, along with the sum of £10. The baby was to be adopted by Mrs Carruthers' sister but Mrs Carruthers had now written to say that they wanted to give the baby back and was prepared to return half the premium. Evans advised his housekeeper that if the matter was distressing her so much, she should get the child back. In due course though, after more letters had passed between Abertillery and Pontypool, Leslie James revealed that the Carruthers family had been unable to refund the £5 they had promised and so had decided to keep the child.

This entire affair had, though, planted an idea in Leslie James' mind. At the end of March, she suggested to David Evans that they should advertise and offer to take in a child for a financial consideration. At first, Mr Evans said he wanted nothing to do with it but Leslie was most persuasive and eventually he agreed. An advertisement was worded and appeared in the *Evening Express* from 20 to 22 March inclusive, and again from 27 March to 3 April. It appeared under 'Miscellaneous Wants' and read: 'Married couple – Christian people, good position, wish to adopt baby entirely as own; every comfort and care; must be healthy; small premium – Apply E44, *Evening Express*.'

Two replies were received; one from Emily Stroud of Abertillery and another from Mrs Lydia English who lived at Ivy Cottage, Fleur-de-lis, near Hengoed. Leslie James replied to both women and heard from Mrs English that her unmarried sister, Maud Treasure was due to deliver a child around May. Of much more interest was Emily Stroud, for she had already given birth to a healthy son on 20 March 1907.

A correspondence was set up between Leslie and Emily, during which a premium of £6 or £7 was mentioned. Agreement was reached and on 10 April, the boy and £6 in cash was handed over at Abertillery. It was the last time that Emily Stroud ever saw her child, though she did receive regular letters from Leslie saying that the boy was doing well.

George Street, Pontypool, where Rhoda Willis lived with David Evans, and where she first had the idea of taking in unwanted babies. (Reflective Images)

David Evans had accompanied Mrs James part of the way on her journey to Abertillery. The couple then went on to Newport to buy some additional clothes for the baby, before returning to George Street, Pontypool. Soon afterwards, Leslie wrote to Lydia English to say that she had now taken in a child and would be unable to assist her when Maud Treasure gave birth. Mrs English was not to be put off though, replying that she wished to see Mrs James, and paid a visit to George Street later that same month.

The two women spoke upstairs for more than twenty minutes and after Lydia had left, Leslie informed David Evans that Mrs English was still very anxious that she take the child when it was born and had offered her £5 cash to do so. Evans advised her to have nothing to do with this second child and suggested that they should concentrate on caring for the baby they had. The thought of all that money was not, however, something that Leslie James could easily dismiss. The problem was that in order to take in this second child, she would have to pass the first on to someone else.

On 7 May, Leslie James received another letter, which she told David Evans was from her cousin, stating that an uncle had died and left her a share of his money, her portion amounting to about £320. She would have to go to Birmingham and in the meantime, would leave the child with a friend at Llanishen.

As Major Emma Chatterton of the Salvation Army left the Army home at 48 Charles Street, Cardiff at 10.15 p.m. on 7 May, she noticed a small bundle near the door, and heard a faint cry. Looking more carefully, Emma found that the bundle was a baby boy wrapped in a piece of red flannel and a piece of sacking. A scribbled note with the bundle read, 'Dear Kaptain do take my baby in i ham won of your girls but gon rong i will come back if you fergie me i bring sum muny [*sic*].'

The police were called and PC Edgar Green attended with Dr Buist. The child was examined and appeared to be well nourished and about six weeks old. The next day, however, the child's condition deteriorated and he began to suffer from vomiting and diarrhoea. The boy was sent to the Union workhouse where he was diagnosed as suffering from exposure. The poor boy held on to life for a week but died on 15 May.

On the day after the baby had been left on the Salvation Army hostel steps, Leslie James was picking up another child. She had received another reply to her advertisement and had consequently agreed to take a child from Mr Stanley Vivian Rees of Salford. He was a married man and said that his wife had given birth to a daughter on 5 May. The problem was that he had now obtained a new position, which necessitated him moving abroad. It would be difficult to take the child with them and so were looking for someone to give her a good home. Leslie met Mr Rees at Pontypool and said she was only too happy to take the child, and of course the £10 that came with her. The agreement was that she would be given £5 immediately and a further £5 at a later date. This, though, presented Leslie with a problem. She couldn't simply return to David Evans' house with a completely different child. The solution was obvious. Leslie would move to a new address.

Hannah Wilson lived at 132 Portmanmoor Road, Cardiff, where she and her husband Robert rented out rooms. On Wednesday, 8 May, she opened the door to a woman who identified herself as Leslie James. Mrs James was alone at the time, and explained that she had a child from a woman who had recently been confined in Bristol and was now looking for both a home for herself and someone to adopt the baby girl. Hannah offered her a room and said she might well be interested in taking the child herself.

Later that same evening, Mrs James returned with a baby which she handed over to Mrs Wilson, having told her that the child was in fact her own. The next day, in consideration of her trouble, Hannah gave Leslie £1.

This situation remained unchanged until 3 June, when two letters arrived for Leslie James. That same morning a telegram also arrived and at 2 p.m., Leslie said that she had to go out and see the father of the baby girl she had given to Hannah. In fact, Mr Rees had contacted Leslie to say that his new job had fallen through and his wife was now pining for their daughter, and would she please return the child. By coincidence, Maud Treasure had given birth to a daughter on 3 June and Lydia English had sent a telegram to Leslie to ask if she would take the child.

At 2 p.m. on 3 June, Leslie James left Portmanmoor Road and travelled to Fleur-de-lis to pick up Maud Treasure's newly-born daughter, catching the 7 p.m. train back to Cardiff. At about 8 p.m., she was seen back at Portmanmoor Road, carrying a small parcel. She told Mrs Wilson that she had seen the baby's father and he had given her £10.

The next day, 4 June, Leslie James went out alone at around noon and by the time she returned, at 2.30 p.m., she was so drunk that Hannah Wilson had to help her up to bed. The next morning, 5 June, Hannah Wilson was in her kitchen, which was directly underneath Leslie's room, when she heard a loud thud. Rushing up to see what the problem was, Hannah found Leslie lying on the floor. However, as Mrs Wilson tried to assist Leslie, she noticed a bundle wrapped in a towel underneath the covers at the foot of the bed. Upon looking inside, Hannah Wilson saw that it was a baby and by the looks of it, the child was dead.

'What is this Mrs James?' queried Hannah, but her lodger only replied, 'Hush! Don't say anything. I will get rid of it tonight.' Horrified, Hannah shouted, 'No my God, you don't. I will go and report you.' This threw Leslie James into a panic and she grabbed Hannah's arm and begged her not to go to the police. Hannah would have none of this, and pulling away, she dashed out of the house to the police station where she reported the matter to Detective Inspector William Davey.

It was 2.15 p.m. when Hannah Wilson told her story to the inspector and by 2.30 p.m., he and PC Charles King were at the house in Portmanmoor Road. Mrs James was lying on her bed, fully dressed, and made no attempt to escape as the inspector searched the room. He ordered PC King to take the body of the child to the police station while he took Mrs James into custody. On the journey to the police station she remarked, 'I am not going to stand all the blame of this. Someone else is in this as well as me.' Later that day she was formally charged with the murder of an unnamed child, to which she replied, 'I did not do it.'

On 6 June, Leslie James appeared before the stipendiary magistrate, Mr Thomas William Lewis at Cardiff. Details of the arrest were given by Inspector Davey, after which Leslie was remanded until 12 June. The next day, 7 June, the inquest on the child opened before the city coroner, Mr Edmund Bernard Reece, where it was revealed that the child had been identified as that of Maud Treasure and that she had died as a result of suffocation. A verdict of manslaughter was returned against Leslie James, who was then sent for trial on the coroner's warrant, to face that charge. Less than a week later, on 12 June, she was back before Mr Reece. Here, it was decided that there was a case of murder, not manslaughter to answer and Mrs James was committed for trial.

Leslie James' trial opened at Swansea on 23 July 1907, before Mr Commissioner Shee. The proceedings lasted two days, during which the Crown's case was led by Sir David Brynmor Jones MP, assisted by Mr Lleufer Thomas. Leslie was defended by Mr Ivor Bowen.

Rose Smith was one of the other lodgers at 132 Portmanmoor Road. She told the court that on the night of 3 June 1907, at some time between 8 p.m. and 9 p.m., she heard Leslie James talking to Mr Wilson, her landlord's son, outside the house. After Leslie came in, she went directly to Rose's room and was seen to be carrying something wrapped up in newspaper. Leslie greeted Rose with, 'I'll take these few things upstairs' and then went briefly up to her room before returning to Rose's room where she stayed that night. The suggestion of the prosecution was that the bundle was the baby, which was already dead.

This sighting was confirmed by David Henry Wilson, Hannah's son, who said that he saw Mrs James alight from a tram car at the top of the street, carrying a parcel wrapped in newspaper in her left arm. Outside no. 132, she asked David if the front door was unlocked. He told her that it was and saw her go into the house.

Hannah Wilson detailed the finding of the child's body on the morning of 5 June. After hearing the thud, going upstairs and trying to lift Leslie back into bed, she had called out for Rose Smith to come and help her. Hannah then went to the bed to straighten the bedclothes and it was then that she noticed a bundle underneath the flock bedspread. Upon unfastening it, she found the body of the child.

Lydia English explained that her sister, Maud Treasure, had found herself pregnant and, being unmarried, wished to have the child taken care of by a decent family. Seeing the newspaper advert, Lydia wrote on her sister's behalf. A few days later she received a reply from Mrs James of 55 George Street, Pontypool and an appointment was made for the two women to meet. At that meeting, Lydia explained her sister's circumstances. Mrs James agreed to take the baby when it was born and said that a premium of £6 up front and £2 later would have to be paid. The terms were agreed.

Over the next few weeks, Lydia wrote a number of times, detailing how her sister's condition was progressing. One of Mrs James' replies stated that she had now moved to 132 Portmanmoor Road and future letters should be sent there. On 3 June, at 6 a.m., a healthy female child was born and a telegram was sent to inform Mrs James. A reply to that telegram was received at 11.30 a.m. and, by arrangement, she met Mrs James at Hengoed railway station at 2.45pm.

The two ladies went back to Ivy Cottage where the child was shown to Mrs James. The child, some baby clothes and £6 in gold were handed over and at 6 p.m., Mrs James left the house, Lydia English having first promised to send the balance of £2 at a later date. A receipt for the £6 had been handed over and this was now produced in court. The scrap of paper read, 'This is to certify that I received £6 from Mrs English for taking baby as my own to entirely adopt for life.' It was signed, 'June 3rd 1907, Leslie James.'

Much of this testimony was confirmed by Mary Treasure, the mother of Lydia English and Maud Treasure, who had been living with her mother during her confinement. Her evidence was of especial import since she was a certified nurse. According to Mary, the child was very healthy and had been fed soon after birth. At 11 a.m., she had handed the girl over to Lydia and later saw her daughter hand it on to Mrs James.

On 5 June, Lydia English received a letter from Leslie James, which had been posted the day before. It read, 'My dear friend, I am leaving by the 12.20 for the north. I gave baby a nice bath, she is lovely. I will write you again in a few weeks time. Your faithful friend, L. James.' The letter carried a short postscript, 'Excuse haste.' Two days after this, on 7 June, Mrs English was called in by the police and made a formal identification of the body found at Portmanmoor Road.

Leslie James' defence was that the child had not been well, and had died from natural causes. Mr Bowen now cross-examined Lydia English, and she did admit that at the time of her visit to Ivy Cottage, Leslie had remarked that there was something oozing from the child's mouth. Lydia was adamant, though, that this was perfectly natural and that the baby girl had been healthy and fit when she left the house with the prisoner.

The body of the child had been examined by Dr James Joseph Buist at the police station. In his initial examination, he confirmed that the child was female, and had been born very recently, with 3 June being the most likely date. The whole of the head and face was discoloured except for a small circular patch of paleness on the right cheek, which might well be indicative of pressure having been applied. The child's back was also discoloured. Dr Buist carried out the post-mortem, which revealed that the lungs were congested, as were the blood vessels in the brain. Death was due to suffocation.

Although Leslie James was facing trial for the murder of Maud Treasure's child, her previous dealings with other women and their babies were held to be relevant, and for this reason, reference was made to the Rees baby and the Stroud baby. David Evans told of the advertisements he had allowed Mrs James to place in the newspaper and of the child who had subsequently lived with them. After Mrs James left his house, on 7 May, he heard nothing more for a few days until she wrote to him, giving him her new address and asking him to bring her coat which she had left behind. On 16 May, Evans had visited Portmanmoor Road and went up to Mrs James' room on the first floor. During his stay, Leslie told him that she had had the Stroud baby adopted by a family named Harrington.

In fact, Leslie James was practising a fairly risky subterfuge. David Evans saw that there was a baby girl in the house and to explain this to him, without arousing his suspicions, Leslie said that it was Hannah Wilson's child. To Hannah though, Leslie had said that David was the baby's father and that if he knew, he might well wish to take it away with him. If David mentioned the child to her, she was to back up Leslie's story that the child was hers, Mrs Wilson's. In this way, Mrs James was avoiding the chance of any awkward questions.

David Evans saw Leslie on one occasion after this, on 23 May when he met her and Rose Smith at Cardiff railway station. Mrs James was drunk at the time and Evans was displeased. He received a letter soon after this, in which Mrs James apologised for her drunken condition. Evans replied to that missive on 4 June, his letter rather affectionately adding that he was looking forward to her return to his house.

The next he heard from Leslie was a letter she wrote to him from Cardiff Prison. Dated simply June 1907, it read:

Dear Mr Evans,
I am in terrible trouble through that woman and her mother that came to see me while I was in your employ. I am almost out of my mind. You will be allowed to see me. I am remanded till next Wednesday. I should like to see you if you don't mind coming here to see me. You are the only friend I have in the world. I cannot say more for my mind is in a whirl.

David Evans did not reply to the letter and consequently he received a second, brusquer one, dated 29 June. It read:

Mr Evans,
What a misconstruction I put on the word friend when I addressed that word to you. Please oblige by sending my things as soon as possible.

The next witness, Emily Stroud, detailed her own involvement with Leslie James. After this, various witnesses from the Salvation Army were called, including Major Chatterton and Ensign Phillip Wilkins. The inference was that the male child abandoned on the steps of the hostel on 7 May was the Stroud baby, and a handwriting expert, David Tempest, testified that the handwriting on a note found with the child was identical to the prisoner's.

Stanley Rees also gave evidence of his arrangement with the prisoner. He told the court that Mrs Wilson had returned the child once she had been made aware of the situation.

Leslie's statement was then read out in court. It began:

I took the room at 132 Portmanmoor Road from Mrs Hannah Wilson under the name of Leslie James. I received the child from Lydia English on the 3rd of June instant. The baby had some froth coming from the mouth before I took it from Mrs English and I asked Mrs English's mother what was the matter with it and she said it was nothing, but only owing to its' being so recently born. They asked me to take the baby home and give it a bath. They wrapped the baby up and gave it to me. When I got to my lodgings I went straight upstairs with it. Then I undid the shawls and found it was dead.

In his closing speech, Mr Bowen asked the jury to decide if the death of the child had been accidental. In his own summing up, Mr Commissioner Shee pointed out that if the jury felt that the suffocation was deliberate, it was murder. If, however, they concluded that it came about from neglect, then it was manslaughter and if they thought it was accidental, then the prisoner should be acquitted. In the event, the jury took just twelve minutes to decide that Leslie James was guilty of murder.

After the trial was over it was revealed that Leslie James was also known as Rhoda Willis. She was born Rhoda Leselles in Sunderland on 14 August 1863, the daughter of a hotel proprietor. When she was 19 years old, Rhoda fell in love with a marine engineer named Thomas Willis and they soon married and moved to Grangetown in Cardiff. They lived happily but in 1895 Thomas fell ill and returned to Sunderland, where he died. Rhoda stayed behind in Cardiff and in due course met another marine engineer, Mr Leslie James, whom she subsequently lived with as his wife. Eventually, differences arose and the couple separated.

A petition was organised for Rhoda Willis, alias Leslie James' reprieve, and thousands of signatures were collected. In the event, it was all to no purpose, and on Saturday, 10 August, the Home Office stated that the sentence would be carried out.

The man Rhoda had lived with, Leslie James, had tried to communicate with her when he discovered she was in prison, but she had said she wanted no contact with him. Now, once she knew her fate was sealed, Rhoda asked to see him and at 8.45 a.m. on 12 August, he arrived at the prison. Their final meeting took place at 11 a.m.

In the early hours of Wednesday, 14 August 1907, Rhoda asked to see her solicitor and when he visited the prison at Cardiff, she made a full confession to him that she had deliberately murdered the child, adding, 'It has been a great comfort to me to tell you this, and I can now die with a clear conscience.'

By 8 a.m., a crowd estimated at 500 strong had gathered for what was to be the first execution of a woman at Cardiff Prison. At the same time, Henry and Thomas Pierrpoint entered the condemned cell, pinioned the prisoner and escorted her to the scaffold. She remained calm, displaying remarkable fortitude as the rope was placed around her neck. It was Rhoda Willis' 44th birthday.

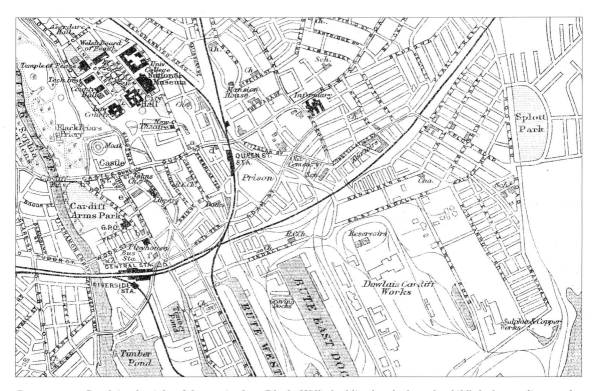

Portmanmoor Road (to the right of the map) where Rhoda Willis had lived and where the child's body was discovered.

6

TEMPER, TEMPER

Margaret Jane Leysham had finished her lunch and, at around 1.15 p.m. on Tuesday, 10 September 1907, left her home at 24 Bridgend Road, Pontycymmer, to return to school. As 12-year-old Margaret passed no. 7, she heard a commotion coming from the house, and stopped to look through the window.

A sewing machine on a table in front of the window blocked Margaret's view somewhat but she could still see what was going on, and this caused Margaret to beckon her older sister, 15-year-old Rebecca. The two girls stood in awe as, inside no. 7, George Stills, a colliery hauler known as 'Notty', battered his mother, 70-year-old Rachel Hannah Stills.

Rachel lay on her back in the far left-hand corner of the room. George, who knelt over his mother, had his back to the window so was unaware that he was being observed. It was only when two neighbours, Sarah Pryor who lived at no. 11, and Mrs Evans, noticed the two schoolgirls looking through the window, and went to see what was going on, that George stopped his attack upon his mother and left the room.

Rachel now lay in the corner of the room, huddled up. Sarah pushed open the unlocked front door to see what assistance she might be able to offer. Immediately, George appeared, his shirtsleeves rolled up and his hands covered in blood.

After what she had heard from the girls, Sarah knew that George had struck his mother and she greeted him with, 'The shame of yourself, beating the poor soul like that.' Stills, replying in Welsh and referring to Sarah and Mrs Evans said, 'If you won't go away from here, I'll give both of you the same.' Then he stormed back inside and slammed the door.

About ten minutes later, while Sarah, Mrs Evans and other neighbours were talking about what had happened, the front door opened and Stills, carrying his mother, came out and laid her down on the pavement. He then pulled Rachel's clothing up over her head and stood watching as the women gingerly moved forward. Sarah Pryor and another neighbour, Ann Davies from no. 17, tried to lift Rachel and carry her back into her house, but Stills slammed the door shut again. Ann Davies pulled Rachel's clothing down, for the sake of decency, while others ran to fetch the doctor and a policeman.

At 1.30 p.m., PC Edward Price Evans arrived at Bridgend Road. He saw Rachel lying on the pavement in front of her house. She was lying on her back, her head towards the gutter and her feet towards the house. Rachel was still bleeding from the nose, mouth and left ear and Evans carried her into no. 7. Dr John Bowen Jones, arriving at about the same time, pronounced that Rachel was dead.

Inside 7 Bridgend Road, PC Evans found Stills sitting on a chair in the kitchen wiping blood from his hands. Evans noted that there was blood on Stills' arms, shirt, waistcoat, trousers and left boot, and he spotted what looked like a fresh wound on his left thumb.

A view of Pontycymmer. (Reflective Images)

Stills' younger brother, John, was also in the kitchen and was in the process of pulling on his boots when Evans asked what had happened. John replied, 'I have done nothing', which was confirmed by George who declared, 'I have done it. I am the man you want.' Stills was then formally cautioned.

At 1.45 p.m., Sergeant Charles George Lane arrived with PC Daniels. Rachel's body now rested in the front room and Dr Jones was completing his examination. Sergeant Lane was appraised of the situation and told Stills that he would be taken to the police station where he would be charged with the murder of his mother. On the way to the station, Stills remarked to Lane, 'I only gave her one blow.' He was then cautioned for a second time but persisted in talking and said, 'I did carry her outside. I was afraid if I left her in, I would do her further injury.'

After depositing his prisoner in the cells, Sergeant Lane returned to Bridgend Road to make a careful search of the scene. He saw a large pool of blood, some 2ft from the corner of the front room. There were other splashes of blood around the room and a broken flowerpot lying underneath the window. Lane returned to the police station and charged Stills with murder, to which he replied 'Not guilty.'

On the day after the attack, 11 September, George 'Notty' Stills made his appearance before the stipendiary magistrate, Mr W.J. Lewis. The prisoner, a short, thick-set man with dark curly hair, heard the evidence of arrest, and the details of his mother's injuries, with his head held in his hands. For the police, Inspector Benjamin Evans then asked for a remand until 14 September.

The inquest opened the next day, on 12 September, before Mr Howell Cuthbertson. Stills was represented by Mr David Llewellyn, but after all the witnesses had been called, the jury took just five minutes to return a verdict of wilful murder against the prisoner.

On 14 September, a further remand was granted and it was not until 23 September that all the evidence was finally heard. During the hearing, Stills fidgeted in the dock and chewed nervously on his moustache as Mr T.J. Hughes detailed the case against him. As expected, the evidence was sufficient to send Stills to the next assizes.

The trial of George Stills took place at Cardiff on 21 November 1907 before Mr Justice Sutton. The case for the Crown was led by Mr J. Lloyd Morgan, who was assisted by Mr A.C. Lawrence, while Stills was defended by Mr B. Francis Williams.

In his opening speech, Mr Morgan related that on the day Rachel met her death, her husband, George, had been in the Ffaldau Hotel enjoying a drink with both of his sons. John was the first to leave, saying that he was going home to bed. Some time later, the prisoner left and though he had been drinking, he was not drunk.

This fact was confirmed by Thomas Jones who lived at 6 Greenhill, Pontycymmer, and who had known Stills for some sixteen years. At 12.50 p.m. on 10 September, Jones was crossing over the railway on the bridge when he saw Stills come out of the Ffaldau Hotel. The two friends passed the time of day and Jones told the court that Stills was not staggering or unsteady on his feet. The last time Jones saw Stills, he was heading back towards Bridgend Road and seemed to be in an excellent mood.

Various neighbours were then called to tell the court what they had seen on the afternoon of Rachel Stills' death. Rebecca Leysham related what she had observed when she looked through the front window. After Mrs Pryor and Mrs Evans had come to the window, Rebecca crossed over to the other side of the road. She was still there when Stills threw open the front door and she saw that his hands were covered in blood. She then heard him say something in Welsh but as she did not speak the language, she could not tell the court what it was.

Margaret Leysham said that she had called her sister over by shouting, 'Oh, look at this man, he is killing the woman!' Margaret added that when she first saw Stills hitting Rachel, he was on his knees, beating his mother about the face with his fists. Margaret had crossed over the road by the time Stills came to the door. Once he had slammed it shut though, she ran off to school.

Another child who had looked through the window of 7 Bridgend Road was 13-year-old Lily Delilah Harris, who lived at no. 34. She was standing near the window of Stills' house when she heard a noise and looked in. Lily noticed the sewing machine, but could still see Stills beating his mother.

Sarah Pryor said that she had called Ann Davies over by shouting, 'Mrs Stills' son is washing his hands in her blood!' In addition to the story she had told at the police court and the inquest, Mrs Pryor was also able to state that she had last seen Rachel alive at 7.30 a.m. that same day and the woman was certainly sober. Sarah denied allegations that Rachel was a heavy drinker and went on to refute the suggestion that she had ever had to put Rachel to bed through drink.

A later sighting of Rachel had been made by another neighbour, Margaret Ann Stone, who lived at 5 Bridgend Road. At 11.30 a.m. she had been at her front doorstep talking to Mr Rees when Rachel came up to them. Finally, Margaret stated that while she had, on occasion, seen Rachel suffering from the effects of alcohol, she was sober that particular morning.

Dr Edward Parry, who had been called to the scene by the police, testified that he had known Rachel for a number of years and though he had seen her 'merry', he had never seen her drunk. When he examined the body, he noted that the jaw was fractured. This blow might have been caused by a fist but equally could have been inflicted with a boot. He ended by stating that if Mrs Stills had been a stronger woman, the injuries she had received might not have proved fatal.

Dr Jones went on to detail the injuries he had observed on Rachel Stills' body. There was a 2in-long wound underneath the chin, which penetrated the flesh down to the bone. A 1in-long cut extended through the lip into the mouth and on the left-hand side of the face, a long gash extended from the eye to the angle of the jaw. The jaw itself was fractured and the whole of the left side of the face was swollen and discoloured. Over the right eyebrow was another cut, irregular in shape and extending down to the bone beneath.

Turning to the rest of the body, Dr Jones said that he had also found a slight bruise in the groin on the left side and there was also slight laceration and bruising of the vagina. He found bruising to the neck which he attributed to 'a direct blow of great severity' rather than strangulation. In summation, Dr Jones said that he believed the wounds on the right eye and under the chin might have been caused by a fall, but that the other wounds would have been caused by either blows or kicks. Rachel Stills was beaten to death in an attack which would, in his opinion, have killed a strong person, let alone a frail old woman. Dr Jones had also examined Stills at the police station and stated that he appeared to be perfectly sober and rational.

Towards the end of the prosecution case, Sergeant Lane stated that the clothing of both the prisoner and his brother, John, had been sent for forensic examination. No trace of blood had been found on any of John's clothing but there were extensive stains on George's.

The time came for the defence to open and the first witness was George Stills senior, the prisoner's father. He began by saying that he had been married to Rachel for forty-six years and that during the last twenty, she had not been a woman but a beast. He went on to clarify this by saying that she had started to drink heavily. This in turn meant that the house was not a happy one and it was largely due to Rachel's behaviour that the prisoner had once left home for a period of three years. George went on to say that Rachel had had a most violent temper and if anyone in the house said something she did not like, he was likely to get a jug, bottle or knife in his face.

In his closing speech for the defence, Mr Williams told the jury that he was not seeking to convince them that George Stills had not taken his mother's life, but that he had done so under such provocation as to reduce the crime to manslaughter. Mr Williams pointed out that witnesses had testified that Stills was in a good frame of mind when he left his father in the hotel.

In his own summation, Mr Morgan pointed out that there was no evidence of any provocation and the jury could not simply assume that it must have taken place. In the event, it took the jury just six minutes to decide that Stills was guilty as charged.

Just over three weeks later, on Friday, 13 December 1907, Stills rose early and partook of a light breakfast of tea, bread and butter. He then smoked a couple of cigarettes.

At 8 a.m., Henry and Thomas Pierrepoint entered the condemned cell at Cardiff and escorted their man to the scaffold as a couple of hundred people waited outside the gates for the notices of execution to be posted.

7

KILLED FOR A KISS

Patrick Collins, 1908

There were seven people living in the house at 5 Aberfawr Terrace, Abertridwr. The house was owned by Mrs Alma Dorothy Lawrence, who shared the premises with her son, William, her eldest daughter, 19-year-old Annie Dorothy, another daughter, 14-year-old Beatrice Maud and two lodgers, John Donovan and 24-year-old Patrick Collins. In addition, Alma's husband also resided at the house but he was a sailor and spent most of his time away at sea and was presently on a voyage to San Francisco.

Two of the men in the house were miners, while the other was a railway worker, and all were used to rising early. Things were no different on the morning of Monday, 17 August 1908. John Donovan rose at 5.20 a.m. and just five minutes later had gone off to his duties at the Aber station of the Rhymney railway. Less than an hour later, just before 6 a.m., William Lawrence was also up and about. He, Donovan and Collins shared the same bedroom, and as Lawrence rose, he saw that Collins was still in bed. Lawrence reminded Collins that it was time to get up but he replied, 'I am going to lose a day to see the boss on top to see for a job on the screen.' Lawrence shrugged his shoulders and went down for his breakfast, knocking on Annie's door as he passed. When William Lawrence left for work, at 6.20 a.m., his sister Annie was the only person downstairs.

Even though she had no job to go to, Alma Lawrence was also not one to lie in bed. It was 6.45 a.m. when she rose but, as she was dressing, Alma heard a shout from downstairs and ran down to see what was happening. Even as she dashed down the stairs, Alma heard her daughter, Annie, shout 'Oh!' from the kitchen.

Alma tried to get into the kitchen but found something was blocking her way. Putting her weight against the door, Alma finally managed to force it open, only to discover her daughter lying on the floor in an ever-widening pool of blood. Nearby stood Patrick Collins who, before Alma could say a word, ran from the back door of the house. Alma dashed to the front door and out into the street screaming for help, and almost ran into Thomas Williams, a neighbour who lived at 1 Aberfawr Terrace.

Williams, a builder, was on his way to work when Mrs Lawrence ran out of her house. Williams tried desperately to calm the hysterical woman down, listened to her story and then went into no. 5 to investigate. He saw Annie lying on her back and was just about to try to raise her when she gave a shudder and fell still. Williams told Mrs Lawrence that he would go for the police but before he left, he noticed two knives lying on the floor. One lay between a table and chair while the other protruded from beneath Annie's body, only the handle being visible.

Even as Williams went off to get the police, another neighbour, Samuel Thorne, who lived at 11 Aberfawr Terrace, also alerted by Mrs Lawrence's screams, had come rushing in to see what he could do. Before the police arrived, Thorne found an empty sheath on the other side of Annie's body.

Abertridwr, where Patrick Collins murdered Annie Lawrence. (Reflective Images)

Lewis Greenway was a railway signalman and his junction box was close to the houses in Aberfawr Terrace. He had also heard the screams, so went to see if he could help. After seeing Annie and realising that there was nothing he could do, Greenway returned to his signal-box and carried on with his duties.

The first policeman on the scene was PC Charles Prosser, who arrived at 6.55 a.m. At about the same time, Dr James Patrick Thomas Burke arrived and pronounced life extinct. PC Prosser retrieved the two daggers, one of which had a broken blade, and then went off to look for Patrick Collins.

At 7.25 a.m., Lewis Greenway was still on duty in his signal-box when he saw a man walking up the line in the distance. As the figure grew closer, Greenway saw that it was Collins, so he left his post again and went to the foot of the signal-box to wait for Collins to arrive. Greenway saw that Collins was sporting a bandage on one hand and that it appeared to be heavily bloodstained. As Collins reached the signal-box he called out to Greenway, 'You can fetch the police when you like. I wish to give myself up.' Greenway saw that there were some platelayers working on the tracks so left Collins with them while he went to find PC Prosser.

Prosser, together with PC Dinwiddi, arrived at the signal-box, and Collins greeted them with, 'Is she dead?' The question was not answered directly but Collins was cautioned and taken into custody. As they escorted their prisoner to the police station, both officers saw that Collins' hands were covered in blood, and that the 'bandage' was in fact a handkerchief that Collins had wrapped around a badly cut little finger on his right hand.

At the police station, Collins asked another officer, PC Samuel Evans, for a cup of water. Evans asked Collins if he might prefer a cup of tea and Collins replied that he would. A few minutes later, as Collins sipped the refreshing brew, he was left alone with PC Evans and began to speak about the crime. Evans, quite rightly, cautioned him again. Collins seemed to ignore this and continued, 'I threatened her six months ago and since, that I should kill her if she would not make it up with me. I had weighed it all up and I knew exactly what I would get after doing it.'

At 11 a.m. that same day, Collins was charged with murder by Sergeant Richard Walters. At this point, the two knives found at the scene were produced by Sergeant Walters. Collins had no hesitation in saying, 'I bought the knives in Cardiff, on Saturday last, halfway down Bute Road in an Italian shop.' Collins was then searched and among the items found on him was a small locket which contained a photograph of the woman he had killed.

The next day, 18 August, Collins appeared at the police court at Caerphilly but after evidence of arrest was given, the proceedings were adjourned for a week. The same day, the inquest opened at the Senghenydd police station where Collins was being held in custody. The coroner was Mr David Rees and Collins was represented by Mr Herbert Samuel. Collins took little interest in the evidence, preferring instead to while away his time reading a book, *Seed Time and Harvest, or Sow Well and Reap Well*.

The first witness was the dead girl's brother, William, who told the court he had made a formal identification of the body and testified that it was his sister, who had only turned 19 on 11 August, six days before she met her death.

When the time came for Alma Lawrence to give her testimony, she averted her eyes from the prisoner and shouted, 'Oh, don't let me see him if he is in the room!' These and all the other witnesses having been heard, the jury took just three minutes to return a verdict of wilful murder against Collins.

On 25 August, Collins was back at the police court when the same evidence was detailed by Mr D.W. Evans for the Director of Public Prosecutions. At the end of the proceedings, when he was asked if he had anything to say, Collins would only reply that he was guilty. Not surprisingly, he was sent for trial at the next assizes.

Patrick Collins appeared at Swansea before Mr Justice Bucknill on 11 December 1908. The prosecution case was led by Mr J. Ellis Griffiths MP, assisted by Mr Clement Edwards MP, and Collins was defended by Mr Ivor Bowen. The case was certainly a curious one for while Collins maintained throughout that he had been romantically involved with the dead woman, and she had spurned him, her entire family swore that there had been no such relationship.

One of the early witnesses was an Italian named Dominico Casale, who ran an ironmonger's shop at 178 Bute Road, Cardiff. He told the court that on 15 August, Collins had come into his shop at some time between 9 p.m. and 10 p.m. and asked to look at some knives. Collins eventually picked out two priced at 3s 11d each, meaning that the total cost should have been 7s 10d. Mr Casale, though, especially remembered Collins because he haggled over the price and eventually paid just 7s 3d for the pair.

John Donovan had, of course, left the house at Aberfawr Terrace long before the incident had taken place, but he was able to say that although Collins and the dead girl had been on friendly enough terms, he had not been aware of any relationship between them. He knew nothing of a trip to Weston-super-Mare that Collins claimed he had made with Annie.

William Lawrence testified that when he knocked on Annie's bedroom door on the morning of 17 August, she had got up to cook his breakfast. Annie was still in the kitchen when he left for work. He too said that Collins and Annie had been friendly towards each other, but there was certainly no relationship. Speaking of the trip to Weston-super-Mare, William explained that while it was true that Annie and Collins had both gone to the resort, there was nothing significant in this. The trip was an outing for the choir and there had been at least thirty people there, including himself.

A letter was produced by the defence, which Collins claimed was an affectionate missive from Annie. This letter had been posted from an address where Annie had previously lived, but William Lawrence said that he did not think the writing was his sister's.

Annie's younger sister, Beatrice, testified that she had heard Annie scream and had gone downstairs after her mother. Asked by Mr Bowen if it were true that Collins had been walking out with Annie, Beatrice replied that she did not think so.

The various wounds were detailed by Dr Burke. He said that upon arrival at the house, he found Annie lying on her back. Her upper clothing was saturated with blood and there was a large pool around the body. Dr Burke found a lacerated, jagged wound on the left side of Annie's neck, which penetrated the large blood vessels, the gullet and part of the windpipe. There was a second, superficial wound some 4ins long, on the right side of the neck and a third on the left lower jaw.

Only these three wounds were visible until the clothing was removed, when further injuries were noted. There was a fourth wound to the left forearm, which was probably a defence wound. There were wounds on the right collarbone, and one below it penetrated deep into the chest cavity. Another penetrating wound lay on the left breast and the blade had gone into the chest cavity, puncturing the heart itself. On the back, three further deep wounds were seen. Upon opening the chest, Dr Burke had found the broken-off piece of one of the daggers, showing that considerable force had been used. In all, seven of the wounds were likely to have been life threatening.

The defence sought to rely on a suggestion that Collins was insane at the time of the attack. Knowing this, the prosecution first called Dr H.J. Cook, the medical officer of Cardiff Prison where Collins had been held.

Dr Cook had been able to observe Collins since his incarceration in August and he said that he had found no signs of insanity, though he did agree that the prisoner was peculiar. The prosecution also called Dr Goodall, superintendent of the Whitchurch Mental Hospital, also in Cardiff. He had examined Collins twice and said that although he was eccentric, brooding, egotistical and obstinate, he was not insane.

When the defence began, they called as a witness 76-year-old Ellen Cronin. She lived at Belle Vue, Cadoxton, and had known Collins' family for many years. She testified that his grandmother was known as being 'a bit soft' and would sometimes talk to herself and throw her food on the fire. Another witness was Mary Ann Griffiths who also lived in Cadoxton. She said that Collins' father was also said to be 'not all there'.

When summing up, Mr Ivor Bowen for the defence tried to use the severity of the attack itself to prove Collins' insanity, saying that anyone hearing of the number and nature of the wounds would have to conclude 'that the man who committed such a crime, must be mad.'

In the event, the jury took just seven minutes to decide that Collins was guilty as charged. Asked if he had anything to say before the sentence was passed, Collins raised his hand and replied,

'When a girl promises to marry any man she did not ought to fall out with him for no reason at all. Because the mother disliked me, she persuaded her to give me up.' The judge then pronounced the sentence of death, but after Collins was removed from the court, Mr Justice Bucknill ordered that the locket containing Annie's picture be returned to the prisoner. It was the day before Collins' 25th birthday.

Over the next few days, something of Patrick Collins' history was revealed in the local newspapers. He had been born in 1883 and had travelled widely, visiting America, South Africa and Scotland. His real name was not Patrick, but Noah Percy Collins, though he refused to answer to that name. He had joined the army and served in the Boer War in the Imperial Light Horse.

A petition was organised for Collins' reprieve. By 23 December, one of Collins' brothers was cycling all over the valleys, gathering as many signatures as he could from the more outlying villages. He reported that wherever he went, people offered him support.

The petition was forwarded on 26 December but two days later, on the 28th, Collins' solicitor, Mr Samuel, received a letter from the Home Office saying that the sentence would be carried out.

On 29 December, a remarkable document was published in the *South Wales Echo*. The letter, stained with tears, was a complete confession, written by Collins in his prison cell. It began, 'I came downstairs with two daggers in my pockets. I intended to persuade Annie Lawrence first, and then, if she would not listen to me, to kill her.'

It continued, 'I said "Good morning Annie, where are my shoes?" She said, "Under the table." After I had laced my boots I noticed that Annie had just finished putting the table ready for breakfast, and she had a blouse in her hands, mending it, and she was quietly humming a tune.

'I said "Give me a kiss Dorothy." She laughed and shook her head. I said "Give me one." She said, "No, you only waited till my brother went out, knowing that I was by myself."' The letter went on to say that Collins had asked for a kiss a number of times, but Annie kept on refusing. Finally, he locked the door and made up his mind to threaten her with the knives. Annie said she would call for her mother and went around the table to the door to unbolt it. Collins was too fast for her though, and pulled her back, raising one of the daggers above his head. Once again he asked Annie if she would succumb to him but again she refused so he struck heavily at her side. As she moaned and fell to the floor, Collins explained how he had struck out again and again until he brought out the other dagger and used that too until one of them broke.

In other parts of the letter, Collins also described how it was pure luck which first led him to lodge at the house at Aberfawr Terrace. He had been hoping to return to America and had alighted at Abertridwr railway station by chance. Taking lodgings with the Lawrence family, he realised that he was falling in love with Annie. He ended by saying that he had gone to Cardiff intending to buy a revolver to shoot her with, but since he did not have enough money, bought two daggers instead.

With all hope now gone, Collins could only wait for the appointed hour. At 8 a.m. on Wednesday, 30 December 1908, Henry Pierrepoint and John Ellis entered the condemned cell at Cardiff Prison, although in the newspapers of the day, the assistant executioner was incorrectly given as Thomas Pierrepoint.

Collins gave a start when he saw the two sombre-faced executioners but soon recovered his composure and walked to the scaffold with a firm step. He was given a drop of 7ft 6in.

8

THE CONFESSION THAT NEVER WAS

William Joseph Foy, 1909

At 2 a.m. on the morning of Thursday, 24 December 1908, Sergeant Charles Hunter was on duty in the High Street at Merthyr Tydfil, talking to PC Richard Henry Lewis. The two men were busily trying to keep warm when a man standing on the opposite side of the road called them over and asked them to lock him up.

Sergeant Hunter asked the man why he should be placed in the cells and was shocked to hear him reply, 'Murder. I have thrown Sloppy down a hole in the old works. She told me she was going to give me away for living on her prostitution and I done for the bugger. If you come with me, I will show you where she is.' Hunter immediately cautioned the man and, together with PC Lewis, walked with him down Castle Street.

The man who had approached the two police officers was 25-year-old William Joseph Foy. 'Sloppy' was the rather unattractive nickname of 33-year-old Mary Ann Rees, a woman known in the area as a prostitute, and whose father, Lewis Rees, still lived in the town.

As the three men walked down Castle Street, Foy put his hand into his pocket and drew out 10*d* in coins which he handed to Sergeant Hunter, asking him to pass it on to his sister and adding, 'I will swing for the bugger.' A few moments later, the group met Detective Constable Edward Jones, who was informed of the situation and joined them.

In due course, the four men arrived at the Ynysfach Works, an old ironworks where there were a number of disused coke ovens. Foy led the police to a 10in-wide plank of wood which rested across an old coal bunker and pointed out one of the coke furnaces at the other side saying, 'That is where I threw the bugger down. She won't worry me no more.'

Sergeant Hunter and PC Jones crossed over the plank with Foy and shone their torches down into the black maw of the furnace. They could see nothing and even when they set fire to some paper and threw that down too, there was no sign of any body. Thinking perhaps the police didn't believe Sloppy was down there, Foy pointed out some marks on the ground and added, 'I caught hold of her and swung her round and dragged her to the hole and dropped her in.'

Still the policemen could see nothing. Becoming rather frustrated now, Foy shouted, 'I will get a bucket of fire to drop it in if you can't see the bugger!' Then, as if to carry out this offer, Foy escorted Hunter and Jones to a second oven where there was indeed a small fire burning inside a bucket. Here, the police discovered that other people besides Foy and Mary Ann had been at the works, for on the ground, lying close to the fire for warmth, was a man and woman.

These two were John Edward Bassett and Mary Greaney, and Sergeant Hunter asked them if they had seen Mary Ann Rees that night. Bassett revealed that Foy had already confessed to them that

High Street, Merthyr Tydfil, at the time of Mary Ann Rees' murder.

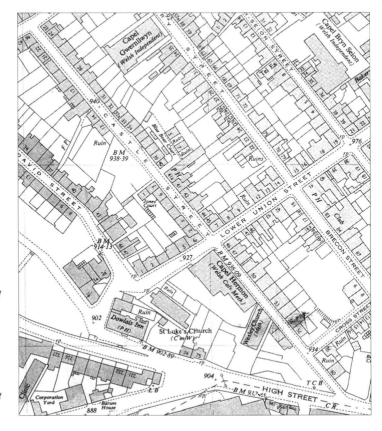

A map of Merthyr Tydfil at the time of Mary Ann Rees' murder. High Street and Castle Street meet at the bottom right-hand corner. It was there that William Joseph Foy first approached Sergeant Hunter and PC Lewis.

One of the coke ovens. Mary Ann Rees was killed in an oven identical to this one. (Old Merthyr Tydfil)

The Ynysfach Ironworks. (Old Merthyr Tydfil)

he had killed Mary, but they had not believed him. Hunter then escorted Foy back to Merthyr and deposited him in the cells before collecting a rope and returning to the coke oven. A lamp was tied to the end of the rope and lowered into the furnace. It was only then that the body of Mary Ann Rees was finally discovered.

Leaving PC Jones in charge, Hunter returned to the police station once again and informed Inspector Arthur Phillips of the situation. Hunter and Phillips then went to the coke ovens together. Going through a culvert at the bottom of the furnace they were able, with some difficulty, to approach the body. Mary Ann lay face down at the bottom of the furnace, which was 39ft 6in deep. Her face and upper body were badly cut and though a doctor would need to make the official pronouncement, it was clear that the woman was dead. Just a few feet away lay Mary's shawl, where Foy said he had thrown it. The body was then removed and taken to Dr Ernest Ward's surgery.

In fact, two doctors performed the examination. In addition to Dr Ward, Dr John Chisholm was also present, and together the two practitioners made their initial examination at 5 a.m. Mary's face was very badly bruised, the skin was torn along the right cheek, and the right upper jaw was broken. There was an extensive haematoma of the left eye and abrasions on both arms, chest, abdomen, thighs and legs. Later, the two doctors performed a post-mortem and found the abdomen full of blood, which appeared to have come from the right renal vein. The injury to the right kidney had caused a rupture and the kidney itself was now loose. All the major injuries were on the right side of the body, consistent with Mary being thrown into the furnace and striking the bottom.

At 9 a.m. on 24 December, Inspector Phillips charged Foy with murder and he made a very brief appearance before the magistrates. Those proceedings too were adjourned, this time until 29 December. On the 28th, the inquest returned a verdict that Mary Ann Rees had been the victim of murder at the hands of William Joseph Foy, and the following day the magistrates reached the same conclusion. Foy was duly sent for trial.

The Cardiff Assizes opened in March, where it was decided that Foy would appear before Mr Justice Bray on the last day of that month. The case for the prosecution was led by Mr W. Llewellyn Williams MP, assisted by Mr Elidyr B. Herbert. Foy was defended by Mr Ivor Bowen.

One of the first witnesses was Mary Greaney, the woman who had been at the coke ovens with the prisoner and John Bassett, on Christmas Eve. Mary explained that she was a married woman but had been living apart from her husband for some time. She, like the dead woman, was a prostitute and had recently been sent to Swansea Prison for that offence.

On the morning of Wednesday, 23 December, Mary was released from prison and was met at Merthyr railway station by Mary Ann Rees. The two friends went to the Wheatsheaf public house to celebrate her freedom. From there they walked together to the Rainbow, where they had a half a pint of beer each. Mary Ann then bought some food and the two women went up to the old Ynysfach Works. By now it was 11 a.m. and when they arrived, they found Foy and Bassett waiting for them.

All four had some food together before going for a walk. Then they returned to Ynysfach, by which time it was sometime between 3 p.m. and 3.30 p.m. They had some more food and then all four walked down to Merthyr, where Mary Ann went with a man and received a shilling for her favours.

They all met up again in the Red Lion pub, where the two men had a pint of beer while she and Mary Ann had a half. Foy and Bassett then left and soon it was Mary Greaney's turn to service a client, for which she too received a shilling. Not long afterwards they met Foy and Bassett again and went to the Rainbow, where more drinks were consumed. They finally left the pub and began the journey back to the works at 10.30 p.m.

A fire was lit inside a bucket and all four settled down for the night. Mary lay down near Bassett and Mary Ann went with Foy, but they had not been together very long when Mary heard Mary Ann shout, 'It is not me you want. It is Polly Gough you want!' Then, in a somewhat indignant mood, Mary Ann pulled on her boots and stormed off. By now it was sometime around midnight.

Merthyr railway station, where Mary Greaney met Mary Ann Rees on 23 December 1908.

The old bridge at Merthyr Tydfil. Mary Ann Rees walked in this area on the day she was killed.

Mary stood and made to go after her friend but Foy told her to lie down, saying that he would go after her and sort things out. Some time later, Bassett went out to look for Foy and she heard them talking outside. Foy told Bassett that he had pushed Mary Ann down a hole, but neither she nor Bassett had believed this.

Much of this evidence was confirmed by John Bassett, who described himself as a labourer. He had had no work for the past fortnight and added that on the Tuesday night, 22 December, he and Foy had slept in the oven at Ynysfach. He said Mary Greaney knew that they were there and on the Wednesday, the two women appeared some time between 10.30 a.m. and 11 a.m., bringing food with them. Bassett related the story of the walk and of later parting from Mary and Mary Ann at the iron bridge in Merthyr.

That night, all four had returned to the disused works together and, after lying down, Bassett heard Mary Ann complain to Foy that he really wanted Polly Gough. Foy had gone after Mary Ann and after fifteen minutes, he had gone out to look for them both. Foy was outside, standing near a second oven, and upon seeing Bassett said, 'Jack, I am after shotting [*sic*] Mary Ann down the hole.' To this, Bassett had replied, 'Don't be silly, come and lie down.' Foy, though, would not be persuaded and said, 'No, come on and I will show you where I shot her down.'

Although Bassett did not believe his friend, he accompanied him to the furnace. He could see nothing down the hole so he lit some matches and dropped them in. All the time Foy was laughing and this convinced Bassett that he was the victim of some sort of joke. Bassett said he had had enough and went back to where Mary Greaney lay. That was the last he saw of Foy until he returned some time later with the police.

After the various police officers involved in the case had given their evidence, the time came for Foy to step into the witness box and give his own testimony. Foy spoke very softly and more than once had to be told to speak up by Mr Justice Bray.

Foy explained that he had worked as a collier and until 24 December, as a labourer at the Cyfarthfa Works. He had for some time been sleeping at the Ynysfach works. Turning to the night of Mary Ann's death, Foy said that when he lay down, Mary Ann came over to be near him but he told her to leave him alone. She had then made the remark about him not wanting her but wanting Polly Gough. After she had stormed off, Mary Greaney made to go after her but Foy said he would go. He found

Mary Ann coming out of the next furnace, caught hold of her arm and asked her to return to the fire. He pulled her back in and Mary Greaney told her to lie down but Mary Ann walked off again and he followed for a second time.

Foy found Mary Ann some distance away and again asked her to come back. Mary Ann refused but finally, after some argument, said, 'Go on, I'll come after you.' He turned and started to walk back but turning round to see if Mary Ann was following, saw her walking off in the opposite direction. Foy ran after her and caught her up by the furnace shaft where they again argued. It was at that point that Mary Ann slipped and fell down the dark hole. It was a pure accident and he never had any intention of harming her.

Mr Bowen for the defence now questioned Foy carefully on the statements he had made to Bassett, Greaney and the police, and which amounted to nothing less than a confession to murder. Foy explained that he was so shocked by what had happened that he did not know what he was saying. What he was trying to explain to them all was that he considered himself responsible for Mary Ann's death, not that he had caused it deliberately. The 'confessions' were nothing of the kind.

The jury though, chose to believe Foy's earlier story, a scenario which appeared to be backed up by the marks near the top of the furnace which were indicative of some sort of struggle having taken place. Foy was adjudged to be guilty as charged and sentenced to death.

The execution was originally set for 20 April, but this was cancelled when Foy announced his intention to appeal. The appeal was heard on 21 April, before Justices Darling, Bray and Lawrance, where it was held by the defence that Foy had largely been convicted on his own statements and that those words should not be looked at as a confession.

Giving the court's verdict, Mr Justice Darling stated that this had to be either an accident or murder, and everything the prisoner had said at the time indicated that the latter was the case. Allied to this, Foy had not sought to get help as he might have been expected to if this had been accidental. The appeal would be dismissed.

A new execution date was now set and at 8 a.m. on Saturday, 8 May 1909 – a beautiful sunny morning – William Joseph Foy, who had eaten a hearty breakfast of beefsteak, was hanged at Swansea by Henry Pierrepoint and John Ellis.

The Cyfartha Works.

9

WITHOUT MERCY

John Edmunds, 1909

At 3.30 p.m. on Saturday, 20 February 1909, 11-year-old Percy Evans and his 10-year-old sister Kathleen left their home at Nant-y-Mailor Farm near Abersychan, to visit a neighbour, 59-year-old Cecilia Harris, who lived alone at Garnwen Farm.

The two children arrived at Cecilia's farm at about 4 p.m. and as they opened the gate, they saw a man standing close by. The man was wearing a dark suit and a light cap, which had a small stripe. Under his left arm he carried a shotgun. Percy and Kathleen knocked on Mrs Harris' door and when she answered, handed over a newspaper she had asked their father for. It was 4.35 p.m. by the time the children left to return home.

Less than an hour later, little Kathleen was back at Garnwen Farm, but this time she was alone, hoping to stay there until her parents returned home from Pontypool. It was 5.25 p.m. and as she got to the gate, Kathleen heard a low groan and immediately saw Mrs Harris, her face a mass of blood. Not surprisingly, Kathleen screamed and ran off home.

William Rees lived at Penyrheol Farm, which was about half a mile from Garnwen. He was sitting in his living room at 6 p.m. when Cecilia Harris arrived in a fearful state. Her throat was gashed and there were other wounds about her head and face. She was covered in blood. Nevertheless, she managed to gasp that Jack Edmunds, the poacher, had done it.

William Rees did not believe that there was any way Cecilia Harris could survive these terrible wounds so, while his daughter Eliza Ann ran for the doctor, he handed Mrs Harris a small scrap of paper and a pencil. Cecilia slowly and painfully scrawled her name at the top of the paper and then added, 'Jack Edmunds shot me and cut my throat he got my money.'

It was 7.40 p.m. by the time Superintendent James James and Sergeant Albert Jones arrived at Penyrheol. Dr McCormack was already there, attending to his patient. Sergeant Jones was handed the bloodstained note Cecilia had managed to write out, and then he and the superintendent proceeded to Garnwen to see what clues they could discover. Cecilia, meanwhile, was rushed to Pontypool Hospital.

Upon their arrival at Garnwen, the two police officers found blood on the gate and along the road that led away from the farm. Inspecting the building itself, they found the front door ajar and half of the kitchen window open, with a pane broken near the latch. Inside, there was a good deal of blood between the kitchen and the front door. Some sacks lay on the floor, and on these Sergeant Jones found a bloodstained knife. Securing the farmhouse behind them, the police officers then went in search of the man Cecilia Harris had named as her attacker.

John Edmunds, known as Jack, lived with his mother at 41 High Street, Garndiffaith, but when Sergeant Jones visited the house that night, Edmunds was not home. A neighbour, William Enoch

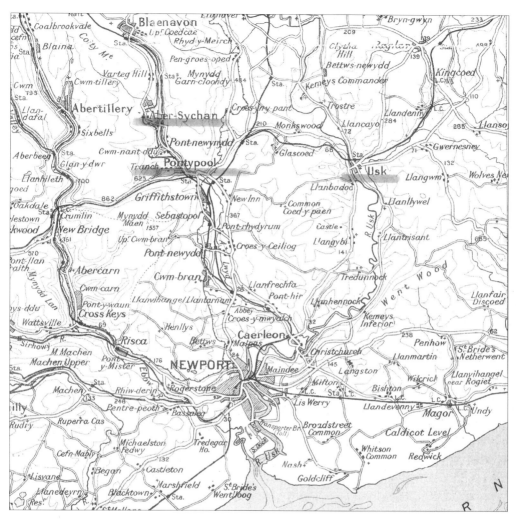

The area where John Edmunds brutally murdered Cecilia Harris. Places mentioned in the narrative are underlined.

Morgan, who lived at no. 40, told Jones that he had last seen Edmunds at 6.15 p.m. When the sergeant made a second visit to High Street, at 1 a.m. on 21 February, Edmunds was there and was immediately cautioned and taken into custody.

At 6 p.m. that evening, Edmunds was interviewed by Superintendent James who asked him to explain his movements between five and six o'clock the previous evening. Edmunds claimed that he was in Garndiffaith all day and at that particular hour, was at home having tea. At about the same time, William Morgan had called at the house to ask him if he was going up to the Aber Theatre that night. Edmunds had replied that he was and left his house at 7 p.m. to do so. At the theatre he was joined by Benjamin Hill, and they had gone out briefly during the interval before finally leaving the premises at 10 p.m.

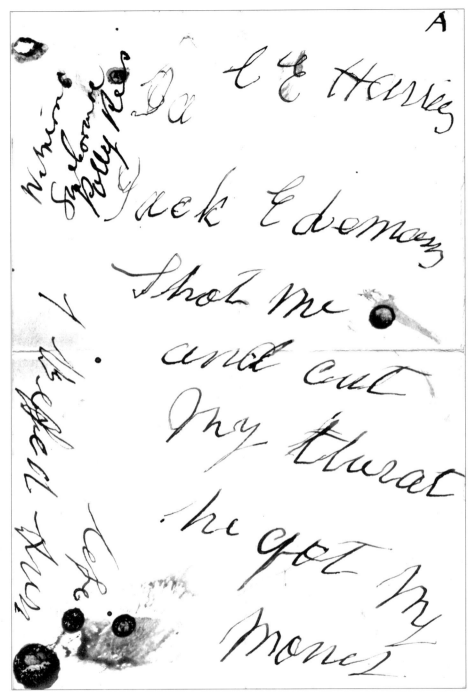

The bloodstained note written by Cecilia Harris after she had been attacked.

To ensure that they had the right man, the police now took Edmunds to the hospital at Pontypool, where a dangerously ill Cecilia Harris positively identified him as her attacker. The police now felt that they had enough evidence to proceed with a case against Edmunds and he was charged with attempted murder. In reply he said, 'I know nothing about it.' Later that same night, a proper deposition was taken from the injured woman.

The next morning, 22 February, Edmunds was brought before the magistrates at Pontypool. Evidence of arrest was given and Edmunds was then remanded until 1 March. Further appearances followed on a weekly basis until 23 April when Cecilia Harris was deemed well enough to attend court and give her evidence. The case for the Director of Public Prosecutions was outlined by Mr Horace Lyne and he informed the court that in addition to attempted murder, Edmunds was now also being charged with rape. All the evidence having been heard, Edmunds was sent to the next assizes on the two charges.

Unfortunately for Edmunds, Cecilia Harris suffered a relapse soon after her court appearance and on Wednesday, 5 May, she died at the hospital. Edmunds was now charged with murder. The inquest opened on 7 May, and resumed on 14 May at Pontypool Town Hall before Mr Norris Roberts-Jones. A verdict of wilful murder was returned and Edmunds was sent for trial on the capital charge.

The trial of 24-year-old John Edmunds took place at Monmouth on 7 June before Mr Justice Ridley. The case for the Crown was led by Mr Cranstoun, assisted by Mr A.J. David, while the prisoner was defended by Mr S.R.C. Bosanquet.

To begin with, a number of witnesses were called to show that Edmunds had been seen either at Garnwen Farm, or very close by, on Saturday, 20 February. William Henry Annetts, a collier like Edmunds, had been walking through Lasgarn with a friend of his, Joseph Jaynes, when, at 3 p.m., they saw Edmunds. The three men fell into conversation for between five and ten minutes and when they parted, Edmunds said he was going to Abersychan and walked off towards Garnwen Farm.

Albert Trumper was a farm-hand at Garnwen and he said that it was about 3 p.m. when he saw a man walking close by the farm. The man was seen again at 4 p.m. and though it did look like Edmunds, Trumper was unwilling to state positively that it was.

Percy Evans, who had visited Garnwen with his sister, described the man he had seen close to the farm. Further, Percy testified that he had attended an identification parade on 22 February and had picked out the prisoner from a line-up of men.

William Rees, to whose farm Cecilia had managed to stagger, had been out earlier that day and had seen Edmunds near Garnwen at 4 p.m. Edmunds had had a gun with him, which he held under his right arm. The two men passed within 30yds of each other but just ten minutes later, Rees saw Edmunds again just 12yds away and staring intently at the farm, with his arm resting on his gun. Rees was also able to say that he knew Edmunds very well because the prisoner's father had worked for him.

William's wife, Polly Rees, confirmed what had happened when Cecilia arrived at Penyrheol Farm. After writing the note, Cecilia had managed to gasp out some more of what had taken place at Garnwen. She had gone on to say that Edmunds had threatened to 'rip her inside out' if she ever told anyone what had taken place.

Other witnesses spoke of Edmunds' movements after the attack had taken place. Cecilia Harris had said that Edmunds stole money from her, including a 5s piece. Mark Williams, a collier who lived in Harpers Road, said that he had seen Edmunds in Mrs Phelps shop in High Street, Abersychan at 7.30 p.m. Edmunds had bought four oranges and paid with a 5s piece.

Mabel Rosser was a nurse at the Pontypool and District Hospital and she told the court that on 20 February, she had helped to remove Mrs Harris' heavily bloodstained clothing, which she had then passed on to another nurse, Jane Burgess. Jane testified that she had passed these clothes on to Sergeant Jones on 22 February, who in turn said that he had passed these, together with Edmunds' own clothing, on to Mr Thompson, the analyst.

George Rudd Thompson confirmed that he had received all the clothing on 23 February. On the male clothing he had found blood on the left breast of the coat and also on the left sleeve. On the coat and vest, he had also found some hairs, all between 1½in and 5in long, and some greyish to golden-brown eyelashes which matched the colouring of the deceased. Seminal fluid had also been found on both sets of clothes. Later, he had also examined the sacks found at the scene and fibres from these had been found on both the male and female clothing. Finally, the blood on the knife was the same type as that of the dead woman's.

Dr Samuel McCormack had gone to Penyrheol Farm to attend to Cecilia on 20 February. She was in a state of shock due to massive blood loss. On the right side of her face, from 1in behind her mouth to the middle line of the lower jaw, was an irregular wound which had been caused by a shot fired from close range and had fractured the lower jaw. There was a clean cut in the throat, some 4in long, and the windpipe had been severed. On 7 May, Dr McCormack had attended the post-mortem carried out by Dr Mulligan, and agreed with that gentleman's findings.

Dr John Watson Mulligan stated that he had attended Mrs Harris at the hospital from 20 February, until her death on 5 May. The post-mortem revealed that death was due to heart failure due to congestion of the lungs but added that this had been brought on by the injuries she had suffered. Put plainly, if Cecilia Harris had not been attacked, she would still be alive.

The most damaging evidence, though, was Cecilia Harris' own deposition. She stated that she was at home at 5 p.m. on 20 February, being helped about the farm by Albert Trumper. At the time she noticed Edmunds, standing on the mountains about 100yds away, and saw that he was carrying a gun. Trumper left and, some time afterwards, Cecilia went outside to dump a bucket of ashes from the fire. Edmunds was now squatting down in her garden and she asked him what he was doing and told him to leave. Edmunds walked out of the garden and sat down near a hayrick, smoking a cigarette. Once again Cecilia told him to go but he came back to the front of the house, raised the gun and aimed it at her. Cecilia went back inside her house and locked the door.

Going upstairs, Cecilia watched Edmunds from the front window. She saw him put the gun down against the wall, go to the kitchen window and break it. Hearing him climbing into the house, Cecilia dashed downstairs and succeeded in getting out of the front door. She managed to reach the front gate but Edmunds chased after her and, as she turned to see where he was, a shot rang out and she was hit near the mouth.

Cecilia fell to the ground near her front gate. Edmunds calmly walked forward, interfered with her clothing and raped her a total of three times. She struggled but Edmunds was much stronger than she was and throttled her. After he had finished, Cecilia tried to calm the situation down by asking Edmunds if he had cut her face much. He replied, 'Yes, it's in a devil of a mess.'

She climbed to her feet and went back into her kitchen but Edmunds followed her, saying that he would get some water and bathe her face for her. Fearful that he might attack her again, Cecilia offered to give him all the money she had if he would leave her alone. He asked her where the money was, whereupon she went to the drawer and took out her purse. It only had 5s 6d inside, which included a 5s piece. Cecilia also told Edmunds that her watch was in the same drawer and he searched for it, found it and took it.

At that point, Edmunds noticed a large white-handled knife on the kitchen table. Without a word, he snatched the knife and cut Cecilia's throat, pulling her head back by her hair as he did so. As she fell to her knees by the back door, Edmunds took hold of her again and banged her head repeatedly against the floor, causing the blood to flow more freely from her wound. Edmunds took up the knife to cut her again but she managed to gasp out, 'For the Lord's sake spare me. Think of your mother.'

Edmunds stopped his attack and Cecilia managed to stagger outside where she saw Kathleen Evans, who ran off in terror. The statement went on to relate how Cecilia had first staggered to Nant-y-Mailor Farm but found no one there, so continued on to Penyrheol.

The defence called no witnesses and having heard all the evidence, the jury had little difficulty in adjudging Edmunds to be guilty as charged. An appeal was entered and this was heard on 18 June before the Lord Chief Justice, Lord Alverstone and Justices Jelf and Lawrance, the single defence issue being that the evidence given at the trial did not show sufficiently that Mrs Harris' death was attributable to the injuries she had received.

Testimony was given that Cecilia Harris had signs of general bronchitis, her heart showed signs of fatty degeneration, and there was some kidney disease. The woman had lived for three months after the attack, and her heart and lungs were in such a state that it was not safe to say that death would not have taken place had these injuries not been received.

The court decided that as far as the cause of death was concerned, there was ample medical evidence that the injuries caused death directly or at the very least, greatly accelerated it, and for this reason the appeal was dismissed.

On 2 July, Edmunds went to bed at 8 p.m. and apparently spent a restful night. The next morning, at 8 a.m. on Saturday, 3 July 1909, John Edmunds was taken from the condemned cell at Usk Prison to the execution chamber. As his ankles were pinioned together, he made some inaudible comment and seemed to be in a state of collapse. He recovered quickly though and managed to smile at those around him before the hood was placed over his head. The trap was sprung and he was hanged by Henry Pierrepoint and John Ellis. It was nineteen weeks to the day since the attack upon Cecilia Harris.

10

A MAN OF HIS WORD

William Murphy, 1910

Gwen Ellen Jones was the wife of Morris, but they had separated and Gwen had taken their two children, a boy aged 7 and an adopted 12-year-old daughter named Gladys, to live with her. In due course, Gwen found a new love in the shape of William Murphy and she went to live with him for a time.

In the last few years of the reign of King Edward VII, work was scarce in Wales and eventually Murphy announced that he was going off to Yorkshire to find employment. Gwen and the children moved in with her father, John Parry, at 21 Cae Star, Bethesda but towards the beginning of November 1909, she left that address and moved into 51 Baker Street, Holyhead, with another man, Robert Jones.

During the middle of December, 49-year-old William Murphy returned to Bethesda and his first port of call was John Parry's house where he asked after Gwen. He was told that Gwen had left and that she might have gone back to her husband, who lived at Beaumaris. Murphy was no fool and surmised, quite correctly, that Gwen had gone off with someone else so he told Parry, in no uncertain terms, that if he saw her with another man, he would kill her.

In fact, it did not take long for Murphy to trace 36-year-old Gwen to Holyhead. After all, he himself had once worked in the Holyhead Local Goods Department, and knew that she had friends there. Robert Jones' house was also easy to find and when Murphy discovered that he could take lodgings in the same street, he was delighted. He therefore moved in with Arthur Bedingfield, at 40 Baker Street, on 19 December, sharing a room with John Griffiths, another lodger.

Murphy paid his first visit to Robert Jones' house on Monday, 20 December 1909. He asked to speak to Gwen and when he saw her, demanded that she return with him to South Wales. When she said that she was content where she was, Murphy showed her a rope and a knife and calmly told her that if she didn't come with him, she would get one or the other. Unaware of this threat, Robert Jones invited his guest to join them for breakfast, which Murphy did.

On Christmas Day, Gwen Jones left 51 Baker Street at 6 p.m., and met Elizabeth Glyn Jones some fifty minutes later. The two women eventually arrived at the Bardsey Island public house, known locally as the 'Bargee'. Murphy was in the same pub, drinking with a labourer, John Jones, who also lodged at 51 Baker Street.

At some time between 8.30 p.m. and 9 p.m., Murphy saw Gwen and Elizabeth, went over to them and said that he wanted a quiet word. When Elizabeth started to follow, Murphy very politely asked her to stay where she was as he wished to speak to Gwen in private. Gwen did not seem alarmed at this request and she too asked Elizabeth to wait for her, saying she would be back in about half an hour.

At around 9.30 p.m., Murphy was back in the Bargee where he was seen by the landlady, Gladys Price Jones, who noticed that his face was scratched. Asked if he had been in a fight, Murphy did not reply, but looked in a mirror and pulled his hand across his face. He left the bar soon afterwards and returned to his lodgings at 40 Baker Street where he went to his cupboard and took out the few food items he kept there. Murphy then shouted, 'Who will give me twopence for this?' The food was sold to a fellow lodger, but the auction was still not over for Murphy then took off his overcoat and cried, 'Who will give me threepence for this?'

Murphy did not stay at no. 40 for long, for by 9.40 p.m. he was at no. 51 again. Robert was not home at the time but John Jones, who had been drinking with Murphy earlier, and Robert's landlady, Minnie Hughes, were. Jones asked Murphy where he had got the scratches on his face and both he and Minnie heard him reply that he had been fighting.

At 10.20 p.m., Robert Jones returned home to find Murphy and the others still in the kitchen. Murphy greeted him with, 'How are you Bob?' but Robert ignored the remark and went upstairs. Not long after this, Gwen's 7-year-old son came into the room. Murphy kissed the boy and, with tears in his eyes, handed the child a penny. Only now did he turn to John Jones and ask him to go with him so that he could show him something.

John Jones decided to humour Murphy and together they climbed a wall at the back of Robert Jones' house and walked through a field until they came upon a drain in Walthew Avenue. Murphy stopped, pointed down into the drain and said that this was where Gwen lay.

John Jones gazed down into the darkness and saw, to his horror, that Murphy had indeed been telling the truth. He ran off to find a policeman, and Murphy followed. At the bottom of Market Hill, Jones found Sergeant Henry Roberts and blurted out what he had seen, but even as the story was being related, Murphy came up and announced, 'Are you looking for me? Here I am.'

Murphy was taken into the guard room where he said, 'I have come here to give myself up as I have killed a woman not very far from Captain Tanner's house, by cutting her throat with a knife, and chucked her body into a sewerage drain.' Completely nonplussed by this confession, Sergeant Roberts contacted his superior, Superintendent Robert Humphrey Prothero, who saw Murphy at 10.45 p.m. Murphy smiled when he saw Prothero and chirped, 'Well, I have done it right enough. You can take my word for it.'

After Murphy had been questioned, Superintendent Prothero went up to the spot indicated by Murphy and began to search for Gwen's body. He found her precisely where Murphy had said she would be; a gaping wound in her throat and her upper body drenched in blood. Returning to the cells, Prothero told Murphy that he would be charged with murder, to which he replied, 'What you say is correct. I walked round with her this evening. We had a good hard fight. I strangled her before I cut her throat.' Later that same night, as he was being locked up, Murphy made a longer, more detailed statement, which was written down by the superintendent.

On the morning of Monday, 27 December, Murphy was brought before a special sitting of the police court. Murphy seemed quite unconcerned and chatted freely with the policemen set to guard him. Details of the arrest were given by Superintendent Prothero. The question of a remand was then discussed, during which Murphy pointed out that he would like to attend the inquest. He then burst out laughing and upon being told that he would be remanded to 3 January, wished everyone in court a good afternoon and added that he would now have another weeks' rest.

The inquest took place on 28 December before Mr Jones Roberts, the Anglesey coroner. There was some confusion over whether Murphy would actually attend or not. He had said at the police court

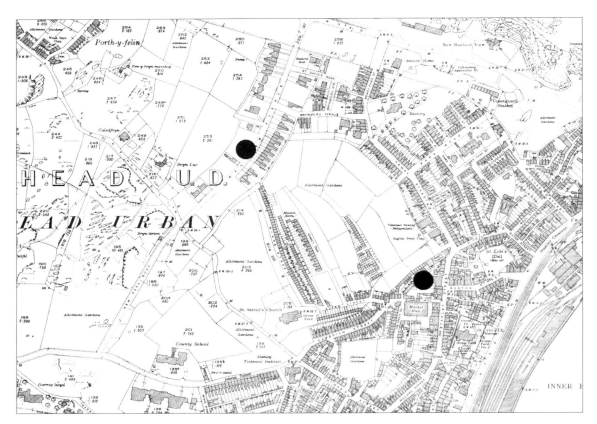

Map of the area where Gwen Ellen Jones was murdered. Murphy and Jones were both living in Baker Street, which runs approximately north–south. The murder took place in Walthew Street and Murphy made his first appearance before the magistrates at the Police Court, which is also marked.

that he wished to be there but then, after hearing that he would not be allowed to view Gwen's body, changed his mind. In the event, Murphy changed his mind yet again, and at the last minute made his appearance in the court.

Elizabeth Jones told the inquest of the encounter with Murphy on the night that Gwen met her death. She also said that Gwen had told her that she had made an appointment with Murphy for earlier that evening, at 7 p.m., but had failed to keep it. Murphy mentioned this when he first saw Gwen but the deceased had told him that she did go and must have missed him. Murphy seemed to be content with this explanation.

After Murphy's various police statements had been read out, Dr Thomas William Clay gave details of the terrible injuries inflicted upon Gwen Jones. The wound on the neck was 5in long and no less than 3in wide. It extended down to the spine and Gwen's head had almost been severed from her shoulders. There was evidence of strangulation, but the primary cause of death was suffocation, followed by haemorrhage. The jury, having heard all this, took just minutes to decide that Gwen Jones had been murdered by William Murphy.

On his way back to prison, Murphy was mobbed by angry crowds who seemed only too eager to lynch him on the spot. At the court, and again at the railway station, it was only prompt action by the escorting police which saved Murphy from the hands of the mob.

On 3 January 1910, Murphy was back before the magistrates, the case for the Director of Public Prosecutions now being detailed by Mr Thornton Jones. Murphy was hissed at as he made his entrance into the courtroom.

Elizabeth Jones elaborated on the evidence she had given at the inquest. After parting from Gwen at the Bargee pub, she had later gone to Gwen's lodgings in Baker Street and found Murphy there. Murphy's face was scratched and his hands and face were covered in blood. She asked him where Gwen was and he told her, 'You have seen Gwen for the last time.' At the time, although she knew that Murphy had threatened Gwen, Elizabeth did not believe that he could have done any harm to her.

Later, when Gwen's little boy was crying for her, Murphy had coldly told the child, 'You have no mother', and then handed him a penny. Soon afterwards, the prisoner stood up and began dancing, and when John Jones asked him if he was drunk, Murphy told him that he had done a worse thing than getting drunk. It was then that Murphy asked Jones to go with him and he would show him something.

The auction of Murphy's goods at his lodgings had been witnessed by a number of people, including John Murray, a fellow lodger there. Before Murphy finally left the house, he turned to Murray and muttered, 'I have done wrong tonight.' He appeared to be sober at the time.

Gladys Price Jones, landlady at the Bargee, told the court that she had first seen Murphy in her establishment at about 7 p.m. on 25 December, when he ordered a pint of porter. She noticed him again at about 9.30 p.m., by which time he had scratches on his face. After she had pointed out his injuries, he had had a single pint of stout, which he drank very quickly. Other customers in the pub at the time, including John Price and Richard Ellis, also said that they too had seen the scratches on Murphy's face and Price had even given Murphy a rag so that he could wipe his face.

In addition to Superintendent Prothero and Sergeant Henry Roberts, another police sergeant, Owen Roberts, said that he had seen Murphy in the cells on 26 December. Murphy had remarked, 'I have made a happy Christmas for myself haven't I?' Sergeant Roberts replied, 'Yes, it seems. I'm sorry for you Murphy.' Hearing this, the prisoner scoffed, 'I'm not sorry for it. I'm damned glad I've done it.' The magistrates quickly decided that Murphy should be sent for trial and stated that it would take place at Beaumaris later that same month. It was to be the first murder trial there since March 1862.

Murphy's trial took place on 26 January before Mr Justice Pickford. The case for the prosecution was led by Mr J. Ellis Griffiths MP, who was assisted by Mr Trevor F. Lloyd. Murphy was defended by Mr Austin Jones.

In addition to the witnesses already referred to, the prosecution called John Griffiths, who had slept in the same bedroom as the prisoner at Baker Street. He reported a conversation he had had with Murphy some days before the attack in which the prisoner had said, 'Well Jack, if she does not come away with me, I'll have her. I'll do her if I can't get her away from that man.'

Murphy's statement to Superintendent Prothero was again read out. It began:

I should have met her tonight between 7 p.m. and 7.30 p.m. at Wynne Street…She did not come. I went into her house and asked for her and she was not there. I went to the Bardsey Inn looking for her. I could not find her.

I was having a pint of porter when a man called me out. He said, 'Here she is' so I went out to her. When I went out she was talking to another ginger piece [Elizabeth Jones]. I said to her, 'Gwen, where have you been?' She said, 'I was there at seven o'clock and did not see you.' I said, 'Are you going to have a walk now?' She said, 'Yes.' We had a walk by Captain Tanner's house.

She was falling against me drunk. We went to look for a certain place to have connection. So, I took her right across the field from Captain Tanner's house. About five yards this side nearer to Captain Tanner's than the stile she told me that she was going to Bethesda tomorrow, and said, 'I like you and we will have a bit before we go.'

I said, 'What road?' [meaning by what method], and she said, 'Any road you like.' I said, 'We'll have a bit back' [meaning rear entry]. I had connection and had a bit back. I said to her, 'Turn round and we'll have a bit front'; so we had a bit front. While we were having a bit front I said, 'Why don't you pull this off?' meaning the ruff around her neck. She said, 'It's hooked underneath.' I then caught hold of her with my left thumb and tried to strangle her.

She screamed and I kept struggling and holding her down with my left hand. She was getting weaker and weaker, until she gave the last kick. I drew my knife from my pocket and commenced to use it by cutting her throat. When I cut her throat I dragged her into the drain. She was still alive, gurgling, when I got her into the drain.

I commenced cutting her throat further, from ear to ear. Then I got my fingers into her throat and opened the wound more. I came up to her head and put my hand under her chin and pulled upwards. Then, after I had done that, I turned her belly downwards and shoved her underneath the water to smother and drown her.

In his closing speech for the defence, Mr Austin Jones said that if Murphy had really intended all along to murder Gwen, he would have done so at the first opportunity he had. In fact, he became possessed by some sort of impulsive mania and was in just such a condition when he committed this terrible deed. His client was not a sane man at the time and consequently could not be found guilty of murder. However, it took the jury just three minutes to decide that Murphy was indeed sane, and guilty as charged.

No appeal was entered, but a petition was drawn up asking for a reprieve. By 4 February, even before the result of the plea to the Home Office was known, Murphy seemed resigned to his fate. He ate heartily, slept soundly and appeared to be totally unconcerned. It came as no great shock to him when, on 13 February, he received notification that the Home Secretary had found no grounds to interfere with the sentence.

At 8 a.m. on Tuesday, 15 February 1910, William Murphy was executed at Caernarfon by Henry Pierrepoint and William Willis, as a large crowd gathered outside the prison. It was the first and only execution at Caernarfon in this century.

11

A LITTLE LOCAL TROUBLE

William Butler (Thomas Clements), 1910

The West family had had enough. For too long now their lives had been plagued by threats from a man who used to lodge with them. It was time to take action and issue a summons. The man who had caused the trouble, 62-year-old Thomas Butler, first appeared in court on Saturday, 6 November, when he was bound over. This appeared to have no effect as other threats followed, so a second summons was issued.

The case came to the Newport County police court on 13 November 1909, and Butler was represented by Mr A.W. Morris of Cardiff. The complainant, 15-year-old Florence West explained that she was a servant, employed by Mr John Ricketts, the stationmaster at Bassaleg. Butler, it appeared, was rather enamoured of Florence and when she had refused to have anything to do with him, had threatened to knock her down, this occuring on 3 November.

Continuing her testimony, Florence explained that each morning and night Butler would be waiting for her when she arrived at work, and when she left. He constantly pestered her to marry him, or run away with him, despite the forty-seven year age gap. On 8 November, frustrated at her ignoring him, Butler had run after Florence and shouted, 'If you don't speak to me I will make you suffer for it!'

Frederick West, Florence's 12-year-old brother, told the magistrates that he had, on more than one occasion, heard Butler calling his sister bad names. Mr Ricketts, the stationmaster, confirmed that Florence had made several complaints about Butler. On 8 November, she had left to go home but returned within minutes, looking pale and frightened. She told him that Butler had threatened her yet again and he had to go and fetch a constable to escort her home. As a result of this, Butler had flown into a rage and told Mr Ricketts what he would do to him if he interfered again.

William Butler denied that he had ever threatened Florence, but the magistrates chose to believe her side of the story and decided to bind him over in the sum of £10, ordered him to find two sureties of £5 each and pay the court costs of 12s 6d. If he did not pay these costs and sureties, he would go to prison for fourteen days. On leaving the court, Butler shouted to Florence, 'I will do the fourteen days!'

In fact, this court case was the second piece of trouble for the people of Bassaleg. On the morning of Friday, 12 November, Frederick West, the same schoolboy who gave evidence against Butler, had found a door key on the sill at the back of his parents' house. It was 8.15 a.m. and Frederick had handed the key to his mother, Elizabeth, who, thinking that her sister had left it by mistake, told Frederick to take it back to her. The boy did as he was told, but soon returned with a message from his aunt to say that it didn't belong to her. It was a puzzle.

There was another puzzle to consider too. As the day progressed, Elizabeth West realised that she hadn't seen her neighbours, Mr and Mrs Thomas who lived in nearby Tank Cottage. Charles Thomas was 82 years old and had been employed as a general labourer on the Tredegar estate. His wife, Mary, was ten years younger and it was strange that they hadn't been seen about.

That evening, Mrs West took her concerns to another neighbour, Alice Llewellyn. Just before 7 p.m., the two ladies went to Tank Cottage where, acting on a hunch, Mrs West tried the key her son had found. The key unlocked the door but when Mrs West called out for Mrs Thomas, there was no reply. Alice Llewellyn, meanwhile, had stepped inside and found that the rooms were in disorder with drawers opened and the contents scattered about. While she waited outside, Elizabeth West went for the police.

PC Thomas Bale arrived at Tank Cottage at 7 p.m., and went upstairs to investigate. There were three small bedrooms, the steep stone steps arching round one corner and leading directly into the main one. The old couple lay in their bed. Charles Thomas was on his back, his head battered to a pulp so that part of his brain protruded. His wife, Mary, was on his right side with her back towards Charles. Her face was covered with a bedsheet but the bloodstains on that sheet left PC Bale in no doubt that she had suffered a similar fate.

Checking around the room, Bale found a satchel on the bed. It too was heavily bloodstained and contained a purse, which held just three bills and a postage stamp. Whatever money had been in the purse had been taken by the killer. The floor of the room was awash with blood. Downstairs, a pane of glass near the door had been broken in the window and removed, showing that the murderer must have gained access that way. Outside that window lay a child's jacket, most probably used by the intruder to prevent himself being cut when he smashed the glass.

Bale immediately contacted his superiors. At 7.15 p.m., he telephoned Inspector John Barry at Newport, who drove to Bassaleg, arriving there at 7.45 p.m. He was shown the child's coat, smeared with dung, which had probably been applied to deaden the sound of breaking glass. When this coat was shown to Elizabeth West, she immediately identified it as one which had belonged to Florence but which she had now grown out of, thus providing the second link between her family and the murder house. Inspector Barry, though, could not accept that any member of the West family had committed this terrible crime. Could it be possible that the real killer was trying to incriminate them? The inspector asked Mrs West if she could think of anyone who might have a grudge against her family – the only name she could think of was William Butler.

The following morning, of course, Butler appeared in court to answer to his threatening behaviour charge. Unable to pay the monies ordered by the magistrates, he was taken into custody to serve his fourteen days' imprisonment. As a matter of routine, he was searched and on him were found eight half crowns, three florins and six 1s pieces; a total of £1 12s. The police also found a glass-cutter's diamond and could not help but recall that one part of the broken window at Tank Cottage had shown a remarkably rounded edge.

On the same day that Butler was sent to prison, PC Bale called at Butler's lodgings, 3 Jones' Terrace, Pye Corner, Bassaleg, and spoke to his landlords, Robert and Cicely Doody. Robert Doody reported that on 11 November he had seen Butler retire at 6.40 p.m. In the night, he heard someone snoring and though he believed this was his 8-year-old son, Samuel, it might well have been Butler himself, in which case, he had not gone out during the night.

Cicely Doody told PC Bale that Butler had been lodging at her house for the past six weeks. They had agreed 10s a week for board and lodgings but in all the time he had been there, Butler had only paid 5s. She confirmed that her lodger had gone to bed at 6.40 p.m. on the 11th and she did not see or hear him again until the next morning when he left the house without any breakfast, saying that he was going into Cardiff. He returned at 6 p.m. on the Friday and mentioned that he had been to see his sister's solicitor. Butler had gone out again that evening but before he did, he handed Cicely six pennies and told her to get some 'supper beer'.

The police knew which solicitor had represented Butler when he had appeared in court on Saturday, 13 November. They now paid a visit to the firm of Lloyd and Cross, where they spoke to the articled clerk, Evan Gibson Davies. He confirmed that Butler had called at the office at 2.10 p.m. on Friday the 12th and had shown him a summons to appear at Newport the next day. Butler asked for legal representation and had handed over two guineas as payment. This money consisted of a sovereign, two half sovereigns and a florin. Yet this same man could apparently not pay his landlady a few shillings rent. Where had he got the money?

The question of Butler's finances became even more important when the police spoke to Caroline James, who also lived at Pye Corner. Her husband, James James, was a friend of Butler's and on 11 November, at 9.15 a.m., Butler had called at her house and asked for a loan of 5s. Caroline told him she could not help, whereupon Butler reduced his plea to 6d so he could send a telegram to his sister, Mrs Mary Jane Andrews, in Cardiff. Officers now traced Mrs Andrews to 96 Newport Road, Cardiff. She had never heard of anyone named William Butler and her brother looked nothing like the man police described to her.

Finally, a piece of real evidence came into the police's possession. George Rudd Thompson – the public analyst for the county of Monmouth – had finished examining Butler's clothes. He found blood on the left sleeve of the shirt and a number of small spots of blood, about thirty in all, on his coat, all of which were on the right side. There was a cut on the sleeve of the coat and when the crime was reconstructed, two vital clues were found. Firstly, a man putting his arm through the broken window touched the broken glass in precisely the same position as the cut on Butler's coat, and a man standing in the correct position to inflict the blows would get small bloodstains on the right side of his jacket.

On 14 November, Butler was interviewed at Newport police station by Superintendent William Porter, who questioned him about the bloodstains found on his clothing. Butler replied that they were paint, though some might have come from a cut thumb which Mrs West had bandaged for him while he was living there. He added that Mr West had killed a pig a week or so ago and he might well have got some blood from that too.

Superintendent Porter thought he had enough evidence to proceed and charged Butler with the double murder. Butler replied, 'Good God! What, me? You know better than that man. I was in bed all night. The people in the house know I was in the house. Don't they say I was in the house?' Told that the Doody's could not confirm this, Butler replied, 'Then they are liars.'

On Monday, 15 November, Butler appeared before the stipendiary magistrate, Dr Garrod Thomas, in the charge-room at the Newport County police court. After Butler described himself as a 78-year-old [sic] Crimean war veteran, and details of his arrest were given, he was remanded until the following day – the same day that Charles and Mary Thomas were laid to rest at the Bethesda Chapel.

The police court reconvened on 16 November when remands followed until 19 November, and then until 26 November. Meanwhile, Butler protested his innocence and wrote letters to friends and acquaintances, telling them that the real killers were the Wests. One letter, written to a friend who was also named Butler, but who was no relation, began:

> Please tell me what has happened to Mr and Mrs Doody, as they do not reply to my letter. They know I did not do the murder, as I went to bed at seven o'clock on the night and rose at the same time as she did on the Friday morning; and little Sammy can say the same. As for murdering poor old Charlie Thomas, I did not do it. I have done many kind turns for the old man. The people in Bassaleg do know who did the murder, and they do know it is those Wests.

On 26 November, the adjourned inquest re-opened at the Tredegar Arms, Bassaleg. After PC Bale had given his testimony, the public analyst, Mr Thompson, told of the various objects, taken from Tank Cottage, that he had examined. A hammer had been found in the cottage, but bore no traces of blood. The same could not be said for a heavy candlestick, which did show minute spots of blood. Mr Thompson also explained that a large number of small blood spots had been found on the wall of the bedroom where the dead couple had lain. There was a gap in these stains on one wall, showing that this was where the assailant must have stood when he battered the Thomases to death. The same sort of blood spotting had been found on Butler's coat. These blood spots were also referred to by Dr Robert Hudson, who examined the bodies of Charles and Mary Thomas at the scene. Dr Hudson believed that all the blows were inflicted from the right-hand side of the bed – as one went into the room – and confirmed that this was where there was a gap in the bloodstaining on the wall.

After listening to all the testimony, the jury concluded that William Butler had murdered Charles and Mary Thomas. Earlier that morning, Butler had appeared before the magistrates again, but was remanded until 6 December, pending the outcome of the inquest.

Thus, on 6 December, the evidence started to be heard. Mr E.W. Pocock represented the prisoner and the case for the Director of Public Prosecutions was outlined by Mr Harold Pearce. Mr Pearce began by stating that it was well known in the district that Mr and Mrs Thomas had had money in the house. Butler had once worked for the old couple, doing gardening and odd jobs for them.

The West family were then called to give evidence. After Frederick West had told of his finding of the door key on the windowsill of his house, which was just a couple of doors away from Tank Cottage, his mother, Elizabeth, took the stand. She stated that Butler had once lodged with her family and while there, always appeared to be short of money. Butler left their house at the end of September, after there had been some trouble over her daughter, and still owed three weeks rent and lodging, a total of 30s.

Butler claimed that the blood on his clothing had come from a pig which Elizabeth's husband, Sidney West, had slaughtered. Elizabeth now confirmed that an animal had been killed, but this had been on 4 November, by which time Butler wasn't living with them anymore, and he had not been present when the slaughtering was done. Mrs West then told of the summons she had been forced to issue against Butler.

The summons was first issued on 5 November and it was served on Butler that same day, but that evening he came to their house, pushed open the front door and, waving the summons in his hand, shouted, 'Yes, you bastard, I got it. I will make you suffer for this. I will ruin this house and bring tears to your eyes before this day week, you bastard!'

After Mr Thompson and PC Bale had given evidence, the case was adjourned again, this time for a week, when the other witnesses would be heard. On 13 December, the Doodys gave evidence. They both said that although they could not be absolutely sure, they were not aware of Butler leaving their house on the night of 11 November. This testimony was, however, seriously weakened by Caroline James, who had already told the inquest that Butler had tried to borrow money from her on the morning of the 11th.

Witnesses were now called to show that Butler had somehow suddenly come into money at around the time of the murder. Elizabeth White was the landlady of the Bush Inn at Pye Corner and knew Butler as a regular customer. The last time she saw him was on 12 November when he had had a glass of beer and had asked for two bottles to take away with him. He had paid for the drinks with a florin and as she went to the drawer for his change, he turned to walk out of the pub. She shouted after him but he seemed to be in a hurry and called back that he would call again for his change.

Lilian Mary Smith was a waitress at the Great Western dining rooms in High Street, Newport. At 8.30 a.m. on 12 November, Butler called and had a cup of tea and some bread and butter. The bill was 3d but he looked so poor that Mrs Smith only charged him 1d. Butler was back, though, at some time between 3 p.m. and 4 p.m. when he ordered tea, ham and eggs, which came to 1s 1d. Butler paid her with a sovereign and told her to take a shilling tip.

PC Gordon Jones had had charge of Butler at the police station and took him his dinner on 15 November. Butler asked him for a newspaper, pointing out that he had plenty of money to pay for it as he had backed the Derby winner last year at odds of 100–1. The bookmakers he used, Frank Smith, had only paid him some of the money but he drew more from time to time. Butler was, of course, explaining where his newfound wealth came from but when the police spoke to Frank Smith, a coal merchant, he told them he had never taken any bets for Butler.

The magistrates ruled that Butler should be sent to the next assizes, which opened at Monmouth in February. Butler appeared before Mr Justice Grantham on the 23rd and, during the two-day hearing, he was defended by Mr Sherwood, while Mr Cranstoun and Mr St John G. Micklethwait led the prosecution case.

After all the prosecution witnesses had been heard again, the defence gave their evidence. They proposed that this was simply a case of mistaken identity. It was pointed out that Butler, as a local man, would have known that PC Bale lived close to the scene and he would therefore not have been silly enough to carry out the attack. However, the jury took just ten minutes to decide that Butler was guilty as charged. At this point, Inspector Munroe of Scotland Yard was called to the witness box to detail Butler's past criminal record.

Inspector Munroe said he had taken the prisoner's fingerprints on 14 November and compared them with the records he had. This showed that Butler was known under a number of different names including George Brown, George Clements, Thomas Palmer and Thomas Butler. He had a long criminal record stretching back to 11 June 1865 when he served six weeks in prison for stealing fowls. He had since been in prison in such places as Gloucester, Brecon, Oxford and Caerleon, serving sentences as long as ten years, all for some form of theft. His real name appeared to be Thomas Clements.

Asked if he had anything to say before the sentence of death was passed, Butler shouted, 'I have not had a fair trial, anything but a fair trial. I consider I have had anything but justice, but you can do what you like, I don't trouble…I have had no trial – anything but justice. But of course, that is a common thing. You never get justice in this country, but I am not afraid to die, and I am not ashamed to live. I am an innocent man!'

Red with rage, Butler then turned to the witnesses and began hurling abuse at Mrs West. As the death sentence was passed, Butler tried to get out of the dock, but was forcibly restrained and hurriedly taken down to the cells.

An appeal was heard on 11 March before Justices Lawrance, Phillimore and Hamilton. There were a number of points the defence wished to make. Butler claimed that certain witnesses had not been properly cross-examined, and that the Doodys' 8-year-old son should have been called to show that Butler was in bed when the murder was taking place. It had been suggested that Butler had stolen money from the Thomas' but there was no evidence to show that any property had been removed from the house. The police had searched Tank Cottage a few days after the murder, forced open a trunk and found more than £154, mostly in gold. Finally, there had been misdirection on the part of the trial judge.

In giving the court's verdict, Mr Justice Lawrance said that he could find no evidence of misdirection. The conviction was right and proper and the appeal would be dismissed. Three days later it was announced that the execution had been fixed.

On 22 March, the Home Office stated that there would be no interference with the sentence and Butler's fate was sealed. Two days later, at 8 a.m. on Thursday, 24 March 1910, a gloomy morning, Thomas Clements (alias William Butler), a native of Nebley in Gloucestershire, was hanged at Usk by Henry Pierrepoint and John Ellis.

12

'FOR THE SAKE OF MY BOYS'

Henry Phillips, 1911

Ann Ace wondered who could be knocking on the front door of her home in Frogmore Lane, Knelston, Gower, at 1.30 a.m. Going downstairs to investigate, Ann discovered her married daughter, 38-year-old Margaret Phillips, with three of her four boys. Margaret complained that, yet again, her husband, 44-year-old farmworker Henry, had struck her and this time she had had enough. She had left the youngest child with a neighbour, packed a few basic items and left him for good.

The date was Thursday, 13 July 1911 and over the next few days, Margaret related further details of the trouble she had endured at her husband's hands. This time she intended to summons him for persistent cruelty. As a result, on Saturday, 22 July, Sergeant David Davies served the summons on Henry Phillips. The document informed Phillips that he was to appear in court exactly one month later, on 22 August. Hearing this, Phillips greeted the policeman with, 'Oh, she has taken out a summons has she?' He then asked the sergeant to read it out to him, after which Davies informed Phillips that his wife needed to get some more of her clothes from their home.

Phillips offered no objection and Sergeant Davies was in attendance later when Margaret called at her old address. Fearful that there might be an incident, the sergeant began by advising Phillips to behave himself, but Henry calmly replied, 'No, I will not touch her Mr Davies.' Margaret went through the house, collecting the items she needed. As she was leaving, her husband asked politely, 'Have you got all the clothes you want?' Margaret replied, 'Yes, for the present', to which Phillips retorted, 'Well, you will get no more as I'll burn the bloody lot.'

Margaret stayed with her mother and sister, also named Ann Ace, until Monday, 24 July, when she took two rooms at the house of a gentleman named Albert Davies who also lived in Frogmore Lane, some 300yds from Ann Ace's home. Margaret had moved from her mother's house because the room she and her children had occupied was needed for a paying lodger, Thomas Casement. For the next couple of days, nothing untoward happened.

The houses in Frogmore Lane did not have running water and this meant that each day, someone in each household would have to walk to the well, situated about half a mile away, and fill containers with enough water to see them through the day. This chore was usually performed early in the morning and the morning of Wednesday, 26 July was no different.

Ann Ace junior, left her home long before 6.30 a.m. and so did not see Margaret arrive at their mother's house at 6.35 a.m. Margaret had two empty water cans with her, and asked her mother if her sister might like to accompany her to the well. Ann Ace senior told Margaret than her sister had already gone and would be on her way back soon. Margaret bade her mother a cheery, 'Good morning' and left, saying she would probably meet her sister somewhere along the way.

In fact, it was just five minutes later, at 6.40 a.m., that Margaret met her sister in Frogmore Lane. The two sisters exchanged the time of day but Margaret did not want to hold Ann up. The full water cans she was carrying were much heavier than the empty ones Margaret had, and anyway, the sooner the water got back to her mother's house, the sooner the house could start to function for the day. Margaret said farewell to Ann and the sisters parted, Ann to return to her mother's home and Margaret to go on to the well.

It was perhaps a minute later that Ann Ace heard a scream and a shout of, 'Oh Harry, Harry!' Turning back towards her sister, Ann saw, to her horror, that Henry Phillips had leapt upon his wife and was attacking her. Ann threw down the water cans she held, ran the rest of the way to their mother's house as fast as she could and cried out, 'Mother! Run!' adding that Margaret was being attacked just up the lane. Thomas Casement also heard these pleas for aid and ran back up Frogmore Lane with the younger Ann.

The couple had gone a few hundred yards when Casement saw Margaret lying on the ground, her head resting on a low bank of grass. A man he had never seen before was kneeling on top of her and even as Casement ran forward, the man made two motions with his right arm as he drew something across the upper part of Margaret's body. The man, seeing Casement and Ann for the first time, jumped to his feet and, after climbing over a low wall, started to run off across a field. Casement followed and, as he did so, heard the man shout back, 'Is the bugger dead?'

Casement chased the man for 100yds or so. Seeing that he was being pursued, and that Casement was gaining on him, the man stopped, turned around and put his hand into his pocket as if to take out a weapon. He shouted, 'If you come any further, I'll blow your bloody brains out!' Thinking that he might well have a gun in his jacket, Casement decided it would be wiser to abandon the chase and return to help Margaret.

Returning to Frogmore Lane, Casement found Ann trying to help her sister. At about the same time, the girls' mother also arrived and Casement left the two women ministering to Margaret while he ran for the doctor. The nearest medical practitioner was Dr Mole, who in turn called out one of his colleagues, Dr Albert Victor Morton from Reynoldston. It was 8 a.m. by the time both doctors arrived at Frogmore Lane. They found Margaret still lying on her left side on the bridge, where she had fallen, her head towards the middle of the road. Gently, the injured woman was lifted and taken to her mother's house where the wound was dressed. Margaret was later taken by ambulance to Swansea Hospital, where she arrived at 10.45 a.m. Despite prompt attention from Dr Peter Chalmers, the house surgeon, Margaret died at 4.07 p.m. that same day.

In the meantime, Sergeant Davies had heard about the attack and arrived at the scene at 7.15 a.m. He spoke to Casement who told him of the encounter with the man he did not recognise, but whom Ann Ace junior immediately identified as Margaret's husband, Henry Phillips.

The first port of call for Sergeant Davies was Fitter's Cottage: Phillips' home at Burry. On his arrival, the door was closed, and when Davies received no answer to his knocking, he tried the handle and found the door unlocked. There was no one in the house, but there was, on a table just inside the door, an empty razor case.

Further inquiries revealed that at 8.30 a.m., Phillips had gone to the Welcome to Town Inn at Llangennith where the landlord, John Thomas, had served him with a pint of beer. After drinking this down, Phillips, who had been a regular customer at the inn for some twenty years, asked for a bottle

The area where the murder of Margaret Philips took place. Places mentioned in the narrative are underlined.

of beer. This too was consumed and Phillips then asked for four more bottles, which he said he would take with him. Before he left, though, Phillips told Thomas that he wanted to speak to him and asked him to come outside. Thomas did so, and once they were alone outside the inn, Phillips said, 'I have done it.' Thomas had no idea what his friend was referring to and asked him what he meant. To this Phillips replied, 'I have killed my wife.' Not believing this for one moment, Thomas told Phillips not to be so foolish, until he showed him a cut on his hand and bloodstains on his trousers. Thomas took a step towards Phillips who cried, 'Stand back! I have got the thing I did it with in my pocket…I am sorry for the children and now I am going to finish myself.' So saying, Phillips took his bottles of beer and walked off towards the Rhossili Downs.

After speaking to Thomas, and knowing now in which direction Phillips had run, Sergeant Davies and one of his colleagues, PC Gannon, began to search the fields around Llangennith. Hours later, at 11.15 a.m., Davies noticed a track through a cornfield and, following it, came upon the sleeping form of Henry Phillips, the beer bottles, all empty, scattered around him. Near Phillips' right hand lay an open, bloodstained razor and, fearful that his man might resist, Davies took hold of Phillips' wrists in a strong grip. Phillips leapt to his feet but offered no resistance whatsoever. He merely asked, 'Is my wife dead?'

Davies did not reply, so Phillips added for good measure, 'I said I would do it, and I did.' He was then handcuffed and taken to the King's Head Hotel, also at Llangennith. There, Davies ordered a pony and trap, which he then used to escort his prisoner to Reynoldston police station. On the way, Phillips again asked if Margaret was dead. This time, Sergeant Davies admitted that when he had last seen her she was in a very serious state. Phillips thought for a moment and then remarked, 'I knew it was going to come to this when you served me with that summons last Saturday.'

At 12.30 p.m. on 27 July, Phillips arrived at Reynoldston where he was charged with attempted murder. Soon after 4 p.m., Sergeant Davies was informed that Margaret had died at Swansea, so he brought Phillips up out of the cells and charged him with murder. In answer to the charge, Phillips only said, 'I can't say anything. I did it for the sake of my boys.'

Phillips made his first appearance before the magistrates at Swansea on 27 July, and, after a hearing lasting just a minute or so, was remanded to 2 August. The inquest took place on 28 July, before Mr John Viner Leeder, when a verdict of wilful murder was returned. The following day, Sunday, 29 July, Margaret was buried at Llandewi, after a short service at her mother's home conducted by the Revd Thomas Davies. As the cortège passed the spot where the crime had taken place, the dead woman's sister, Ann Ace, collapsed and had to be supported by her brother.

On 2 August, Phillips made his second visit to the Magistrates' Court, which this time convened at the Penmaen workhouse. The evidence having been heard, the prisoner was sent for trial.

Phillips faced trial at Cardiff on 10 November 1911, before Mr Justice Channell. The case for the Crown was led by Mr Clement Edwards who was assisted by Mr H.O.C. Beasley. Phillips was defended by Mr T.R. Jenkins.

Ann Ace, the dead woman's mother, told of Margaret coming to live with her on 13 July, after Phillips had hit her. This was not the first time he had done so in their thirteen-year marriage but Margaret told her that on this occasion, Phillips had accused her of having had other men to the house while he was out at work. That same day, Margaret had gone to Swansea to take out a summons. Ann also confirmed that there were four children still alive, all boys ranging in age from 3 to 13, and that two other children had died.

Ann went on to explain that her daughter had worked as a cleaner and washer for a local farmer, Andrew Thomas, at Lake Farm, which was in Knelston. Phillips also worked there from time to time. He worked on the land while Margaret worked inside the house. She had been there, on and off, for the past three years.

Ann Ace junior said that after hearing Margaret call for help on the morning of 26 July, she had turned to see Phillips kneeling on top of her sister. Margaret was on the ground and his knee was on her chest. One hand was keeping her down and that was the situation when she ran to her mother's house. By the time she and Casement got back, Ann said she was just in time to see Phillips drawing something across Margaret's throat. She shouted at him and when Phillips turned and saw them coming, he ran off across the field. As Casement hurried after him, Margaret got up from the ground and staggered towards her sister. Ann caught hold of her and held her up until they reached the bridge, where she collapsed, blood streaming from her throat.

After Thomas Casement had given his evidence, the prosecution called Francis George Clement, a 17-year-old farm servant who also worked at Lake Farm for Andrew Thomas. At 6.45 a.m. on 26 July, he was in the old lane which led from Burry to Knelston when he saw Phillips walking towards him, across a field which was in the direction of Frogmore Lane. Clement knew Phillips well and asked him how he was. He replied, 'All right' and after Clement asked Phillips if he had been out doing some hoeing, he replied, 'Go down and tell Andrew that I've cut Maggie's throat.' He then said goodbye and walked off towards his house at Burry. Clement had thought he must have been joking.

Dr Chalmers, who had tended to Margaret at Swansea Hospital, said that when she was admitted, she had collapsed and was suffering from loss of blood. There was an incised wound in her neck, which ran from behind her right ear across the neck to a point 2in beyond the middle line. It was a clean cut and the larynx was severed. The tips of the fingers on Margaret's left hand were also cut, as were the backs of the fingers on her right, both being defence wounds. One finger had actually been severed and was later found near the location of the attack. Margaret had bruises on her right forearm, right thigh and left thigh, which were consistent with someone kneeling roughly upon her. Dr Chalmers also performed the post-mortem and the cause of death, not surprisingly, was shock and loss of blood.

The only defence possible was one of insanity and Phillips stepped into the witness box to say that he was addicted to drink and had no recollection of the attack upon Margaret. He did not remember being in Frogmore Lane on 26 July and knew nothing of the crime until he found himself in a police cell.

Medical evidence was called to support this claim. Dr W.L. Griffiths of Swansea had examined Phillips that very day and he testified that while he was certainly not suffering from any mental disease now, he was certain that judging from Phillips' conduct at the time of the murder, he was not sane.

The trouble was that Phillips had confessed his guilt to both John Thomas, the landlord of the inn at Llangennith, and to Francis Clement, and as such, there could be little doubt that he had been fully aware of what he had done, and what the consequences would be. The jury took just ten minutes to find the prisoner guilty and he was sentenced to death.

An appeal was heard on 25 November, on the grounds that the trial judge had misled the jury on the subject of insanity. It failed, as did a petition for a reprieve bearing some 7,000 signatures.

At 8 a.m. on Thursday, 14 December 1911, Henry Phillips was hanged at Swansea by John Ellis and William Willis as a crowd of a few hundred, one of whom was the condemned man's brother, waited outside the prison.

13

ONE FOR THE POT

Hugh McLaren, 1913

In the years before the First World War, work was hard to come by for the men who spent their days around the docks in Cardiff. Many lived a precarious existence, surviving only by doing odd jobs when the ships arrived. One such man was 22-year-old Spaniard Julian Biros, who, although he had been in Cardiff for two years, didn't have a fixed home and often slept at the Crown Patent Fuel Works, as did others.

Another of those workers was John McGill who lived at 3 Riverside, Merthyr Tydfil, and he too sometimes slept at the Fuel Works when he was in Cardiff. He knew Julian Biros well and also knew yet another dockside labourer, 29-year-old Hugh McLaren.

At some time between 8 p.m. and 9 p.m. on Saturday, 22 March 1913, McGill met McLaren in Bute Road when the latter asked McGill if he had seen Biros. The question, though, was filled with venom, for McLaren asked, 'Do you know that dago? I shall cut him from lug to lug.'

Patrick McGuirk also slept at the Fuel Works on the night of 22 March and he and Biros both rose at 7 a.m. on the morning of 23 March, which happened to be Easter Sunday. The two men did not know each other very well, but nevertheless chose to walk together down to the Roath Dock to watch the SS *Dee* berth in the basin, hoping perhaps that they might be able to pick up some casual work. At 8 a.m., Biros and McGuirk were joined by James Walsh, a marine fireman, and the three soon fell into conversation outside an old railway carriage which the men used as a canteen.

Some twenty minutes after Walsh had joined the group, Hugh McLaren approached from the direction of the Alexandra Dock where the Fuel Works was situated. He greeted the three men with, 'Don't you know this is Easter Sunday boys? We'll make some tea.' At this, McLaren brought out a packet of tea from his pocket. Julian Biros immediately recognised the packet as one that he owned and shouted, 'It's my tea!' and tried to take it from McLaren.

In the brief struggle that followed, McLaren grabbed Biros by the necktie and placed his left hand around the man's throat. Then, without warning, he drew out a dagger with his right hand and plunged it into Biros' side. McLaren then ran off towards the East Docks, wiping blood from the blade as he went.

In addition to McGuirk and Walsh, a third man, Alphonso Burke, a seaman who was on the SS *Dee*, had also witnessed this attack. He saw the argument, watched the two men struggle with each other and saw McLaren strike Biros in the side. Though Burke had observed nothing in McLaren's hand, he saw Biros place his fingers to his side and blood trickle from between those fingers. As McLaren ran off, Biros tried to follow him but had gone no more than a few paces before he collapsed.

Cardiff Docks, where Julian Biros was murdered by Hugh McLaren.

Another view of the docks area.

Alphonso Burke called for help from his shipmates and a group of men now went onto the docks to offer aid. Patrick McGuirk, meanwhile, ran to find a policeman and discovered PC John Lewis on duty near the Pier Head. Meanwhile, another officer, PC John Ashman, had also heard about the incident and was the first to arrive on the scene. By now, the men from the SS *Dee* had placed Biros on a stretcher. Ashman contacted his headquarters and asked them to send more officers and an ambulance.

PC Ashman accompanied Biros in the ambulance and tried to question him on the journey. Biros made no replies to the questions and was unconscious when he was admitted to the hospital. The stricken man was attended to by Dr Joseph Henry Whelan, who noted a single stab wound in the region of Biros' heart. He was still bleeding profusely and was given an immediate blood transfusion. Despite Dr Whelan's ministrations, Julian Biros died from his injury at 2.15 p.m.

Even before Biros passed away, McLaren had been picked up. The police knew that he often lodged at 58 Adam Street and it was to that address that PC Lewis was despatched. McLaren wasn't there but as the constable left, McLaren approached from down the street. He was immediately cautioned and offered no resistance as he was taken into custody. At 10.25 a.m., McLaren was told that he would be taken to the hospital where Biros was being treated and where he would make a dying deposition. McLaren was indeed taken to the hospital, but the deposition was never completed. No sooner had Biros given his name than he collapsed into unconsciousness, from which he never recovered. McLaren was taken back to the police station where he was charged with 'stabbing a Spanish man whose name is unknown.'

The Pier Head. It was here that one of the witnesses, Patrick McGuirk found PC Lewis and told him of the attack upon Biros.

In due course, Biros' identity was established and once he had died, the charge against McLaren was amended to one of wilful murder. In reply, McLaren said, 'I got nothing to say. I could kill a dozen dagos like that – they could not touch me for it.' Later, McLaren claimed he wasn't responsible for Biros' death and it was the hospital treatment that killed him. He exclaimed, 'It was not the knife that done him – it was the chloroform them chaps gave him down there.'

McLaren appeared before the magistrates on 25 March when details of his arrest were given by Detective Chief Inspector William Henry Harries, after which McLaren was remanded until 26 March. The next day, the inquest, before Mr William Lougher Yorath, ruled that Biros had been murdered by McLaren and at the police court, later that afternoon, McLaren was remanded again, this time until 28 March. On that day, all the witnesses gave their evidence and McLaren was sent for trial.

Hugh McLaren appeared at Swansea before Lord Coleridge on 18 July 1913. The prosecution was led by Mr Ivor Bowen who was assisted by Mr Clem Edwards, while the prisoner, who appeared in court scruffy and unkempt, was defended by Mr Ernest Evans.

Patrick McGuirk told the court what he had witnessed on the morning of 23 March. After bringing PC Lewis to the scene, McGuirk had taken the officer to Rickett's lodging house at 58 Adam Street where McLaren was known to stay. McLaren wasn't there but as he and the constable were leaving, James Walsh came to the door to say that the man they wanted was coming down the street. McGuirk heard Lewis caution McLaren and saw him take a knife from his jacket pocket. McGuirk added that he

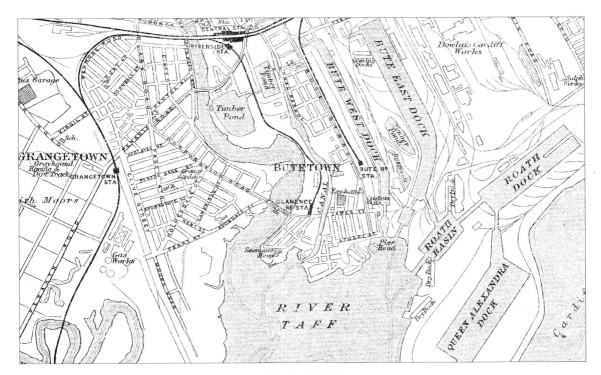

Map of the area where Julian Biros was murdered by Hugh McLaren.

had picked up the packet of tea at the scene of the stabbing and had given this to PC Lewis with the comment, 'This was what the bloody row was about.'

Alphonso Burke, who had witnessed the stabbing from the SS *Dee*, confirmed that he had known neither man before this incident had taken place. At 10.30 a.m. on 25 March, he was taken to the police station to attend an identification parade and, without hesitation, had picked out McLaren from twelve other men.

Inspector Harries stated that at 10.35 a.m. on 23 March he had gone to the hospital with Mr Isaac Samuel, a Justice of the Peace and Mr Edward Hayward, the Clerk to the Justices, in order to take Biros' dying deposition. The procedure had been explained to McLaren and the entire group then went to number one ward, where Biros was lying. An interpreter was also present but Biros only managed to give his name before he became unconscious. An attempt was made to revive him, but to no avail. At 5.35 p.m. Inspector Harries formally charged McLaren with murder.

In addition to treating Biros upon his admission, Dr Whelan had also performed the post-mortem after his patient had died. He reported a 1½in-long wound, which was situated 1in below the left nipple and positioned over the fourth rib. This wound had split the fourth rib and the cartilage and had caused two wounds to the heart. One was superficial, on the left ventricle, but the other was across the septum of the ventricle, laying both ventricles open. The direction of the stab had been upwards and backwards and the direct cause of death was shock and loss of blood.

McLaren's defence contended that the wound he had inflicted had not been the cause of Julian Biros' death, but that the treatment given at the hospital was. After Biros had been stabbed, he had walked after McLaren and some witnesses reported that he took as many as thirty paces, which implied that he could not have been mortally injured. The jury, though, rejected that explanation and returned a verdict that McLaren was guilty of murder.

Hugh McLaren had killed without hesitation, shown calmness at his trial and now, in the condemned cell at Cardiff Prison, showed the same indifference to his fate. He slept well, ate heartily and gave no signs that he was afraid of what was to come. He rose early on the morning of Thursday, 14 August 1913, a beautiful sunny day. At 8 a.m. he was taken to the execution chamber where he was hanged by John Ellis and William Willis.

14

THE GIRL NEXT DOOR

Edgar Lewis Bindon, 1914

Maud Mulholland, an attractive 20-year-old shop assistant, lived at 80 Theobald Road, Canton, in Cardiff. Next door, at no. 82, lived the Bindon family, the youngest member of which was 19-year-old Edgar Lewis Bindon, an insurance agent, who soon found himself falling in love with Maud.

For a time, the two young lovers walked out together but were often quarrelling. Bindon had become violent and on one occasion had threatened Maud's father with a razor. Maud had leapt to his defence and had obtained a nasty cut to her hand in the process. Eventually, partly at her parents' request, and partly because she had become frightened of him, Maud gave up Bindon and in October 1913, started seeing another man, Bernard Campion. Edgar Bindon decided that enough was enough.

At 10.30 p.m. on the night of Tuesday, 4 November, Bindon called at Maud's house. The door was opened by Maud's father, Captain Samuel Mulholland, a master mariner. Bindon told Captain Mulholland that he wished to speak to him and was courteously invited to come into the front room. Only when Bindon sat down did Mulholland notice that he held a revolver in his right hand. Bravely, Mulholland held out his hand and insisted, 'Give me that revolver.' Bindon offered no resistance and handed the weapon over. Captain Mulholland broke open the weapon and discovered, no doubt to his relief, that it was not loaded.

Turning back to Bindon, Samuel Mulholland told him, 'Maud has told me that she doesn't want to keep company with you any more.' Bindon, nevertheless, asked to speak to Maud so Captain Mulholland called her into the room, told her not to be afraid and to tell Bindon how she felt. Maud hesitated for a few moments and then said, 'Edgar, I don't wish to hear any more from you.' Captain Mulholland then escorted his visitor to the front door but as Bindon went back to his own house, he called out, 'You will be sorry for this.'

On Sunday, 9 November, Bernard Campion called at Maud's house at 3 p.m. and stayed for tea. At around 6 p.m. they went out together for a walk. The couple returned to Theobald Road at 10 p.m. and by 10.35 p.m., Campion was bidding his young lady goodnight. Campion had wanted Maud to stay at home but she insisted on walking him to the tram and he finally parted from her at the corner of Church Road.

Randolph Howe, a 15-year-old schoolboy, was in his bedroom at the back of 1 Eton Place when he heard what sounded like a shot at 10.50 p.m. Rushing to his window, Randolph heard a second shot and upon looking out onto Denton Road, saw a woman running down the street, pursued closely by a man who, when he was directly opposite Randolph's window, raised a gun and fired another shot at the woman's back. As the boy watched, the woman reached the corner of the street, staggered against the wall and cried out, 'Oh don't!' The man was now upon her and fired two more shots at close range.

At this time, John Hoskins was in Cowbridge Road. Hoskins had just posted a letter and was returning to his home in Alexandra Road when he heard shots. Turning, he saw a young lady stagger out of the road at the back of Eton Place. She was immediately followed by a man who fired two shots at her. The man then ran directly towards Hoskins who, naturally fearful for his own safety, hurried off towards St John's Crescent in search of a policeman.

Henry John Griffiths also lived in Alexandra Road and he too was in the area of the shooting at the time. Passing down Church Road towards Eton Place, Griffiths heard two loud reports. Curious as to what the sound might be, he walked towards where they had apparently come from and in the darkness heard another report, saw a flash and a woman's body fall to the pavement. Dashing towards the stricken woman, Griffiths now saw her attacker step forward, point at her body and there was another flash as a bullet was fired directly at her still form. Griffiths whistled, hoping the attacker would think he was a policeman, and this subterfuge seemed to work as the man started running away.

Going to where the woman lay, Griffiths found her lying on her back but she groaned and rolled onto her left side as he bent down and tried to assist her to sit up. Another man, Windsor David Thompson, then arrived, helped Griffiths to gently lift the woman and together they carried her to Dr Hesketh Evans' surgery. That gentleman was out so Maud was carried to Dr Cownie's surgery, which was also in Cowbridge Road. The efforts of Thompson and Griffiths proved to be in vain. The young woman was still alive when she reached the surgery, but died within four minutes.

Meanwhile, back at 80 Theobald Road, Maud Mulholland's family were growing somewhat concerned that she hadn't returned home. Maud's sister, Sarah Gertrude Mulholland, said that she

Cowbridge Road, Cardiff. Maud Mulholland's body was brought here after she had been shot. (Relective Images)

would go out and find Maud and walked down Theobald Road without finding any trace of her. Sarah then turned into Cowbridge Road and saw a small crowd of people collected outside Dr Cownie's. Sarah crossed over to the surgery and asked one of the men what was the matter. The man replied, 'Oh, there has been a terrible murder. A young woman from Theobald Road has been shot, and she has died inside.' Terrified at what she would find, Sarah pushed her way into the surgery and there her worst fears were confirmed. There lay her sister, Maud, covered in blood, having already breathed her last.

The man who had shot Maud Mulholland had not run very far. He watched from around a corner as Thompson and Griffiths carried Maud to the surgery and, seeing the first police officer to arrive, PC Patrick Ford, he marched forward and gave himself up. The revolver was handed over without protest and, asked his name, the assailant readily replied, 'Edgar Lewis Bindon'. The prisoner was then escorted to the police station where he was charged with wilful murder.

On the morning of Monday, 10 November, Bindon was brought up before the magistrates, the only witness being PC Ford who stated that he had been on duty in Denton Road at about 10.50 p.m. when he heard shots coming from the direction of St John's Crescent. Going to investigate, Ford arrived in Cowbridge Road about five minutes later and immediately saw Bindon walking towards him from the direction of Earle Place. Bindon greeted him with, 'Arrest me constable, I've shot a girl.' He then handed over a revolver and added, 'I've done it with this.' This evidence having been given, Bindon was then remanded until the next day.

The inquest opened the following morning, 11 November, before Mr William Lougher Yorath, Bindon being represented by Mr Harold Lloyd. Captain Mulholland was the first to give evidence.

Mulholland said that the prisoner had been seeing Maud for between eighteen months and two years but that recently his daughter had called off the relationship and started walking out with Mr Campion, a young man she had first been seeing a couple of years before.

Sarah Mulholland told the court that when Bernard Campion left their house on the Sunday night, Maud had insisted on going to the tram stop with him, despite the protestations of both her mother and Campion himself. Maud had said she would be back in about five minutes but when she had still not returned by 11 p.m., her mother became worried and so Sarah went out to look for her.

Maud's insistence that she go out with Campion was held to be highly significant, for a letter was now produced in court and Sarah confirmed that it was in her sister's hand. The letter began:

Dear Edgar,
I am very sorry, but I am afraid I cannot meet you, as you know, if I go out, mother will want to know where I am going, and then she will not let me go alone.
   I don't think I shall be going out tonight unless I make an excuse, and leave B down the street a little way, and then that won't be until about half past ten. Then, kiddie, if you wish to say goodbye to me, it will be by St John's Church, Canton, ten thirty. Hope this will suit you. Hope to see you there. St John's Church, 10.30. I remain yours as always,
Maud

This letter, though undated, had been found in Bindon's possession and fitted with the known facts. It appeared that Maud had agreed to meet Bindon, and had used the excuse of seeing Campion to his tram in order to get out of the house.

St John's Church, where Edgar Bindon met Maud Mulholland before shooting her. (Reflective Images)

Bernard Campion told the court that he had first met Maud in February 1912, and they had started walking out together. In July 1912, they parted but he had started seeing her again some two weeks before her death. The Sunday of Maud's death was the first time he had visited her home.

After the various witnesses to the shooting itself had given their evidence, Dr J.F. Cownie, who had performed the post-mortem, described six bullet wounds in Maud's body, including one over the heart, a second over the lower ribs on the right side, a third in the ribs on the left and a fourth to the scalp. Two of the wounds were exit wounds, meaning that she had been shot a total of four times, the fatal wound being the one close to the heart.

The jury deliberated for a very short time before returning the expected verdict of wilful murder against Bindon, who was then sent for trial on the coroner's warrant. That same morning he was back before the magistrates when another remand was granted, this time for eight days.

On 19 November, Bindon was again in court when he appeared before the stipendiary magistrate, Mr H.C. Bailey. Mr Harold Lloyd again represented the prisoner while the case for the Director of Public Prosecutions was detailed by Mr D.S. Brown.

Other letters found in Bindon's possession when he was arrested were now read out in court. One of these, addressed to his mother and apparently written on the day of the shooting, read in part, 'I have got a seven chambered revolver fully loaded in my pocket, so tonight I will end everything. I will see Maud at 10.30, and that will be the last goodbye she will ever wish anyone.' The other letters cast doubts on Maud's morals but Dr Cownie had already confirmed that when Maud died, she had been virgo intacta.

Further police evidence was given by Superintendent William Burke, who had interviewed Bindon at the police station. The revolver was checked and it was seen to contain six empty cartridge cases and one live cartridge, and as Burke examined the weapon, Bindon handed over four sealed envelopes which he asked be given to his mother. In addition, the prosecution called PC Miles who had had charge of Bindon in the cells. At one stage Bindon had said to him, 'It's all right. I have had my revenge and will die with a good heart.'

The matter of the weapon used to shoot Maud was now cleared up. After the incident of 4 November, when Maud's father had taken a revolver from Bindon, he had needed to purchase another. Robert Bevan, a gun dealer, stated that Bindon had come into his shop the very next day, 5 November, and picked out a seven-chambered revolver. In the view of the magistrate, this was more than enough to send Bindon to face his trial at the next assizes.

The trial of Edgar Bindon took place at Cardiff on 6 March 1914, before Mr Justice Rowlatt. The case for the prosecution was led by Mr W. Llewellyn Williams MP, who was assisted by Mr Wilfred Lewis. Bindon was defended by Mr Ivor Bowen and Mr Hugh Jones.

The only hope for the defence was to show that Bindon was insane at the time of the shooting. After the prosecution case had been heard, Mr Bowen called the prisoner's elder brother, James Harry Bindon. He stated that for some time before the shooting, Bindon had suffered from sleeplessness and irritability and had only eaten sparingly. Their father had died some years before from some sort of brain trouble and two other members of the family had been confined in lunatic asylums.

Dr Brierley said that he had treated Bindon for pleurisy in March 1913 and subsequently for depression. At that time, the prisoner's mind was certainly abnormal and having read the letters found on Bindon, he believed that his actions were those of someone with an unsound mind.

To counter this testimony, the prosecution called Dr E.G.G. Cook, the medical officer of Cardiff Prison, who said he had found no signs of insanity in Bindon. This was confirmed by Dr Martin Craig, an expert from London, who described Bindon as perfectly rational.

It took the jury an hour to return their verdict and when it came it was that Bindon was guilty but a strong recommendation to mercy was added.

By 12 March, Mr Lloyd, Bindon's solicitor, announced that it had been decided not to enter an appeal but to draw up a petition for a reprieve instead. The petition became available the next day and quickly collected over 1,000 signatures. Over 27,000 names had been added by the time that petition was handed in but on 23 March, the Home Office announced that no grounds for interfering with the sentence had been found.

On 24 March, Bindon was said to be in a state of virtual collapse. At 8 a.m. the next morning, Wednesday, 25 March 1914, Bindon was hanged at Cardiff by John Ellis and William Willis, as a crowd of around 200 gathered outside the gates.

15

A CAT AND DOG LIFE

Daniel Sullivan, 1916

In 1909, 31-year-old Daniel Sullivan, a labourer, married Catherine Colbert, a widow with two young children, 6-year-old Frederick John and Bridget Ann, who was just 2. Almost from the first day, Sullivan was cruel towards his new wife and if he wasn't actually beating her, he was abusing her verbally. Despite this, two more children were born to the union and in 1913, the expanded family moved into 20 Cwmcanol Street, Dowlais, Merthyr Tydfil.

Hannah Grant was Catherine Sullivan's sister and lived opposite at 5 Cwmcanol Street. The two women were quite close and Hannah grew to be fully aware of the problems Catherine was enduring. More than once Hannah advised her sister to leave but for one reason or another, Catherine stayed where she was.

At 8 a.m. on Saturday, 8 July 1916, Hannah Grant saw Catherine cleaning the front windows of no. 20. The rest of that day seemed to pass without incident, largely due to the fact that Sullivan was out of the house. Catherine stayed at home all day, with her four children, the eldest, Frederick, who was by now 13, announcing at 7.30 p.m. that he was going out to see some of his friends.

Frederick returned to his home at 9.30 p.m. and found, to his horror, that not only was his stepfather at home but that he was busy kicking Catherine who lay on the floor near the door which linked the front and back rooms. Frederick wasted no time in running across the road to fetch his aunt, Hannah Grant.

Unfortunately, Hannah was out at the time, so Frederick ran to Pond Street, hoping to enlist the help of Mrs Woods, a family friend, but she was asleep and Frederick was unable to rouse her. Seeing little other alternative available to him, Frederick returned home to find that Sullivan was still kicking Catherine as hard as he could. Frederick called for him to stop and then, when Sullivan threatened him, he ran out again and headed for the police station.

It was not long before Sergeant Thomas Davies arrived at the house. Catherine still lay on the floor between the two rooms. She was wearing nothing but a man's flannel shirt and was bleeding from a number of wounds. Sergeant Davies summoned two neighbours: Mrs Mary Ann Ryan of no. 4 and Mrs Collins, who helped him carry the unconscious woman to bed. Throughout this time Sullivan remained in the kitchen, and when cautioned by Sergeant Davies replied, 'My wife is always drunk.' The sergeant noted that Sullivan himself was rather the worse for drink, before leaving the house to fetch the doctor. In the meantime, Inspector John Granville Lamb had arrived on the scene.

By 10 p.m., Hannah Grant had returned home and, hearing what had happened, went over to no. 20. Catherine remained in bed that night and, despite the ministrations of Dr Cecil Francis Williams, died from her injuries at around 3 a.m. on Sunday, 9 July. Sullivan, who had previously been charged with inflicting grievous bodily harm, now found himself facing a charge of murder.

Cwmcanol Street, where Daniel Sullivan murdered his wife, Catherine.

Sullivan made his first appearance before the magistrates on 11 July, being represented by Mr J.W. Lewis. The hearing was very brief and after details of the arrest had been given, Sullivan was remanded to 14 July. On that date, all the witnesses having been heard, Sullivan was sent for trial. Catherine Sullivan was buried that same day.

Daniel Sullivan's trial took place at Swansea on 22 July, before Mr Justice Ridley. The case for the prosecution was put by Mr J.A. Lovat Fraser and Sullivan was defended by Mr St John Francis Williams.

Hannah Grant told the court of the marital troubles Catherine had endured, claiming that although Sullivan was especially cruel to her when he was drunk, he had beaten her when he was sober too. According to Hannah, Catherine was not a heavy drinker and appeared to be under the influence when she had had very little alcohol. After going over to no. 20 and sitting by her sister's bedside, Hannah heard Catherine call 'Dan' twice but she was only semi-conscious at the time and never came round properly before she died.

Bridget Colbert, who was by now 9 years old, said that after Catherine had had her tea on 8 July, she had gone to bed, taking the baby and the other child with her. Bridget was in the kitchen when Sullivan came home and demanded to know where Catherine was. Bridget told him that her mother was in bed to which Sullivan remarked, 'There will be a corpse leaving this room tonight.'

Sullivan stormed into the bedroom and struck Catherine in the face with his fist. He then demanded that she get up and make his supper, dragged her out of bed and began kicking her. The kicking continued until Catherine was forced through the doorway, and it was then that Bridget ran from the house to find her brother, Frederick. Luckily, as she went to the front door, Frederick opened it on his way in. After her brother had gone for help, Bridget ran off crying, looking for her Aunt Hannah, but couldn't find her.

The next witness was Mary Ann Ryan, the neighbour from 4 Cwmcanol Street. She reported that she had been called to the house by Sergeant Davies at around 9.30 p.m. Catherine was lying on the floor and there were lots of bloodstains about the various rooms. Sullivan was sitting in a corner of the room with the baby in his arms.

Mary also stated that she had been in Catherine's house earlier that day, at 4.30 p.m., when Sullivan came home from work. He was sober at the time and handed Catherine £1 and asked her to go out and get it changed. She was out for ten minutes before she returned and handed the money over. Sullivan then turned to Mary and handed her a half-sovereign to pay for some furniture he had purchased from her earlier in the week. They both seemed to be happy enough at the time. Finally, Mary Ryan said that she had often seen Catherine drunk.

Sergeant Thomas Davies told of his visit to Cwmcanol Street on the night of 8 July, and what he had found upon entering no. 20. The sergeant confirmed that he had often visited the house before, usually to do with domestic disputes, but added that both Sullivan and Catherine had been in trouble for being drunk.

At 11 p.m. on 8 July, another police sergeant, James Bevan, had also called at 20 Cwmcanol Street. Sullivan was in an outhouse at the back and it was there that Bevan cautioned him. Sullivan was most abusive and had to be forcibly removed. Bevan needed help to get his man to the police station, but once there, he was charged with causing grievous bodily harm. At 3.35 a.m. the next morning, Sergeant Bevan heard that Catherine was dead, took possession of Catherine and Sullivan's clothes for scientific examination and, at 7.45 a.m., charged Sullivan with murder.

Inspector Lamb said that when he arrived at the house, at around 9.45 p.m., Catherine was unconscious and her face was covered in blood and coal dust. The downstairs rooms were paved in stone and there were many splashes of blood on these and congealed pools between the paving stones. Lamb confirmed that both husband and wife had been in court for drunkenness.

The final witness was Dr Williams, who, in addition to attending to Catherine, had later performed the post-mortem, when he was assisted by Dr Brennan and Dr Lewis. He found a scalp wound 1½in long at the back of the head, which extended down to the bone. Over the right eyebrow was another wound, ¾in long. He saw many bruises, including two on the forehead, one near the left ear, others on the left cheek and some on the chin, left shoulder, forearm and hand. The right hip was covered in bruises and abrasions, as was the right thigh. A boot could have caused all of these injuries, and the cause of death was shock and loss of blood. A great deal of violence had been used.

In his summing up, Mr Justice Ridley told the court that this was 'one of the most brutal assaults I have ever heard proved in a court of justice', and added that drink was no excuse. The jury took those words to heart and, after an absence of fifty minutes, ruled that Sullivan was guilty as charged. Asked if he had anything to say, Sullivan replied, 'Can I make an appeal?'

An appeal was entered and a petition for a reprieve was also drawn up. The appeal itself was heard on 22 August before the Lord Chief Justice, Lord Isaacs, and Justices Bray and Darling. There were four main grounds: that there had been no malice aforethought; that the verdict was against the weight of evidence; that Sullivan had been too intoxicated to be responsible for his actions; and finally, that Bridget had misheard Sullivan when he was supposed to have made his statement about a corpse leaving the room that night. All this led the defence to ask that a verdict of manslaughter be substituted.

In giving the court's verdict as to why the appeal would be dismissed, Lord Isaacs said that Bridget had been sure of her evidence and added that the murder was as brutal as could possibly be conceived. The only real question was whether Sullivan could appreciate what he was doing at the time, and his statement to Bridget showed that he did.

On the morning of Wednesday, 6 September 1916, Daniel Sullivan was hanged at Swansea by John Ellis and George Brown, Ellis later reporting that Sullivan had gone to the gallows in sheer terror.

16

FIENDISH FURY

Alex Bakerlis, 1917

The city of Cardiff has always had strong seafaring connections and sailors of many nationalities have visited the port and stayed in lodging houses. In the dark years of the First World War, one such house was situated in Bute Road, Cardiff, and was run by George Fortt.

It was around summer 1914 that Fortt admitted a new guest, a Greek sailor named Alex Bakerlis, who was just 22 years old. From the very beginning, Bakerlis appeared to be rather enamoured of one of Fortt's daughters, Winifred Ellen, who, in 1914, was aged 17. The two became very friendly but what should have been a pleasant relationship was marred by the fact that Bakerlis was insanely jealous and objected when Winifred even spoke to another man. This situation was not made easier as Bakerlis was often away for long periods of time and became increasingly jealous of the other lodgers in the house, imagining Winifred might be involved with them.

George Fortt had two other daughters, Olga and Marion, and in September 1916, Olga went to her father and reported that Bakerlis had shown Marion a gun and told her that it was his intention to kill Nell, the name by which Winifred was known. Upon hearing this, George took the story to the police and on 22 September, PC Porter interviewed Bakerlis, took a revolver from him and charged him with being an alien in possession of a loaded firearm. For that offence, Bakerlis was fined £10.

A couple of days after PC Porter had arrested Bakerlis, George Fortt saw his troublesome lodger in the shipping office at the docks and asked him why he had behaved in such a manner when he and his family had shown him nothing but kindness. Bakerlis replied that he had intended no harm and would not have used the weapon. Fortt was far from satisfied and told Bakerlis that he thought it would be better if he did not return to the house. As a result, Bakerlis took fresh lodgings at a house in Wharf Street, owned by George Antonio. Meanwhile, Winifred, realising that her father did not want her to have anything more to do with Bakerlis, gave the ring that he had given her to a friend, Rhoda Heard, for safe keeping. She did, however, keep some letters, which Bakerlis had written to her, in a box in her bedroom.

On Monday, 25 December, Winifred and Rhoda went to a Christmas party. It was 9.30 p.m. and already dark by the time the two young ladies started to make their way back to Winifred's father's lodging house. As they crossed the canal bridge on Bute Street, Bakerlis appeared and asked Winifred for the return of his letters and the ring. Winifred did not have the letters on her, but the ring was still being worn by Rhoda. At Winifred's request, Rhoda removed the ring and handed it to her, and she in turn handed it over to Bakerlis.

Once again Bakerlis asked for the return of the letters and Winifred said she would go home to fetch them. She started to walk towards the lodging house, with Bakerlis following a few steps behind.

They had only gone a few feet when Bakerlis suddenly jumped forward and struck out at Winifred. The assailant had something in his hand, and at first Rhoda thought it was a stick but now, as a light caught the blade, she saw to her horror that Bakerlis was holding a knife which he repeatedly plunged into Winifred's helpless form. Bravely, Rhoda grabbed at Bakerlis' coat and tried to pull him from her friend, but he was far too strong for her.

Seeing that there was little she could do to stop Bakerlis, Rhoda ran to Winifred's house for help. On the way she saw a policeman, PC Arthur Moss, and as Bakerlis finally stopped his murderous assault and made to escape, Rhoda shouted, 'Stop him! He's got a knife in his hand. He has killed a woman.' PC Moss saw the fleeing figure, ran after him, and stopped Bakerlis within a few yards. Bakerlis immediately admitted, 'I have killed Nellie' and Moss noticed that Bakerlis had a large, bloodstained carving knife gripped tightly in his right hand. The knife was confiscated; Bakerlis was escorted to the Bute Street police station and there told that he would be charged with cutting and wounding. Later that same night, the charge was amended to one of attempted murder.

On 27 December, Alex Bakerlis made his first appearance before the stipendiary magistrate on a charge of attempted murder. Only the briefest details of the arrest were given before it was stated that Winifred Fortt was still in hospital, but was improving slowly. Bakerlis was remanded until 29 December but by the time he made his second appearance, the charge had once more been changed. At 8 p.m. on Thursday, 28 December, Winifred had succumbed to her injuries and died. Bakerlis now found himself facing a charge of wilful murder and he was consequently remanded again, this time until 2 January 1917. One further remand followed and it was not until 10 January that the evidence

A view of the area where Winifred Fortt was attacked. (Reflective Images)

was finally detailed by Mr George David for the Director of Public Prosecutions, after which Bakerlis was duly sent for trial.

Bakerlis' trial took place on 6 March at Cardiff, before Mr Justice Bailhache. Mr Marlay Samson defended the prisoner, while the Crown's case was led by Mr W. Llewellyn Williams MP, who was assisted by Mr J.A. Lovat-Fraser.

Rhoda Heard told the court what she had witnessed on the night of 25 December and confirmed that she had known that the ring she had worn for two months had been given to Winifred by Bakerlis. There were other witnesses to the actual attack and they were now called one by one by Mr Williams.

Jane Redquist had been walking down Bute Street and was opposite St Mary's Church when she heard someone screaming, 'Oh Alex, Alex, don't, don't!' She turned and saw, opposite the school, Bakerlis kneeling beside a figure, which he stabbed twice with a long knife. Jane had her baby with her at the time, which she handed to a passing soldier before running to the police station to summon help.

Another witness had been William Gale who said that he saw a man stabbing a woman close to the church at about 9.30 p.m. He heard the woman scream and went over to see what help he could give. Bakerlis ran away at that moment, heading towards the police station, and Gale saw him being intercepted by PC Moss.

The next witness was Dr Razzak, the house surgeon at the King Edward VII Hospital. He testified that Winifred Fortt was conscious when she was admitted to the hospital. Her clothing was soaked in blood and he noted eight stab wounds of varying size on her back, another at the top of her shoulder, one on her left thumb, one on the right arm and other superficial cuts to the right hand.

Dr Razzak, continuing his evidence, said that on 27 December Winifred had developed signs of septic poisoning and that this was the direct cause of her death. He added that the wounds had, in his opinion, been inflicted with a fiendish fury.

After PC Moss had given his evidence, the prosecution called George Fortt, the dead girl's father. He told the court of the troubles his daughter had had with Bakerlis and of the incident with the gun reported to him by his other daughter, Olga. Turning to the night of the attack upon Winifred, Fortt said that Winifred and Rhoda Heard had been in his house until 8 p.m. when they went out to a party.

The King Edward VII Hospital, where Winifred Fortt died.

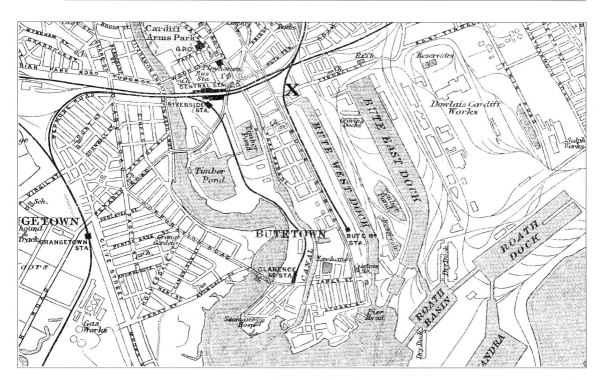

The spot – marked with a cross – where Alex Bakerlis stabbed Winifred Fortt.

Just after 9.30 p.m., Rhoda returned alone. She was hysterical and screaming. Fortt had then gone out and found his daughter lying on the pavement. Fortt gently picked his daughter up and carried her back home where he arranged for an ambulance to be called.

Detective Chief Inspector William Henry Harries said that he had seen Bakerlis in the Central police station at 9 p.m. on 28 December. He informed the prisoner that Winifred Fortt had died from her injuries and that he would now be charged with murder. Bakerlis replied, 'I do not understand at all.' The charge was repeated to Bakerlis, through an interpreter, and he said, 'I had no intention to kill her. I don't know where I got the knife from. First of all I don't know what I was doing because I was paralytic drunk.'

In reference to the knife used to stab Winifred, the prosecution then called George Antonio, the owner of the house Bakerlis had moved to. Mr Antonio said that the knife produced in court belonged to him, showing that Bakerlis had deliberately taken it with him when he left Wharf Street on the night of 25 December.

Two final police witnesses were Sergeant John Harries and Detective Sergeant Pugsley. Sergeant Harries stated that when Bakerlis was first brought to Bute Street police station, he was perfectly sober and not 'paralytic drunk' as he had claimed. Sergeant Pugsley reported that he had searched the prisoner and his room. Among his belongings were a number of letters of an affectionate nature, which the dead girl had written to Bakerlis.

The final witness was Dr Davies, the prison surgeon at Cardiff who said that he had examined Bakerlis a number of times. During their talks, Bakerlis had expressed remorse for killing 'Nellie' but added that he felt justified in doing so.

Under cross-examination, Dr Davies confirmed that disappointment in love was one of the primary causes of insanity and that a person of emotional temperament, brooding over such a disappointment, could have his reason overthrown. The doctor added that even in such a state, a man would still know right from wrong.

The jury took just twelve minutes to decide that Bakerlis was guilty of murder, and he showed no emotion as Mr Justice Bailhache sentenced him to death. An appeal was entered and heard on 26 March by the Lord Chief Justice, Lord Isaacs, and Justices Ridley and Atkin. The grounds of the appeal were that on the day of the attack, Bakerlis had been drinking heavily and the defence could now produce witnesses to this effect. It was also claimed, somewhat obtusely, that if Bakerlis had intended to commit murder, he could have used his own knife and had no need to take one from his lodgings. Lord Isaacs, in giving the court's judgement, said that there was no point in calling further witnesses and that Bakerlis' guilt had been correctly decided by the court. Consequently, the appeal would be dismissed.

In the condemned cell, Bakerlis was attended by a Greek priest, who walked with Bakerlis on his final journey to the execution chamber at Cardiff Prison. It was the morning of Tuesday, 10 April 1917 and snow fell heavily. Bakerlis walked firmly to the scaffold, where he was supported by two warders as John Ellis and Edward Taylor finished the pinioning process. Despite the inclement weather, a sizeable crowd gathered outside the prison at the fateful hour.

17

THE GRAMOPHONE

Thomas Caler, 1920

In 1915, Gladys May Dibble, a native of Caerphilly, married an Egyptian named Ahmed Ibrahim. Soon after the ceremony, Gladys and her new husband moved to 52 Christina Street, Cardiff, and there they opened a refreshment house, largely frequented by Arabs. By all accounts, the relationship between Ahmed and Gladys, who was then just 18 years old, was a most happy one and two children were soon produced. In 1916, May Ibrahim was born and in the early summer of 1919, Ahmed and Gladys were blessed with another daughter, Aysha Emily Ibrahim.

It transpired that the refreshment business was most popular. So successful did Ahmed become that he and his wife decided that they would move from Cardiff and set up a similar establishment in London. It was for this reason that on Friday, 12 December 1919, Ahmed Ibrahim travelled down to London to look for suitable premises. His doting wife, now 22, and his two young daughters were left behind at Christina Street, Ahmed having told them that he would be back on the Saturday night.

At 10 p.m. on Saturday, 13 December, Gladys Ibrahim was seen at her front door by a neighbour, Alice Ali. Gladys told Alice that she was expecting her husband back at any moment, and was looking out for him, though she had no idea what time the train might arrive. Alice said she had a railway timetable, went to her home to get it and then went inside no. 52 where she saw little Aysha lying in her pram in the kitchen, May having already been put to bed upstairs. Alice Ali stayed for just a few minutes before returning home.

Around noon on Sunday, 14 December, another neighbour, also named Ali, was disturbed by the sounds of a child crying in no. 52. Edie Ali was the wife of Hossan Ali, who kept a boarding house at 264 Bute Street, and was a close friend of Gladys and often called at the house in Christina Street.

At 12.15 p.m., Edie knocked on Gladys' front door but found that the only sound from within was the eldest child, May, crying. Trying the front door, Edie found that it was unlocked so, calling out for Gladys, she walked down the small passageway and into the middle room.

Gladys Ibrahim lay on her back with her head towards the fireplace, her clothes pushed up above her knees. Beside her lay the body of her youngest daughter, Aysha, and both she and Gladys bore terrible wounds to their throats. Edie dashed to fetch Alice Ali who in turn alerted other neighbours. One of those neighbours, Ahmed Said, who ran a butcher's shop in Christina Street, was the first to venture upstairs where he found the other daughter, May, crying loudly. The room she was in was locked though, and Ahmed thought it better to wait for the police to arrive and take charge.

A number of police officers were soon on the scene, including Acting Inspector Sidney Adams, PC Jesse Hayes and Inspector William King. Inspector Adams made a careful examination of the room where the two bodies lay. By now, one of the neighbours had thrown a shawl over the lower half of

Gladys' body but Adams saw that there was a good deal of blood between Gladys' legs. On the table lay signs of a meal having been taken quite recently. There were two cups, which had contained tea, one half full and the other almost drained.

Inspector King searched the downstairs front room of the house and found a large gramophone horn. Questioning some of the neighbours who knew the house quite well, King discovered that there had been a gramophone there. It appeared that the killer had taken this, but left the horn behind.

Meanwhile, PC Hayes had gone upstairs, where there were four bedrooms, only one of which was locked. The remaining three were unfurnished and when he forced the single locked door, he and Ahmed Said found May, still crying. Said wrapped the child in a blanket and handed her to his wife who had followed him upstairs. The girl was taken downstairs while PC Hayes examined the bedroom. Drawers had been thrown open and the contents of a suitcase scattered about the room. Yet if robbery had been the killer's prime motive, he had certainly missed some cash, for in plain view on the mantelpiece Hayes found two £1 notes and 5s in silver. It looked, though, that an attempt had also been made to kill May as the gas bracket had been left turned on and the room smelled strongly of gas.

By 1 p.m., Dr James Joseph Buist had arrived and he confirmed that both Gladys and Aysha were dead. He noted that there was a single wound on Gladys' throat. Across her left arm, and off to the side lay Aysha, also with a single deep cut to the throat, which stretched from ear to ear. Gladys' legs had been stretched wide apart and her clothing pushed up above her knees. The garments over her chest were torn and there were three superficial cuts on her chest. There were obvious signs that Gladys had been raped. The doctor's initial examination put the time of death at around 1 a.m. Dr Buist was, though, able to give the police one other valuable piece of information. Though the cuts to the throats of both victims were quite clean, they did show signs that the weapon used to inflict them had a rather jagged edge.

PC Hayes' search of the bedroom had revealed one other clue. Among the items scattered around the floor was a small suitcase, the contents of which were disarranged. When this case was examined, a number of letters were found inside addressed to one Thomas Caler, and there was also an open and empty razor case. Enquiries were made, which revealed that Caler was known in the area, and worked as a fireman on the SS *Fountains Abbey*, which was at present tied up in Cardiff Docks. As a matter of routine, Detective Inspector Thomas Hodges paid a visit to the ship to interview Caler.

Thomas Caler, a native of Zanzibar, explained that he had been in Cardiff on the night of Saturday, 13 December, but had returned to his ship at 10 p.m. Asked if he had a razor, Caler had no hesitation in showing Inspector Hodges the one he normally used for shaving. Hodges could not fail to notice that the blade had a rather jagged edge and that the inside of the handle bore stains that looked like blood. Finally, Inspector Hodges spoke to one of Caler's shipmates, Said Mohamed, who said that he had seen Caler going ashore at 3 p.m. on 13 December. He added that Caler did not return until 2 a.m. on the 14th, four hours after Caler had stated. Further, when Caler had finally come back on board, he had been carrying a gramophone and some broken records wrapped up in a wet coat. These items were now in Said's cabin and when Inspector Hodges examined them he saw that the horn from the gramophone was missing. On the strength of that evidence, Caler was cautioned and taken back to shore for interview. Caler was charged with murder by Inspector Hodges that same evening.

At 2.30 a.m. on Monday, 15 December, Ahmed Ibrahim arrived back in Cardiff only to be met at the railway station and told of the terrible tragedy. He was then taken directly to the mortuary to view the

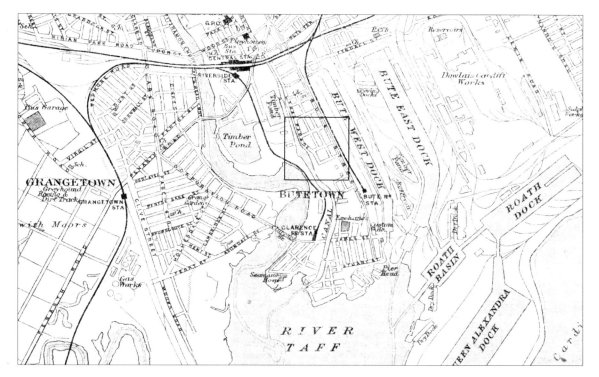

Christina Street (marked with a box) where Thomas Caler murdered two people.

bodies, after which he was spoken to by the police. Ahmed confirmed that he did know Thomas Caler. The man had been a fairly regular customer at his refreshment house over the past five months or so.

It was also on 15 December that Caler made his first appearance at the police court when, after evidence of arrest had been given, the proceedings were adjourned until 23 December. The next day, 16 December, the inquest opened before Mr William Lougher Yorath.

After Alice Ali had given her evidence of seeing Gladys and Aysha alive and well on the Saturday night, and being one of those neighbours who had entered the house on Sunday and saw the bodies, Ahmed Ibrahim stepped up to give evidence. Ahmed made an immediate dash for Caler and had to be restrained. Nevertheless, he was then able to take the stand and explain that before he had left for London, he had given his wife a canvas bag containing a £10 note and a wallet which held twenty £1 notes. He was also able to confirm that there was £2 5s on the mantelpiece.

After the medical and police evidence had been given, Caler was asked if he had anything to say. He made several totally unintelligible remarks before becoming very excited and bringing his hands down violently on the brass rail of the dock. He then shouted, 'This woman and child have been killed, but I know nothing.' The jury then retired and had no trouble in returning a verdict of wilful murder against Caler who was committed for trial on the coroner's warrant. On 23 December, all the evidence was heard again in the police court, and a similar verdict was reached.

Thomas Caler stood in the dock at Cardiff on 15 March 1920. The judge during the two-day hearing was Mr Justice Salter. Caler was defended by Mr T.W. Langman while the prosecution case was led by Mr Marlay Samson, who was assisted by Mr H.O.C. Beasley.

An important witness for the prosecution was Ahmed Fellah who lived at 183 Bute Street. He claimed that at 8 p.m. on 13 December, he had seen Caler leaving 52 Christina Street, which ran parallel to Bute Street, to the west. Later that same night, at 11 p.m., Fellah saw Caler again, this time at a coffee house at 15 Maria Street, a thoroughfare which lay at right angles to the top of Christina Street. The two men stayed at Maria Street for perhaps ten minutes before leaving together. They separated at the junction of Maria Street and Christina Street and the last time Fellah saw Caler, he was walking down Christina Street, towards no. 52, at around 11.15 p.m.

Pridu Rahn went on duty as a nightwatchman on the SS *Fountains Abbey* on 13 December and he testified that it was 2 a.m. when he rowed out to the shore to pick up Caler. The prisoner was carrying a gramophone and some records wrapped up in a coat and he either dropped or threw these into the water. Rahn retrieved them and noticed that the gramophone did not have a horn.

At 12.40 a.m. on 13 December, James Mandrell, who had been serving as a special constable on the docks, saw a coloured man trying to hail the *Fountains Abbey*. The man, who was holding a parcel, shouted, 'Fountains Abbey Ahoy!' and when he saw Mandrell, appeared anxious to avoid being seen as he turned his face away. Mandrell later saw a boat come alongside the quay and pick the man up.

Attempts were now made to link the gramophone found on the ship with the one missing from the Ibrahim household. To begin with, the instrument was identified by Helena Jervis, who worked for a gramophone dealer in the Morgan Arcade. She said that on 15 August she had sold the gramophone to Mr Ibrahim.

Inspector Hodges testified that he had taken the horn from Christina Street and tried to marry it to the gramophone found on board the SS *Fountains Abbey*. The two fitted precisely and the various records found had been identified as the property of Mr Ibrahim.

Throughout, Caler had insisted that the gramophone found on the ship belonged to him. It was true that he had once owned just such an instrument but the prosecution now produced Mohamed Ali who also lived in the boarding house at 264 Bute Street. He testified that the gramophone Caler had once owned had been sold to him on 27 October 1919, and produced a receipt to that effect. Caler's mark on that receipt had been witnessed by two people.

Medical evidence was given by Dr Buist who confirmed that Gladys Ibrahim had been raped after death and also that the razor found in Caler's possession was exactly the type of weapon he would expect to have caused the injuries he had seen.

When Caler gave evidence on his own behalf, he denied having even passed through Christina Street on the night Gladys Ibrahim and her daughter met their deaths. He had spent much of the evening in a public house before going on to a coffee-house in Maria Street. The gramophone and records were his own and he had stored them in the railway cloakroom from where he retrieved them before returning to his ship. He reached the docks at about 11.30 p.m. though it took him some considerable time to attract the attention of the nightwatchman on the ship. At one stage, he had even thrown the records down in frustration at being kept waiting for so long, and this was why they had been broken. Finally, he had only heard of the murder much later, when three of his shipmates boarded and spoke of an Egyptian having murdered his wife and child. In short, Caler was suggesting that Ahmed Ibrahim was the killer.

The jury were out for more than an hour and when they returned they announced that Caler was guilty of murder. An appeal was heard on 30 March, before the Lord Chief Justice, Lord Isaacs, and Justices Bray and Avory.

Caler's defence claimed that the verdict was against the weight of evidence, that the judge had misdirected the jury and that whatever evidence there was had been purely circumstantial. The Lord Chief Justice said that he and his colleagues did not agree, that the conviction was safe, and that consequently the appeal would be dismissed.

At 8 a.m. on Wednesday, 14 April 1920, Thomas Caler was hanged at Cardiff by John Ellis and William Willis. As the condemned man approached the scaffold, Caler sagged at the knees and had to be briefly supported, but he soon recovered his composure and stood alone as the trap was sprung.

18

RACE RELATIONS

In March 1920, Lester Augustus Hamilton, also known as Joe Bascombe, a Jamaican marine fireman, was living at a seamen's boarding house in Maria Street, Cardiff, and frequented a Japanese restaurant close by. It was at this establishment that he first met 17-year-old Doris Appleton, who worked there. The two started seeing each other, despite the fact Hamilton, at 25, was eight years her senior. The attention that Hamilton paid to Doris was not, however, welcomed by her family and they told him that he was not to call at 57 Cwmdare Street, the house that Doris shared with her mother and siblings.

At about 7 p.m. on the evening of Saturday, 12 February 1921, Doris and her mother, Rose Appleton, were enjoying a quiet drink together in the Universal Hotel on Bute Street. The two women left together some time before 8.30 p.m. and parted at Cathays Bridge. Doris went straight home to Cwmdare Street where her sister, 14-year-old Edna, was sitting in the kitchen. The sisters had not been together for very long when a knock came on the back door.

The events of the next few minutes would be described in very different ways by the people who witnessed them. What is certain is that the caller was Lester Hamilton, and soon after Doris had answered the door, he fired an automatic pistol into her face. Hamilton then took a few steps into the street, raised the gun once again and shot himself in the head. Badly injured, Hamilton asked a passer-by, Evan Tooby, where the nearest police station was, and staggered towards it, only getting as far as May Street, where he found a uniformed constable and gave himself up.

For Doris Appleton it was already too late. The police arrived at Cwmdare Street at around 9.40 p.m., just as Rose returned home. They found Doris lying seriously ill. She was taken to the King Edward VII Hospital, but died at around midnight. Hamilton was also rushed to the hospital where his condition was judged to be very serious. Indeed, little hope was held out for his recovery.

The funeral of Doris Appleton took place on 17 February. After the prayers had finished and the Appleton family climbed back into their carriages, some of the crowd began to boo and hiss. The family returned to Cwmdare Street, but there were further demonstrations there and several large stones were thrown into the back garden of no. 57. It was plain that the Appleton family were held partly to blame for what had happened.

On 15 March, Hamilton was pronounced fit enough to be discharged. He was then escorted to the police station where he was formally charged with murder, making his first appearance before the stipendiary magistrate, Sir Thomas William Lewis, later that same morning. Hamilton was now paralysed down his left side and had to be carried into the dock by a warder. The prisoner was remanded for eight days.

That afternoon the inquest reopened, the first witness being Rose Appleton, the dead girl's mother. Rose stated that Doris had known Hamilton for about the last six months, having met him in the Japanese restaurant which she had first visited, accompanied by her eldest sister, Marion. Rose went on to say that soon afterwards, Doris had run away from home and she had assumed that at the time she must have lived with Hamilton, though she was not sure. Eventually, Doris had returned home to Cwmdare Street.

Referring to her own knowledge of Hamilton, Rose claimed that he had last visited her house on the Monday before the shooting, 7 February. Hamilton had called at 11 p.m. and she had demanded to know what he was doing there at that late hour. Hamilton explained that he wanted to see Doris, and Rose had tried to get him to leave by saying that her daughter didn't live there any more. To this, Hamilton said that he knew Doris was home, insisted on coming in and was eventually given some supper and a cup of coffee. He finally left at 1.30 a.m., but before he did, Hamilton said that he believed Doris was seeing a Japanese man and if he saw them together, he would do her in.

After Rose Appleton had finished giving her evidence, 14-year-old Edna was called and she told the court that when Hamilton arrived at the house on 12 February, he had another coloured man with him. As Doris opened the door, Hamilton tried to get into the house with his companion but Doris said she did not like the look of the stranger and refused them admission. Hamilton then claimed that as Doris had opened the back door, the Japanese man she had been seeing had been let out of the front door. Doris had denied that there was any truth in this but Hamilton drew out a gun, forced her back into the kitchen and shot her in the face before running out into the street and shooting himself.

Evan Tooby, who lived at 6 Edmund Street, told the court that he was walking down Minny Street when he saw Hamilton coming towards him. As Hamilton drew near, Tooby saw that the front of his shirt was covered in blood and was shocked to hear him say, 'Mister, mister, I have shot myself. Take me to the police station.' Tooby duly escorted Hamilton to the station, and on the way, Hamilton handed over the revolver.

The next witness detailed a remarkable coincidence in the case. Detective Chief Inspector Thomas Hodges had been on duty at the police station when Hamilton was brought in. Hamilton immediately recognised the officer and called out, 'I know you. You are the man who took Tom Caler from my ship, the *Fountains Abbey*.' It seemed that Hamilton had worked with and known Thomas Caler, who had been found guilty of murder that same month (see Chapter 17).

Chief Inspector Hodges said that Hamilton had made a full statement in which he said, 'I worked all my life for the girl and it is more than I can bear. Her mother has brought her up to be so. Last night she took a Japanese fellow home. He was in the house when I shot her.'

Having had all this evidence detailed to them, the coroner's jury had little difficulty in returning a verdict that Doris Appleton had been murdered and that Hamilton was responsible. On 23 March, the Magistrates' Court reconvened, the case for the prosecution being detailed by Mr D.S. Brown and Hamilton being defended by Mr Burnett Janner. It being decided that there was a case to answer, Hamilton was once again committed for trial.

The case of the Crown against Lester Hamilton took place at Swansea before Mr Justice Salter on 25 July. The proceedings lasted just one day, during which Hamilton was defended by Mr T.W. Langman. The prosecution was led by Sir J. Ellis Griffith, who was assisted by Mr Wilfred Lewis. There was one woman on the jury.

Doris's sister, Edna elaborated on her earlier testimony. According to Edna, Hamilton had called at the back door and when Doris had opened it, asked his friend to come in with him. There followed a brief argument over where Doris had been that night. Doris had then again referred to Hamilton's companion and after saying that he shouldn't invite a man like that into her mother's house, Hamilton had remarked, 'Who are you insulting?' before drawing out the gun and shooting Doris.

Continuing her testimony, Edna said that she then ran from the house but turned and saw Hamilton leaving. She saw him raise the gun to his head and fire again. In all, she had heard four shots fired. Once Hamilton had gone off down the street, Edna returned to Cwmdare Street where she found Doris, bleeding from her face, eye and head. Edna brought a cup of water to Doris but it seemed to offer her little comfort. Finally, Edna denied that there had been any Japanese man at the house on the night of the shooting, nor on any other occasion.

For the defence, Uriah Erskine, the owner of the lodging house where Hamilton lived in Maria Street, stated that he knew Hamilton as a respectable man and was aware that he was courting Doris Appleton, contrary to what her mother had told the court. He also knew that the prisoner was giving money to Doris.

Confirmation that the Appleton family was perhaps not all that it should be was given by PC Lister who stated that the girl's house at 57 Cwmdare Street was known as one which was not respectable and that Rose Appleton had in the past given the police some trouble.

Hamilton then gave evidence on his own behalf, saying that on one occasion when he had come home from sea, he had found Doris living in her mother's house in a terrible condition. Hamilton went on to say that he was a regular visitor to the house and had received no trouble from the family until he was out of work on 23 November 1920. Soon afterwards, Doris had admitted to him that she had been living an immoral life by saying, 'Look, I am sorry, forgive me because I stopped up at my mother's house with a Japanese fellow.'

Turning to the night of the shooting, Hamilton said that he had followed Doris into the kitchen to talk to her about the Japanese man he thought she was seeing. As they were speaking, he lost his temper, took the pistol from his pocket and fired. He had no idea how many times he shot Doris, but seeing what he had done, he walked outside and shot himself.

In his summing up, Mr Justice Salter was scrupulously fair. He told the jury that the charge of murder could be reduced to manslaughter if they believed that it was a sudden act, committed under intolerable provocation. He added that if they believed Hamilton's statement in its entirety then this was great provocation. In the event though, the jury, after deliberating for almost an hour, held that the case of murder had been proved but they did add a recommendation to mercy.

Hamilton's defence advised that there were no real grounds for an appeal. They had never sought to deny that Hamilton had fired the shot which took Doris Appleton's life, but had sought to show that he had been sorely provoked. Now the only real hope lay in a petition for a reprieve. One was organised and by 9 August it held over 2,500 signatures. By 15 August though, the Home Secretary had considered all the circumstances of the case and advised that he saw no reason to interfere with the sentence.

At 8 a.m. the next day, Tuesday, 16 August 1921, Lester Augustus Hamilton, still suffering from some degree of paralysis, had to be helped to the scaffold at Cardiff Prison where he was hanged by John Ellis and William Willis.

19

A GENTLEMAN OF THE ROAD

William Sullivan, 1922

Some five miles north of Pontypool, and a similar distance south of Abergavenny, lies the hamlet of Pen-groes-oped. One of the houses in this small village stood out because it was painted white, but to everyone in the area it was known by its name: Lapstone Cottage. In 1921, there were two people living in Lapstone Cottage; David Thomas, a 60-year-old labourer who worked on the Llanover estate of Lord Treowen, and his wife, 48-year-old Margaret.

On the morning of Wednesday, 26 October 1921, David Thomas rose at his usual early hour of 6 a.m., and at 6.30 a.m. enjoyed a light breakfast with Margaret. Just ten minutes later, David left for the Ffawydden quarry, where he was working that day. At the time he walked out of the cottage, Margaret was still at the breakfast table, eating bread and butter and drinking a cup of tea.

David Thomas finished his duties at around 5 p.m. and by the time he got back home it was 5.30 p.m. He was surprised to find the front door locked. Further, the blind was down at the kitchen window. David knocked on the door a number of times, but he received no reply.

Thinking that his wife might be seeing to some of the animals they kept, David took a walk down to the pigpen, only to find that the animals there had not even been fed. The chickens too had not been attended to. Puzzled, David returned to Lapstone Cottage to find that the door to the kitchen was on the latch. The kitchen was not actually part of the cottage itself and entry to the main part of the house could not be gained through here but David could collect some food for the ravenous pigs.

After feeding them, David tried once again to gain entrance to his home. He noticed that the front bedroom window was partly open so, collecting a ladder from the coal shed, David climbed up and finally got inside the cottage. The bedroom was the one he shared with Margaret and appeared to have been disturbed with clothing scattered about the room. David then went downstairs and, walking into the kitchen, discovered why Margaret had failed to answer his calls. She lay on the floor between the window and the fireplace, her body covered with a quilt and a mat. There was a large pool of blood close by and a heavy iron bar, also bloodstained, lay in the crook of Margaret's left arm.

David left the house, again via the bedroom window, and ran towards the house occupied by the local constable, pausing only to tell his neighbour, Mrs Evans, what he had found. On the way, he met the postman, told him what had happened and despatched him to the officer's house while he returned to Lapstone. It was 6.30 p.m by the time PC Owen Preece arrived at the scene. He entered the house with David Thomas, saw the body and noted that drawers in the kitchen had been ransacked.

It was 9 p.m. by the time Dr Thomas Edward Lloyd attended. After pronouncing life extinct, he made notes on the position of the body. A quilt covered Margaret from the backs of her knees to up over her head. A hearthrug, which was partly underneath the body, had been wound around so that it covered her from the waist upwards. Both articles, like Margaret's clothing, were saturated in blood. The heavy iron bar, which was a door bolt, lay on the left side and had obviously been used to batter Margaret to death. Dr Lloyd saw eight wounds on Margaret's scalp, three more on her face and others around her right ear. The right side of her skull had been fractured.

Very soon after his arrival, PC Preece was joined by Superintendent John Barry and Sergeant Prosser, and some uniformed constables. The police saw that the breakfast things were still on the table and, knowing that Margaret Thomas had been a most tidy and fastidious woman, surmised that the attack had taken place very soon after she had eaten breakfast. Interviews with the husband and some of the neighbours soon gave the police a possible suspect; a stranger had been seen in the area.

David Thomas explained that the previous Friday, 21 October, a tramp had called at the house and Margaret had kindly given him some bread and cheese to eat. Now, though, when the neighbours were spoken to, it was discovered that this same man had not only been seen by them on the 21st but had also been observed in the area on the morning of the murder.

George Henry Smith was a milkman. On 21 October, he had seen this same tramp between 4 a.m. and 5 a.m. walking along the banks of the Brecon and Newport canal, heading towards Abergavenny. The man was carrying an overcoat over his arm and asked Smith for a drink of water, producing an old tin to hold the liquid. The man explained that he had come from Newport workhouse and was now heading for the one in Abergavenny. This information was of especial interest to the police for they had found, inside Lapstone Cottage, an old tin which looked very much like the one Smith was describing.

Smith, though, had seen the tramp another couple of times. The next occasion had been on 22 October, at around 7 a.m., when he saw the man walking towards Pontypool. The third sighting was on the morning Margaret Thomas was battered to death. Smith had seen the tramp, again on the canal side, at some time between 5 a.m. and 5.30 a.m. The tramp came up behind Smith and bade him good morning before striding off towards Abergavenny again.

This tramp had also been seen by George Smith's wife, Florence. She had seen him on the canal a number of times and had noticed him last at between 8.30 a.m. and 9 a.m. on the 26th. Now the tramp was coming from the direction of Abergavenny, was walking quite quickly and was wearing an overcoat and cap. The police now began to search for this mysterious stranger.

David Thomas told the police that certain items were missing from his cottage, including a navy blue suit of clothes, two razors, two watches, a pair of boots, and some loose change. Margaret had had four £1 notes and had changed one of these. The other three notes were still loose in her jacket pocket, the killer having missed those, but the change, which amounted to 19s, which she kept in a purse, was gone. On 28 October, though, while David was looking for something suitable to wear for his wife's funeral, he moved the bed upstairs and found an old handkerchief by the side of the bed. Since this did not belong to either him or his wife, it was logical to assume that it had been left by Margaret's killer. Later that same day, however, there was a further dramatic development.

Sixty-two-year-old John Coughlin was known to have been travelling around the area for the last few weeks. He had been seen close to the cottage on the evening of Friday, 28 October and it could not help but be noted that his trousers, which were navy, appeared to be new. He was taken in for questioning and informed that he would be charged on suspicion of causing the death of Margaret Thomas. Coughlin made an appearance before the magistrates and was remanded until Monday, 31 October.

On Sunday, 30 October the body of Margaret Thomas was laid to rest, the service being conducted by the Revd L.C. Edwards. Hundreds of people gathered along the route and many more visited the graveside after the service had finished.

The following morning, John Coughlin was back before the magistrates but by now the police had realised that they had arrested an innocent man. Superintendent Thomas for the police offered no evidence and the 'suspect' was released without further delay.

The resumed inquest opened on 10 November. The first suspect in any murder case is usually the spouse and it had not escaped public notice that David Thomas himself had been closely questioned by the police. Witnesses were now called who confirmed that they had seen him walking to work, wheeling a barrow at the quarry, and generally going about his duties. William Williams, a fellow worker, had seen David in the quarry, as had his son, William Alfred Williams.

Further details of the aftermath of the crime were then given. After finding his wife's body, David Thomas had first run to a neighbour's house, that of Elizabeth Evans, and told her what he had found. After this, he went to Henry Jones' house for help and it was Jones, along with David himself, who took an axe and broke down the door of the cottage so that an easier entrance could be gained when the police and the doctor arrived.

Medical evidence was given by Dr Lloyd, who surmised that Margaret had been standing, facing the breakfast table and with her back to the door, when her assailant came upon her from behind and struck her once with the iron bar. This blow would have knocked her to the floor and left her partially paralysed while the killer rained down more blows until she was dead. After hearing this testimony, the jury did not even bother to retire before returning the verdict that Margaret Thomas had been murdered by a person or persons unknown.

It was not until Thursday, 17 November, that a second suspect was arrested. This man, 41-year-old William Sullivan, had been seen trying to sell a pair of navy blue serge trousers. David Thomas subsequently identified these as the ones that belonged to his suit. As a result, Sullivan was charged with murder and made his first appearance before the magistrates on 18 November. Once again, only evidence of arrest was given before Sullivan was remanded, to Monday, 21 November.

Further remands followed until 25 November and then to 3 December, but it was not until 9 December that all the evidence was given by Mr Ross Pashley for the Director of Public Prosecutions. Sullivan was represented by Mr W.J. Everett.

The important evidence was that which showed a link between Sullivan and the crime. To begin with, Sullivan had been picked out at an identify parade by George Smith and his wife as the tramp they had seen on the canal side on more than one occasion. Further, Mr Smith had described the water tin which the tramp had as having little black and white patches on it. The tin found at Lapstone Cottage had subsequently been positively identified by Mr Smith as the one the tramp, Sullivan, had in his possession.

The handkerchief found by David Thomas close to the bed in Lapstone Cottage was a red and white one and another witness, Tudor Evans, who had also seen Sullivan on the canal, said that at the time the man wore just such a handkerchief around his neck.

Other items had also been found by David Thomas, and these included an old, dirty pair of pyjamas and a pair of worn down boots. The boots were identified by both George Smith and his wife, Florence, as having been the ones Sullivan was wearing when they saw him. Yet, at noon on 26 October, by which time the crime had already been committed, Sullivan was seen by Annie Jones, the landlady of the Forge Hammer Inn at Cwmbran, wearing a new pair of boots. Further, Sullivan was now spending money freely. He ordered himself a pint of beer and paid with a half-crown. Having left the pub, he returned a little later with his brother, Michael Sullivan and his brother-in-law, Nick Kellow, and ordered three more pints. The group also asked for two packets of cigarettes and Sullivan paid with a £1 note. Annie also swore that at the time, Sullivan was wearing a blue serge suit, and did not have an overcoat on or a handkerchief around his neck.

It was now shown that on the day after the inquest had returned its verdict, 11 November, Sullivan knocked on the door of 54 Albion Road, Pontypool. He had visited that house once before, in August, when he asked for, and received, a cup of tea from the occupier, Lily May Groves. This time, the door was answered by Mrs Groves' 14-year-old daughter, Hannah Eliza, and Sullivan said, 'Ask your mam if she will buy a jacket and a pair of boots.'

As it was only 8 a.m., Hannah asked Sullivan to call back later and he did so, at 6 p.m. that evening. He saw Mrs Groves and told her that the items had been given to him as payment by an old lady he had done some work for. The transaction was completed and two days later, Sullivan was back, this time seeking to sell a blue serge waistcoat and trousers for 3s. Mrs Groves haggled and got the price down to 2s 6d, which she handed over to Sullivan. In the meantime, she had heard about the murder and seeing that she now had an almost new blue serge suit like the one that had been reported missing, she handed this over to police the same day. The suit was shown to Mr Thomas, who said it looked like his suit. To be sure, Mr Thomas tried the suit on and it fitted him like a glove. He then had no hesitation in identifying it as his property.

Sullivan was taken to Cwmbran for interview. He was asked to give an account of his movements and stated that on both 25 and 26 October, he had been with a man named Stewart. Unfortunately for Sullivan, when Frederick Stewart, a fellow tramp, was traced, he said that he hadn't seen Sullivan since August.

The evidence was circumstantial, but it was more than enough for the magistrates who ordered that Sullivan be sent to the next assizes. His trial opened at Monmouth on 7 February 1922, before Mr Justice Darling. The hearing lasted for two days, during which Sullivan was defended by Mr S.R.C. Bosanquet while the case for the prosecution was led by Mr Arthur Powell, who was assisted by Mr Lort Williams MP.

The first witness was David Thomas, the dead woman's husband, and even now it seemed that he was not free from suspicion. A good deal had been made of the fact that he said he had left his home at about 6.40 a.m. and arrived at work an hour later, at 7.40 a.m. That evening he left work at 5 p.m. and arrived home at 5.30 p.m. A journey that took him only half an hour at night had apparently taken him twice as long in the morning. At the inquest he had explained this by stating that the outward journey was uphill. When cross-examining Thomas, Mr Bosanquet pointed out that the county surveyor had stated that the outward trip was not uphill at all. David Thomas maintained that he must have walked 'quietly' to work in the morning, that is to say he walked at a leisurely pace.

After all the prosecution witnesses had been heard, Sullivan stepped into the witness box to defend himself against the charge. He began by stating that he was 42 years old and had served in the army from 1901 until 1919. Since then he had spent much of his time travelling up and down Monmouthshire and on 25 October, the day before the murder, was with Frederick Stewart.

They were together at about 6 a.m. on 26 October and walked towards Pontypool, and parted on the way. He branched off towards Cwmbran, getting to the Forge Hammer Inn close to noon. At the time he had about 9s on him, which was money he had earned.

The drinks he had purchased for himself, his brother and his brother-in-law, along with the cigarettes, came to about 6s in all and Sullivan denied that he had ever tendered a Treasury note as payment. He went on to deny that he had been on the canal bank on 26 October at any time, had never met Mr or Mrs Smith and that the tin found at Lapstone Cottage was not his. The red handkerchief was also not his property and he had not sold any clothing to Mrs Groves. Finally, he had never been near Lapstone Cottage in his life.

Sullivan's fellow traveller, Frederick Stewart, was now recalled, having already given evidence for the prosecution. He maintained that Sullivan had not been with him on the night of 25 October, since he was at a lodging house in Tredegar.

Annie Jones, the landlady of the Forge Hammer was also recalled. Again she said that Sullivan had paid for the second round of drinks with a £1 note, but under cross-examination, wilted somewhat and said that she couldn't be sure it was a pound, but was certain it was a note of some kind.

In his summing up, Mr Justice Darling again referred to the suggestion that David Thomas had killed his wife and asked the jury to consider whether they accepted all of his evidence. The jury retired at 4.45 p.m. on 8 February, and did not return until 7.10 p.m., with the decision that Sullivan was guilty of murder. Asked if he had anything to say before the death sentence was passed, Sullivan replied, 'I am not guilty, and I have always said so.'

An appeal was entered and this was heard on 7 March before Justices Avory, Sankey and Salter. For the defence, Mr Bosanquet again referred to the evidence being purely circumstantial, and the trial judge had recalled witnesses after the prisoner had given evidence and even after the counsel had made their closing speeches. For the prosecution, Mr Powell in rebuttal claimed that the recalling of the witnesses had been done as much in Sullivan's interests as that of the Crown. Giving the court's judgement, Mr Justice Avory said that there was no irregularity and the appeal would be dismissed.

The defence were still not prepared to give up and an application was made to the Attorney General for permission to take the case to the House of Lords. On 20 March it was announced that permission had been refused. Sullivan's fate was sealed.

At 8 a.m. on Thursday, 23 March 1922, William Sullivan was hanged at Usk by John Ellis and Thomas Phillips. Sullivan's last words were, 'I am innocent.'

20

'TWO SIDES TO EVERY STORY'

George Thomas, 1926

On the A469 road just south of Rhymney, which is itself just a few miles east of Merthyr Tydfil, lies the village of Pontlottyn. It was in this village, in December 1924, that George Thomas fell in love. By coincidence, the object of his affections was also surnamed Thomas, though they were not related. Marie Beddoe Thomas, at 19, was George's junior by seven years but that was no problem. She returned his love and, for a time, the relationship flourished.

In March 1925, Marie wrote a letter to Thomas, which he considered to be rather insulting. As a result, on the 26th of that month he went to her home in Wine Street to ask her what it was all about. The door was answered by Marie's mother, Ann Jane Thomas, who explained that her daughter did not wish to see him. Instead, Ann handed over a note which read, 'I am sorry' and was simply signed M.B. Thomas.

The romance was finished; both Marie and Thomas started seeing other people and both became unofficially engaged to their new partners. Everyone believed that a chapter had closed but in reality, the relationship was far from over. Letters began to pass between George Thomas and his ex-girlfriend, many carried by a mutual friend, Angelina Mary Francis, who acted as a go-between.

There was certainly a good deal of passion in the letters Marie now sent to Thomas. An early one began, 'It isn't wrong for us to write to each other, is it? Oh I know we are both engaged and all that but there can be no harm in our just asking after each other's health now and again, can there?' The messages, though, did not stop at polite inquiries after Thomas' health and another read:

> Aren't you happy? I met your pal, Bert Jones, last night, and he said that when he saw you on Easter Monday night you looked very miserable. Is that so?
>
> Well, you are not alone in your unhappiness. I would give everything just to soothe and comfort you again as I did long ago when we were sweethearts. Do you remember in the clubhouse one rain swept night when the wind howled and wailed outside? But that night, anyway, we were very happy together, weren't we? Does it come back to you sometimes? The memory of how happy we used to be before other people butted in and tried to arrange our affairs. I shall never be sorry I met you.
>
> Happiness is too elusive and fragile a thing to catch and hold roughly or lightly. We held it lightly and it flickered away from us like some brilliantly hued butterfly of golden summer moments – never to return again... Has your love died? Will you never even think of me again? Now, close your eyes for a moment – I am going to kiss you. Goodbye, please burn this, it is wiser.

Perhaps such letters were bad enough but Marie had also told Thomas a lie. Maybe it was to encourage feelings of love and protection within him, or simply to make him jealous, but she had said that the new man in her life had been beating her. The stories were totally untrue but it had the desired effect.

Eventually, Marie confessed to Thomas that she had not told him the truth. In an undated letter, but which must have been sent that same summer, she told him that she had lied and begged for his forgiveness.

Thomas did forgive Marie. His replies to her show, though, that the situation was preying heavily on his mind. In one he penned, 'I am hoping the mist will roll away, so that I may enjoy with my friends what little life has to offer us.'

Other letters were addressed to 'Lena' (Angelina Francis) so that she could pass the details on to Marie and as the days turned into weeks and the weeks into months, the tone of those letters became more and more depressed. In one he wrote '...everything seems so impossible. There is only one thing in my heart – my love for Marie, and I pray that the day will not be long before I shall repay in full the great wrong and injustice which has been done to me.'

Summer turned into autumn which in turn gave way to winter and still Thomas' plans to be with Marie had failed to materialise. He became more and more desperate. The pressure took its toll and on Friday, 4 December 1925, George Thomas called at an ironmonger's shop in Bargoed where he was sold a new butcher's boning knife by the proprietor, David Sallis.

It was just before 6 p.m. on Sunday, 6 December, when Harriett Maud Lewis called at Marie's house in Wine Street, so that they could walk to the chapel together for the evening service. The two young women walked off together and it was not until they passed the back of the General Picton Hotel that Harriett first saw Thomas, a man she knew by sight as Marie's ex-boyfriend.

A few moments later, as they approached the chapel, Marie appeared to stumble and as she regained her footing, Harriett looked around to see that there was a man close behind them. They took another couple of steps before Marie stumbled again but this time she fell forward to her knees. Only now did Harriett realise that the man behind them was George Thomas and he had something in his hand. Before Harriett even knew what was happening, Thomas too fell onto the road, his hand held to the side of his chest. He had stabbed Marie in the heart and then turned the knife upon himself.

Lewis Woods, an ambulance officer, was inside the chapel at the time. The service had just started when he heard a scream and ran out to see what had happened. He saw Marie lying on the ground and upon checking her pulse, realised that she was already dead. The young man was alive, but unconscious. Woods helped to carry him into the house of Mrs Pugh, who lived opposite to the chapel. Once inside, Thomas regained consciousness and was heard to utter the words, 'Let me die.'

Thomas was rushed to the Aberbargoed Hospital where it was discovered that the knife had hit a rib, or the wound might well have proved fatal. He soon began to respond to treatment. Meanwhile, four days after the attack, on 10 December, the inquest opened before Mr Rees Jenkin Rhys. Here it was stated that a number of letters had been found on Thomas, which showed that the crime was deliberate and planned. One read, 'Dear Everybody. Please forget this as quickly as possible. There are two sides to every story. Locked away in my heart is one. I die perfectly happy.'

Once all the witnesses had given their evidence, Mr Rhys, in his summing up said, 'If anything had been premeditated in this world it was the deed that Sunday night.' The jury returned a murder verdict without leaving the box. Later that same day, the body of Marie Thomas was laid to rest in the cemetery at Rhymney.

Thomas was discharged from hospital on 28 December and that same day appeared before the stipendiary magistrate, Mr T. Price, at Pontlottyn. Thomas, who seemed calm but somewhat drawn, was represented by Mr Edward Roberts who made no objection to a remand until 1 January 1926.

On 1 January, Thomas appeared before a bench of magistrates, presided over by Mr R.A. Griffith, as the evidence was described by Mr John Evans on behalf of the Director of Public Prosecutions. Mr Evans began by reading all the letters found on Thomas after the attack had taken place. In addition to the 'Dear Everybody' letter, there were three others; one addressed to a friend, Justus Pugh of Chapel Street, Pontlottyn, a second to the dead girl's mother and a third, to 'Lena' Francis. Each of these documents showed that the crime was premeditated and that Thomas intended to take his own life after the event.

The letter to Ann Jane Thomas read in part, 'This is your hour of sadness and sorrow. The same with my dear mother, because after all, to you both we always remain children, never growing up. Forgive me and forget if you can, and pray for us both.'

After Harriett Lewis had given her testimony, other witnesses who had been in or near the chapel were called. William Rees, a colliery timberman who lived in Duffryn Street, said that he and his sister, Mrs Jane Jones, were walking up the street near the chapel when they saw two women running along the street apparently being pursued by a man. He heard a scream and saw one of the women fall. Going to her aid, he found to his horror that she was already dead and his sister cried out, 'Look out William, he's got a knife.' Only then did Rees realise that the dead woman had been stabbed and as he turned to face Thomas, he saw him open his waistcoat, raise the knife again and plunge it into his own chest.

Medical evidence was given by Dr John Jones who said that he first saw Marie at 6.20 p.m., by which time she had been taken into a nearby house, 15 Chapel Street. She was dead and he observed two wounds on her back. The more serious of these was 1½in long, 4in deep and was positioned 4in from her spinal column, and had penetrated a lung. Marie would have died almost immediately and great force had been used to inflict the fatal wound.

PC Ambrose said that he had arrived at the scene at 6.30 p.m. Marie was still lying on the pavement near the chapel and the prisoner was lying close by. Mr Rees handed a knife to him and identified Thomas as the man who had stabbed the woman. The 'Dear Everybody' letter was found and this bore the prisoner's name and his address: 47 McDonnel Road, Bargoed. Soon afterwards, Dr Jones and Inspector John Clinch arrived and Thomas was escorted to the hospital.

Thomas was committed to take his trial at the next assizes and they took place at Cardiff in February. On the 16th of that month, Thomas faced Mr Justice Fraser and a jury of nine men and three women. His defence rested in the hands of Mr T.W. Langman while the case for the prosecution was given by Mr Artemus Jones and Mr John Grace.

David Thomas, the dead girl's father, confirmed that after March 1925, any meetings between the accused and Marie had been unknown to him. He claimed that he had had nothing to do with the original breaking off of the relationship between them. Ann Thomas said much the same but did admit that she had told her daughter that she had better have nothing to do with the prisoner as she did not approve of their being sweethearts. Mrs Thomas refused to give her reasons for her disapproval.

The Cardiff Law Courts, where George Thomas, and many others mentioned in this book, faced their trials.

Further letters were then read out in court, including one, dated 4 January, which Thomas had sent to the dead girl's mother while he had been in prison awaiting trial. This letter began:

My dear Mrs Thomas, it cut me to the heart on seeing you both on Friday, and with me there is no tears to fill, because my heart is quite dead within, quite cold.

My days are numbered. How pleased and happy I shall be on that morning. Think of the joy and happiness to be mine for ever to wander hand in hand with Marie in the Great Beyond.

The defence was one of insanity. David Millward, Thomas' brother-in-law, gave evidence that the prisoner had never been the same after the war. Thomas' widowed mother gave evidence that her son often complained of headaches and sleeplessness and behaved oddly. In fact, one night she had heard noises and went out to find her son claiming that he was throwing bombs. She went on to say that her daughter had gone off her head after her father's death, and had later died in an asylum. The defence believed that this could well have been the reason that the dead girl's mother wanted the relationship to end.

The jury took fifty minutes to arrive at their verdict – guilty, but with a recommendation to mercy. Thomas did not appeal against his sentence and, twenty-one days later, at 8 a.m. on Tuesday, 9 March 1926, he was hanged at Cardiff by Robert Baxter and Thomas Phillips, as a crowd of a few hundred people gathered outside the gates. The newspapers of the day incorrectly announced that Thomas Pierrepoint had been the hangman, but he was busy at Maidstone Prison, executing Henry Thompson who had murdered Rose Smith at Chatham.

George Thomas had been quite prepared to die. In his last interview with his relatives, on the night before he was hanged, Thomas said, 'They can take my body, but they cannot take my soul. My body will be buried here, but my soul is with Marie.'

21

A DAY AT THE RACES

Edward Rowlands & Daniel Driscoll, 1928

In his prime, David Lewis, better known as Dai, had been a promising boxer and rugby player. He had won medals and a silver cup and had fought in rings as far away as Canada and America. By the mid-1920s he was describing himself as a bookmaker's assistant at Monmouth racetrack, but he was still interested in athletics and kept himself fit.

The term 'bookmaker's assistant' was, however, nothing more than a euphemism for a protection racket, which Lewis ran. Using the threat of his muscle, he would rent out racetrack items such as stools, chalk and blackboards to the local bookmakers and undertake to ensure these against unforeseen accidents. Unfortunately for Lewis, there were other men who sought to offer the same sort of service.

On Wednesday, 28 September 1927, Lewis was back at Monmouth racetrack and it was there that he was seen by the two brothers who controlled the gang who were his rivals; John and Edward Rowlands. Lewis may have felt he was stepping on some very dangerous toes and chose, wisely, not to go home that night to Ethel Street, Canton, Cardiff, but to book into Barry's Hotel in St Mary Street.

On Thursday the 29th, Lewis returned to the racetrack but when he had finished for the day, he still did not go straight home. Going back to Cardiff and walking into the Blue Anchor pub, also on St Mary's Street, Lewis found several members of the Rowlands gang standing around the bar and was quite relieved when they all joined him in a drink.

Closing time came but Lewis and the others did not leave the pub until almost 11 p.m. No sooner did Lewis go outside than he was surrounded. A fight followed, a knife appeared and Lewis fell to the floor, a stab wound in his throat. He was rushed to the Cardiff Royal Infirmary, but refused to name any of the men who had attacked him.

Over the next couple of hours, there were two telephone calls to the hospital, asking how Lewis was faring. Each time when the duty nurse asked the caller for his name, he rang off. This information was of great interest to the police and when the caller rang for a third time, he was kept talking while the call was traced. The number was for the Colonial Club in Custom House Street, a known base of operations for the Rowlands gang.

Early the next morning, five members of the gang were picked up. At 1 a.m. on 30 September, PC Albert Davies and other officers visited the club in Custom House Street and took 34-year-old Daniel Driscoll and John Hughes, who was 54, into custody on a charge of attempted murder.

Less than two hours later, at 2.45 a.m., Inspector Davies, PC Bishop and other police officers, went to 39 Stanway Place, Ely, where they picked up 43-year-old William Joseph Price. Fnally, at 3.15 a.m., PC Albert Davies made the third and fourth arrests of the night when he went to 37 Turner Road, Canton, where he found 40-year-old Edward Rowlands and his 30-year-old brother, John.

On Friday, 30 September, all five men appeared in the police court, charged with attempted murder. No sooner had they been remanded to the following Tuesday, 4 October, that news was received from the hospital that Dai Lewis had died from his injury, at 11.35 a.m. The charge was immediately amended to one of murder.

On 4 October, the five were back before the magistrates when, after a very brief appearance, they were all remanded until 12 October. By this time, William Price and John Rowlands were being represented by Mr Harold Lloyd while the other three had all engaged Mr C. Stuart Halliman. On the 12th, a further remand followed, this time until 19 October.

The evidence finally began to be heard on 19 October, outlined by Mr G.B. Paling, the proceedings lasting for two days. The first witness was William Charles Lynes, who lived in Easton Road, Bristol and had worked as Lewis' partner. Together they supplied bookmakers' stools and had both been at the races on 29 September. Edward Rowlands was also there and at one stage he went up to Lewis and said, 'You are a desperado.'

George Dyer, a commission agent, testified that John Hughes worked for him as a clerk. On 29 September, he had gone to Monmouth races in company with Edward Rowlands and John Hughes. They drove back together and went into the Blue Anchor pub for a drink. When Dyer left, just before 10 p.m., Hughes, Edward Rowlands and Driscoll were all drinking with Dai Lewis and they seemed to be on friendly enough terms.

The dead man's wife, Annie Lewis, was then called briefly to confirm that her husband had never carried a knife. Mr Paling then called Frederick Forrest, a taxi driver who said that although he had not seen the fight in St Mary Street, he did see a policeman running up the street and go to the assistance of a man lying on the ground. The man, who was lying only a yard or so from his cab, was bleeding badly from the neck.

Towards the end of the first day, Inspector Davies produced a statement made by John Rowlands. When Rowlands was first taken into custody, his wife had visited him and he had said to her, 'I had nothing to do with it. Hong Kong [William Price's rather curious nickname] and I had been drinking in the Blue Anchor. Hong Kong went out because he was going to be sick. Lewis hit him.' Later, though, Rowlands handed a note over, 'I hereby state that John Hughes, Ted Rowlands and Danny Driscoll were never in my company on the 29th. I also state that W.J. Price, Driscoll and Hughes had nothing to do with causing the death of David Lewis, as I stand solely responsible.'

On the second day, Dr Arthur Richards Culley, a house surgeon at the Cardiff Royal Infirmary, gave evidence on the injuries Lewis had sustained. There were two wounds. One on the left side of his face extended from 3in above his ear and went downwards for 7¼ins. There was another cut on the right side of his face but this was largely superficial and had probably been caused by a glancing blow. Dr Culley had performed the post-mortem, observed by Dr James Joseph Buist and both men agreed that the cause of death was a haemorrhage.

David Lewis had made a dying deposition, but it did not carry the case forward very far. It began: 'I do not know how I have been injured. I do not remember how it happened. There was no quarrel or fight as far as I am aware. Nobody did anything to me. I do not know I have been cut. I did not see anyone use a knife.'

At the end of the evidence, the magistrate asked what evidence there was against John Hughes. Mr Paling replied that while Hughes had been seen inside the Blue Anchor, none of the witnesses had

St Mary Street, Cardiff, where David Lewis was beaten to death by a group of men. The attack took place outside the Blue Anchor pub, which is at the bottom right of the picture.

Another view of St Mary Street.

picked him out as being present when the altercation took place in the street outside. The magistrate thought that there was no case to answer in regard to that prisoner and Hughes was then discharged. The other four were all told that they would be sent to the next assizes to answer the charge of murder.

The trial of the Rowlands brothers, William Price and Daniel Driscoll opened at Cardiff on 29 November before Mr Justice Wright. The prosecution was led by Lord Halsbury, who was assisted by Mr T.W. Langman. For John Rowlands, Mr C.H. Goodman Roberts MP appeared, and was assisted by Mr Matebele Davies. Edward Rowlands was defended by Mr Lawrence Vine and Mr Francis Powell. Mr O. Temple Morris appeared for Price, and Mr Artemus Jones, assisted by Mr Trevor Hunter, represented Driscoll.

It was crucial for the prosecution to show that the men involved in the fight with Lewis were the same men who were now standing together in the dock. Margaret Sullivan was one of the barmaids at the Blue Anchor and she confirmed that John Rowlands, the shortest of the men and whose nickname was consequently 'Tich' had been in the bar with Lewis and Driscoll. She had heard no argument or cross words between them.

Lillian Huggins was in St Mary Street at some time after 10.30 p.m. on 29 September and she saw a man whom she recognised as Lewis quarrelling with a number of others. The group closed around Lewis and one of them struck a blow at him. Lewis staggered back and the next she knew, all the others were on top of him. Lillian had since identified the prisoners as the men who had attacked Lewis.

William Callagher, a driver, said that he too saw the fight. There were four men in the street; three quite tall and one short, and the shortest one seemed to want to fight one of the others. Callagher saw him push the man and then strike him about the head and neck. Eventually, the short man and two of the tall ones ran off, leaving the other lying on the ground and Callagher saw that he was bleeding from the neck.

While Callagher had suggested that three men were responsible for the attack upon Lewis, another witness, Margaret McNeil, claimed that there were five or six men arguing and that one of them was followed across the road until he reached a taxi cab before he was attacked by the others. This number of assailants was also sworn to by Eileen Lashford, who had rushed to Lewis' aid and torn strips off her clothing in an attempt to staunch the bleeding. She knew Edward Rowlands by sight and swore that he was one of the men involved in the affray.

Beatrice Manley, who was standing outside the Playhouse, did not see the attack but did see some men running off down the street. She identified one of them as John Rowlands, claiming that he had nearly knocked her down.

The next witness, PC Evans, said that he was on duty in St Mary's Street on the night of the stabbing and saw the four prisoners standing outside the Blue Anchor pub at about 11.10 p.m., and decided to keep an eye on them. Lewis was standing nearby and suddenly the five began to struggle. Evans ran forward to stop the fight and saw Driscoll holding Lewis' hands. While he did so, Edward Rowlands ran forward and slashed at Lewis' face with a knife. As soon as they saw Evans, the four ran off and Evans went to assist Lewis who mumbled, 'I am all right. Leave me alone.'

When Lewis had given his deposition at the infirmary, the prisoners had been escorted there by Detective Sergeant Broben who later took their clothing for examination. In the left-hand pocket of John Rowlands' trousers, he found smears of blood. Rowlands was known to be left-handed and the inference was that he had put the bloodstained knife into that pocket after the stabbing.

The defence opened on the second day of the trial. The first of the defendants to step into the witness box was Edward Rowlands. He outlined his movements on the day in question, stating that he had gone to Monmouth races and later been in the Blue Anchor, with Lewis and others. At 11 p.m., he, Driscoll and Lewis left the pub together and stood talking on the pavement outside. John Hughes was also there and he suggested that they might all go to the Kit-Kat Club in Custom House Street. Rowlands told Hughes that he had had enough 'booze' and was going home. The group split up but he hadn't walked very far when he saw Lewis hit William Price, who was just coming down the street. A scuffle followed but Rowlands denied taking any part in it.

John Rowlands then took the stand. He claimed that on the night of 29 September, he had met Price in St Mary Street soon after 7 p.m. and they went on to several public houses together. At 11 p.m. they were both in the Express café when Price said he felt sick and went outside. Rowlands followed Price outside and was talking to two women when he saw an argument between Price and Lewis which ended with Price being knocked to the ground.

Rowlands walked over to Lewis and demanded to know why he had hit Price but Lewis told him to mind his own business and aimed a kick at him. The kick missed but Lewis then took out a knife and brandished it towards him. Rowlands grabbed Lewis' wrist and in the struggle that followed, both men fell to the ground. Seizing his chance, Rowlands then picked up the weapon and, since Lewis was a much bigger man, used it to defend himself. He had no intention of injuring him seriously and certainly did not intend to kill him.

William Price now took his turn in the witness box. He confirmed John Rowlands' story that they had been in the café when he said he felt ill and went outside. He was just about to hail a taxi to take him home when Lewis came up to him and struck him. He knew nothing more of the fight until he stood up and saw a crowd of people gathering, but he felt too ill to investigate so simply walked away and went home.

The last of the four, Daniel Driscoll, now gave his testimony. He agreed that he had been in the Blue Anchor, and that the group broke up outside. Walking off, Driscoll heard a noise, which sounded like a loud crack and upon turning around, saw that Lewis was standing at the back of a taxi cab while Price was lying on the ground. He took no part in the fight that followed.

The closing speeches took up most of 1 December. The defence disputed the prosecution's arguments that the four men had conspired to murder Lewis. If this had been the case, the prisoners could surely have selected a more secluded spot. It was also their belief that it was Lewis who owned the murder weapon, a knife other witnesses had said he always carried. This knife was not among his possessions when he was admitted to hospital, showing that it was he who drew it during the affray. Most of the defence barristers quoted the statement of John Rowlands, which indicated that he alone was responsible for the death of David Lewis, and asked that their clients should be acquitted. For Rowlands himself, Mr Roberts suggested that at worst, he should be convicted of manslaughter or that the jury might see fit to agree that he had acted in self-defence.

The jury retired at 12.32 p.m. on 2 December and were out for less than an hour. The verdict was that William Price was not guilty, but that the other three were. Asked if they had anything to say before the sentence of death was passed, Edward Rowlands and Driscoll both replied, 'I am innocent.' John Rowlands made no comment but appeared to be on the verge of collapsing.

All three men entered an appeal, which was heard before Lord Hewart, the Lord Chief Justice, and Justices Avory and Branson on 11 January 1928. John Rowlands was too ill to attend, but the two other condemned men stood in the dock to hear their counsel pleading for their lives.

For Driscoll, Mr Artemus Jones claimed that his client's chance of a fair trial had been seriously prejudiced by the suggestion that he was part of 'a murderous gang'. He also held that the judge, in his summing up, had never put Driscoll's case adequately.

Edward Rowlands' defence argued that the verdict against him was against the weight of evidence. In his opening speeches, Lord Halsbury had spoken of a determined effort by a ruthless gang to eliminate a rival and yet witnesses had been called who swore that the group were all together in the Blue Anchor, behaving in a friendly manner towards each other. A policeman who had been on the scene said that he saw Edward Rowlands strike the blow and yet other evidence showed that it had been John.

For John Rowlands, Mr Roberts claimed that the language used by the judge in his summing up had suggested to the jury that once it had been established that his client struck the fatal blow, they could do nothing else but find him guilty of murder. He also claimed that in the prosecution's opening speech, they had called the crime premeditated and stated that Lewis and the men had argued, none of which they had been able to substantiate. Mr Roberts submitted again that Rowlands had acted in self-defence.

In giving the court's judgement, Lord Hewart agreed that the jury might have come to the conclusion that a verdict of manslaughter was possible but they had decided that such a verdict was not the correct one and that the men were guilty of murder. All three applications were dismissed.

In fact, although the sentence had been confirmed on three men, very soon, only two were facing the hangman's noose. John Rowlands had set out to attend the appeal court hearing but on the way, had gone berserk in the van and had to be forcibly restrained. He was adjudged to be insane, the death sentence respited and he was sent to Broadmoor.

Petitions were now organised for the two remaining prisoners. On 21 January a document bearing 51,700 signatures, pleading for the life of Daniel Driscoll, was handed into the Home Office. All of these names were collected in Birmingham, Driscoll's home city, and it was announced that a second petition there, and another from Cardiff, bore between 100,000 and 150,000 more names.

Two days later, the number of names had risen to well over 200,000 but on 24 January, the Home Office announced that no reason for interfering with the sentences had been found.

Still, the efforts to save the two men continued. On 26 January, two of the jurymen who had served at the trial travelled down to London accompanied by the local Member of Parliament, Mr T.P. O'Connor, in an attempt to secure a reprieve. The two jurymen were not granted admission to the Home Office but Mr O'Connor was seen and was allowed to hand over a request, signed by eight of the jury, asking that the death sentence not be carried out.

These last appeals did not move the Home Secretary to change his opinion and, at 8 a.m. on Friday, 27 January 1928, Edward Rowlands and Daniel Driscoll were hanged side by side at Cardiff.

As the two men entered the execution chamber, Driscoll saw the two ropes and asked, 'Which is mine?' Rowlands was unable to speak as the four executioners, Robert Baxter, Thomas Phillips, Lionel Mann and Robert Wilson carried out their grim task. Meanwhile, a crowd approaching 5,000 waited outside the gates. Four of Driscoll's brothers were among the group, tears streaming down their faces.

22

A WOMAN IN TROUBLE

Trevor John Edwards, 1928

Edgar Cook and his wife, Annie Elizabeth, had no objections to the young man their 21-year-old daughter Elsie was seeing. Trevor John Edwards, a colliery fitter, was also 21 and the couple had been walking out together for some months. An engagement had been discussed, though no definite arrangements had been made, but the consensus of opinion was that Trevor and Elsie would tie the knot some time in early July, 1928.

In April of that year, Annie Cook had to be admitted to hospital where she stayed until the 20th. When she returned to the family home at 4 Gwawr Street in Aberaman, she noticed that Elsie seemed to be showing something of a tummy bulge and, after questioning her daughter, discovered that there might be a baby on the way. Annie marched Elsie around to Dr Farquhar's surgery where the tests were carried out and the pregnancy was confirmed.

On Saturday, 2 June, Annie and Elsie Cook went to 24 Aman Street, Aberdare where they saw Edwards and his mother, Mary Jane Whitbread. Annie asked Mrs Whitbread if she knew that her son had been seeing Elsie and had made her pregnant. Mrs Whitbread said she was of the same mind as Annie Cook; the only real solution was for Edwards and Elsie to marry.

Mary Whitbread suggested to her son that he arrange to call on Annie on Wednesday, 6 June, to discuss the marriage plans. The meeting took place as arranged. Edwards arrived at around 6 p.m. and after some discussion, he said that he would try to put the banns in the following Tuesday, which was 12 June. There was, however, one small problem which Edwards had neglected to mention, and that was that he was in love with another woman, and had no intention of being tied down to Miss Cook.

Edwards and Elsie had agreed to meet up again on Saturday, 16 June. That day, Elsie left her parents' house some time between 5.20 p.m. and 5.30 p.m. when her mother saw her go. Elsie was wearing a brown felt hat, a brown coat with an astrakhan collar, a black skirt, a pink knitted jumper, white stockings and blue shoes. She carried no handbag but had in her hands a pair of gloves.

At 6 p.m., a collier named Thomas George Thomas met Edwards, a friend of his, outside the Cwmneol Inn in Aberdare. They went into the pub together and Edwards bought a pint for himself and his friend. Edwards drank up quickly and told Thomas that he was in a hurry as he was going to meet his girl.

Elizabeth Mary Morgan was the landlady of the Brynffynnon Hotel in Llanwonno and at some time before 8.30 p.m. on the evening of 16 June, she served a young man with a pint of beer and a glass of cider. This seemed to be a strange order for a man on his own so Elizabeth asked him who the cider was for. The man replied that he had his young lady with him, but she was outside and didn't want to come in.

A short time later, the man returned with two empty glasses, asked for a refill of the pint and also ordered a flagon of beer to take away. He then downed the pint quickly and as he left the bar with the flagon, Elizabeth called out that if he returned it when he had finished it, he could have 2*d* back. The young man replied that he wouldn't be bringing it back. As he walked away, Elizabeth Morgan went to the door and saw the woman he was with. She was only a couple of yards away and wore a brown hat and coat.

The young man and his lady friend were of course, Edwards and Elsie Cook. Elizabeth Morgan later made a formal identification of Edwards, but the couple were also seen by Percy John Down. Percy knew Edwards, and saw them about half a mile from Llanwonno Church, at some time between 8 p.m. and 8.30 p.m. Edwards asked Down what time it was but Percy said he didn't have a watch. Down noticed that Edwards was carrying a flagon of beer and saw the couple walk off together. They were heading off over the mountains.

At 10.15 a.m. on Sunday, 17 June, David Griffiths, a collier, was quietly sitting on the mountainside at Llanwonno when he heard footsteps. Turning to look over his shoulder, Griffiths saw a man with bloodstains on his coat pass him and walk off, away from Llanwonno. Griffiths assumed that the man had slipped on the mountainside and hurt himself.

Five minutes after this, William John James, a coal cutter, was sitting near the Aberaman bridge, waiting for a friend he had arranged to meet there, when the same young man that Griffiths had seen, came over the bridge, approached James, and asked him for a match. James recognised the man as Trevor Edwards and saw that he had blood on his chest, neck and face, along with what looked like dried fern on the side of his face.

James asked Edwards what had happened to him and Edwards calmly replied that he had cut his throat. Somewhat startled, James told Edwards to sit down. Edwards did as he was told, then took out a notebook and scribbled, 'How far off is the police station?' James said it wasn't very far.

The two men sat together for a few minutes before Edwards said something about a girl. James asked Edwards if he was saying that he had left a young girl up on the mountainside. Edwards said that he had and that she was lying after the first clump of trees, on the side of the road. It was now that James saw a man cycling past, stopped him and asked him to stay with Edwards while he went for his friend. James soon returned with his friend, Charles William Gubb, and they now helped Edwards to his feet and escorted him to the police station.

By this time, Albert Edward Roberts, another man who had seen Edwards, had called at the police station and informed Inspector Andrew Poolman that there was an injured man near the bridge and a doctor would be needed. The inspector sent PC Archibald Ivor Thomas to get the doctor and then went out with Roberts to see the injured man. He met James, Gubb and Edwards on a footpath close to the police station, took hold of Edwards' right arm, and helped him back to his office. By the time Inspector Poolman arrived, PC Thomas was already there with Dr Frederick Charles Bullen.

Edwards was placed gently into a chair and Dr Bullen began his examination. He had a handkerchief around his neck and once this was removed, Dr Bullen saw an incised horizontal wound over the front of the neck. The wound was 3in long and 1in deep at one point over the windpipe. The wound had largely stopped bleeding and no arteries had been severed so Dr Bullen found it a simple task to dress it. Inspector Poolman then began to question Edwards.

Edwards made a brief statement, which was written down by the inspector. It consisted of: 'Last night we went over to Llanwonno and on the way back I done her in and tried to do myself in. It's failed. That was near enough to ten o'clock last night.' He then went on to describe exactly where the body would be found. Edwards signed the statement, was searched and then taken off to hospital for further treatment.

Inspector Poolman now notified Superintendent Jones of the matter. In the meantime, Poolman, Charles Gubb, William James and Albert Roberts all went up the mountain to the spot described by Edwards. There, precisely where Edwards had said, they found the body of Elsie Cook, at 11.32 a.m. Elsie lay on her back, with her skirt resting just above the knees. Elsie's head had been almost severed and in the grass nearby was the clear impression of where a second body had lain. To the right of the body lay an open razor, the blade of which was heavily bloodstained and scattered around were a number of cigarette ends and spent matches. Finally, close by Elsie's feet lay the broken fragments of a beer flagon.

The inquest on the dead girl opened on 20 June at the Aberdare police court, before Mr Rees Jenkin Rhys. Edwards was still in hospital, but was represented by his solicitor, Mr A.J. Prosser. Evidence of identification was given by Edgar Cook, and details of the arrest were given by Inspector Poolman. After this, Dr Christian Balfour Fotheringham Millar, who had been treating Edwards, told the court of the injuries he had suffered.

Dr Millar said that he had arrived at the hospital at 11 a.m. on 17 June. He removed the dressing, which had been applied by Dr Bullen, and made his own examination of the wound in Edwards' throat. Edwards was trying to speak at the time, but Dr Millar told him not to. An immediate operation was ordered to close the wound properly and after this was done, Dr Millar next saw his patient at 11 a.m. on 18 June. Edwards' condition had already improved and continued to do so over the next couple of days.

At the end of this testimony, Mr Rhys remarked that it was a pity that Edwards was recovering from his injuries as a rather bad time awaited him. He added that the inquest would have to be adjourned until after the magistrates had dealt with the case.

Edwards' condition continued to improve and by 22 June, he was fit to be discharged. He was immediately escorted back to the police station where he was charged with the wilful murder of Elsie Cook. A number of Magistrates' Court appearances followed, the evidence not being finally heard until 11 July. Mr W. Thomas appeared for the Director of Public Prosecutions during the two day hearing, after which Edwards was sent to the next assizes to face his trial.

The next assizes were at Swansea in November, and it was on the 22nd of that month that Edwards appeared before Mr Justice Branson. Throughout the two days that the case lasted, Edwards was defended by Mr Morgan Evans while the prosecution lay in the hands of Mr Godfrey Parsons.

Edgar Cook, the dead girl's father, began by saying that Elsie had turned 21 on 28 October 1927. He told the court that he had last seen his daughter alive at 5.30 p.m. on Saturday, 16 June. He expected her to return home that night and when she had still not come home by the next morning, he went to Thomas Whitbread's house to see if he knew where Elsie was. Thomas told him that he had not seen Elsie and that Edwards had not come home either. Later that same day, two police officers called and escorted him to the mortuary where he had identified Elsie's body.

Annie Cook was the next witness and she told the court of her meeting with Edwards and his mother, after she had discovered that Elsie was carrying his child. After this, Harriett Cook, Elsie's sister, said that they had left the house together on 16 June and walked down Jubilee Road together. Elsie seemed perfectly normal and happy when they parted.

The next witness was 16-year-old Annie Prothero who now lived at 20 Princes Street in Swinton, but who used to live near Edwards and had been out with him a number of times. They had started seeing each other in January 1927 and had continued doing so until August of that same year, when Annie moved away. They still kept in touch by letter though, and when Annie went back to Wales on Easter Sunday, 8 April, she met Edwards, by accident, and went for a walk with him.

They talked together and Edwards confessed to her that he had been seeing Elsie Cook and thought he had got her into trouble. He said that he was in 'a fine mess' and even talked of committing suicide. Annie told him not to think of such a thing. She returned to Swinton soon afterwards and the next she heard from Edwards was on 12 June, when she received a letter from him. In this missive, he told her that the trouble he feared had come true and continued '...by the time you come home next, I shall have a wife or a coffin.'

Thomas Frederick Whitbread was Edwards' stepbrother and now lived in Bristol, but from the end of 1925 up to 19 May 1928, he had lived with his father, also named Thomas, in Aberdare. When he left Wales, Whitbread forgot to pack his razor, which had his initials and a star-shaped mark on the handle. He now identified the razor found near Elsie Cook's body as the one he had last seen on a shelf in his father's house.

In addition to giving details of Edwards' comments in the police station and his subsequent arrest, Inspector Poolman said that when he searched the prisoner, he found a sealed envelope in his wallet which contained three photographs. On the outside of the envelope was written, 'Please bury this with me.' The photographs were of Edwards and Annie Prothero together, and separate shots of them both, all taken at Barry Island the previous year.

PC Archibald Thomas said that he had accompanied the prisoner to the hospital on 17 June. During the day, Edwards spoke to him about the crime. Thomas cautioned him and said that he would write down whatever he said. Edwards spoke in short sentences and there were long gaps between various parts of the narrative, which meant that it was only completed at around 4 p.m. The statement began:

> I hit her on the head with a flagon. I planned all this out before. I knew what I was going to do when I went out on Saturday. There's only one thing I am sorry about is that I didn't finish the job properly but the razor wouldn't cut me. I must have blunted it on her. Perhaps I smashed the flagon on her head, fancy that, you wouldn't believe that her head would have been so hard but she had a felt hat on.
>
> I had it all planned. I bought the flagon on purpose to hit her on the head, to stun her, as I thought not for her to kick up a row. When I hit her, the flagon didn't stun her and she struggled as much as she could. I overpowered her, first of all choked her into a weakened state, then I finished her with a razor. I afterwards finished the letter to my mother which I had started earlier in the night, then smoked two cigarettes and attempted but failed to do myself in.

Dr Millar, in addition to attending to Edwards, had also performed the post-mortem on Elsie Cook. He reported a large transverse cut across her throat, running from one ear to the other. This had cut through all the large blood vessels, the windpipe and the gullet and a great deal of force had been needed to inflict this wound. On the top of the head was a small wound corresponding to a cut in the

The Brynffynon Hotel. Trevor John Edwards had a drink in the hotel before buying a flagon of beer – which he used to attack Elsie Cook before cutting her throat on a nearby mountainside. (Rhondda Cynon Taf / Aberdare Library)

A modern view of the Brynffynon Hotel.

hat. This was only ½in long and was surrounded by a recent bruise. The post-mortem showed that Elsie was indeed pregnant and the foetus, a boy, was between 4 and 5 months old.

An attempt was being made to show that Edwards was suffering from some mental problem and so was not responsible for his actions. Dr Millar said he did not detect any signs of insanity in the prisoner but confirmed that Edwards' father had been in an asylum some thirty-three years before and that his sister had committed suicide, seventeen years ago, by drinking carbolic acid.

Dr Bullen disagreed with Dr Millar as to Edwards' mental condition. He told the court that twelve months before the crime, Edwards had received a severe blow to the head. This blow could have been enough to set up an irritation on the surface of the brain, which might have predisposed Edwards to insanity. This, allied to the fact that there was a history of insanity in the family, led Dr Bullen to conclude that it was very likely that Edwards was suffering from impulsive insanity.

The entire matter now lay in the hands of the jury and, after a short deliberation, they concluded that Edwards was guilty of murder, but did add a strong recommendation to mercy on account of his age.

There was no appeal and in due course, despite the jury's recommendation, the Home Office advised Edwards' defence that the sentence would not be respited. Just a few days later, at 8 a.m. on Tuesday, 11 December 1928, a crowd of around 200 people gathered outside Swansea Prison as Trevor John Edwards was hanged by Robert Baxter and Alfred Allen. The proceedings were not without incident. Baxter had moved very quickly to pull the lever, which would spring the trap and end Edwards' life. Allen was still on the trapdoors and as they sprang back, he fell headlong into the pit, though fortunately he was not injured.

23

A STATE OF FRENZY

Although he was only 22 years old at the time, William John Corbett, a miner, fell in love with Ethel Louisa Jones, who was 21, early in 1917. It did not matter to him that she already had a 3-year-old daughter, Florence Matilda. In April of that year, the couple married and over the next thirteen years, six more children were born to the union. To all intents and purposes, the marriage was a happy one until, in November 1930, Corbett lost his job.

This, coupled with the financial concerns it brought, preyed heavily on William's mind, and at one stage he even threatened to commit suicide. There were other concerns for the family too; Ethel Corbett accused her husband of seeing other women and this caused several rows.

Florence, who was known as Thora, had never been told that Corbett was not her real father. Once she left school, Florence entered into service at a house in Llanishen, but once Corbett lost his job and her mother announced that she was expecting yet another child, Florence returned to the family home, a bungalow at 48 Caer Bragdy, off Lawrence Street, Caerphilly, to help Ethel.

It was close to 2 p.m. on Wednesday, 25 March 1931, and most of the Corbett children were at school. In the kitchen sat Corbett, Ethel and Florence and in an adjoining room, the youngest child, a 9-month-old baby, slept soundly. It was that moment that Ethel Corbett chose to bring up the matter of something that had happened the previous Thursday, 19 March.

On the 19th, Corbett had been alone in the house with Florence when, without explanation, he had seized her around the waist. Corbett then hit Florence, released his grip and went to the door. Florence took her chance to run out of the house and was seen crying by her sister, Margery. She in turn told her mother what she had seen, but not until 23 March.

The next morning, 24 March, Ethel Corbett asked her daughter what had happened between her and her father. Florence told her the whole story and was informed by her mother, for the first time, that Corbett was not her real father. Later that morning, Ethel asked Corbett why he had made Florence cry and he had replied, 'Nothing', and asked her to forgive him.

Now, though, on 25 March, the matter was brought up again. Florence was dressed up, ready to go out, and Corbett asked her where she was off to. Florence told him that she was going over to Llanishen to see Mrs Williams, the woman she had been in service with, to ask for her job back. Corbett objected to this and said that if she went, he would go over there and fetch her back. It was then that Ethel told Florence to go to the police if her father followed her. That seemed to cause something to snap inside Corbett for he shouted, 'That's the last', and struck Ethel in the mouth.

Seeing her mother hit, Florence leapt forward and tried to intervene. Corbett now turned his attention towards her. He struck her in the face a number of times, cutting a lip and giving her a black eye. Florence fell and Corbett, far from stopping his attack upon her, now began to kick and beat her. Now it was Ethel's turn to try to save her daughter but Corbett knocked her to the couch, took a razor from his pocket and drew it across her throat.

Florence tried to run from the house but Corbett, the razor still in his hand, caught her, threw her down onto a mat, put his hand under her chin and pulled her head backwards. There was little doubt that he intended to cut her throat too. The razor was raised high above Corbett's head and as it came down, Florence somehow managed to grab the handle. The struggle continued and Corbett was getting the upper hand. Seeing this, and despite her own terrible injury, Ethel threw herself onto Corbett's back in an attempt to save her daughter's life.

The plan worked, for Corbett loosened his grip on the razor and Florence was able to take it from him as he turned and struck Ethel yet again. While his back was turned, Florence hid the bloody weapon in her clothing. When Corbett faced her again and demanded to know where the razor was, she gasped that it had fallen on to the floor somewhere and while Corbett was searching for it, she finally managed to make good her escape.

Florence ran to fetch the police but PC William Bowen was not at home. Returning to her street, she then sought help from a neighbour and by the time they entered her home, Ethel was dead and Corbett was nowhere to be seen. In fact, Corbett had snatched up another weapon, a table knife, gone to a woods nearby and slashed his own throat. He was found there, later that same day, by PC Bowen. After receiving treatment to his throat, Corbett was charged with the murder of his wife.

Corbett made his first appearance before the magistrates on 26 March, his neck heavily bandaged. No evidence was offered but after hearing details of the charge, the magistrates set his next court date to 31 March when he was remanded again, until 8 April. On that date, Corbett appeared before three magistrates; Mr E.S. Williams, Mr Thomas James and Mr Evan Brinson. Mr C.S. Goodfellow acted for the Director of Public Prosecutions and Corbett was represented by Mr C. Davies-Jones.

After Florence Jones had given her testimony, Dr J.R. McManus was called. He stated that he had known the prisoner for twelve years. He described Corbett as physically sound but depressed. He was temperamental but Dr McManus did not expect that he would commit a crime of this nature.

One of the final witnesses was PC Bowen who stated that once he had heard of the crime, he went to look for Corbett and found him an hour later, in the woods. He was bleeding badly from a wound in his throat and when he saw Bowen he said, 'Is she dead? I intended to do myself in and the rest of the children.' Told that Ethel was indeed dead, Corbett continued, 'She was a good woman and I am sorry for what I have done.'

Sent for trial, Corbett appeared in the dock at Swansea, before Mr Commissioner Walker, on 2 July 1931. Mr Walter Samuel MP, and Mr Ellis Lloyd MP appeared for the prosecution while Corbett was defended by Mr Trevor Hunter and Mr Matebele Davies.

Florence Jones repeated her story of what she had witnessed on 25 March but also confirmed that she had heard Corbett threaten to kill himself more than once. Her mother had taken two razors from him and hidden them because she thought he had been 'acting funny' and was very worried about his finances. He only got 38s a week in benefits and the rent and other bills were getting into arrears.

After PC Bowen told the court of Corbett's arrest and his subsequent statements, Inspector Coles stepped into the witness box. He testified that at the police station, Corbett looked wild and said to him, 'During the past twelve or fourteen weeks there had been nothing over my head but a dark red cloud, worrying over my children and for my wife.'

Confirmation that Ethel had been concerned over Corbett's behaviour was given by a neighbour, Dorothy Well, who said that on the day before the tragedy, 24 March, Ethel had spoken to her and told her that she was worried as Corbett had threatened to kill himself and was asking where his razors were.

Another witness was John Venn, one of Corbett's friends, who said since Christmas 1930, he and others had taken to calling Corbett 'Looney' due to his odd behaviour. Venn said he had also spoken to Ethel and she had told him that Corbett was behaving strangely at night, roaming about the house.

Dr McManus gave details of the wound in Ethel's throat. There was a single cut, 5in long and deep enough to completely sever her windpipe and almost cut through the jugular vein. Death was due to haemorrhage and shock.

For the defence, Mr Hunter said that it was not in dispute that Corbett was responsible for his wife's death; what was at issue here was his frame of mind when the crime was committed. Mr Hunter claimed that the attack was carried out in a state of frenzy and to give credence to this, he now called his client to the witness box.

Corbett said that he could not remember anything of the crime. He maintained that the first he knew of the death of Ethel was when Inspector Coles charged him with murder. Mr Samuel for the prosecution pointed out that when charged, Corbett replied, 'I plead guilty; I tried to do it on myself. I done it' and surely this showed that he knew exactly what he had done, but Corbett continued to say that he couldn't remember anything.

The judge's summing up took an hour and Mr Commissioner Walker advised the jury to decide for themselves whether Corbett's behaviour had been a form of abnormality of a man so depressed through unemployment or whether it was simply anger. It took twenty minutes for the guilty verdict to be decided and, asked if he had anything to say, Corbett announced that his case had not been clear and he wished to appeal. Told that he could do so, he thanked the judge before the death sentence was passed.

Corbett's appeal was heard on 27 July, before the Lord Chief Justice, Lord Hewart and Justices Avory and Acton. The main thrust of the defence was, once again, that at the time he killed his wife, Corbett was insane and suffering from melancholia.

The court called Dr McGowan, the superintendent of the Cardiff City Mental Hospital, who testified that all people suffering from melancholia were potential suicides and that they might also commit homicide.

A letter which Corbett had written to the court, and which was dated 17 July, was now read out, as it was believed to throw some light on the possibility of a motive. In this document, Corbett claimed that Ethel had continually thrown at him the way in which she had fooled him into marrying her in the first place by telling him she was a widow with a child, when in reality she was a single woman and Florence was illegitimate.

Giving the court's judgement, Lord Hewart pointed out that in a case where insanity was the reply to a charge, it was the duty of the defence to prove that the prisoner was insane at the time the crime was committed. It was not for the Appeal Court to decide on a prisoner's sanity. This was a matter more properly handled by the Home Office. The appeal was dismissed.

Just sixteen days later, on Wednesday, 12 August 1931, William John Corbett was hanged at Cardiff Prison.

24

SMALL CHANGE

The party at 69 Ferry Road, Cardiff, had been a great success. Everyone had had a great time that Saturday night and, by the time the festivities began to break up, it was the small hours of Sunday, 4 February 1940.

At 2.45 a.m., 38-year-old Arthur John Allen left no. 69 with a group of friends. In addition to Evan Lewis, there was also Lewis' wife, mother and sister, her boyfriend and a gentleman named George Sheppard, his wife and their two sons.

They all strolled as far as Kent Street where Arthur Allen said he was going to go home. Evan Lewis' mother said she wanted Arthur to come to her home and spend the night there as she couldn't forgive herself if something happened to him, wandering the streets at this hour. It was at that moment that another man who had been at the party, 29-year-old George Edward Roberts, came upon the group, threw his arm around Arthur Allen's shoulder and announced, 'You don't want to worry about him. I'll see him home.' The two men then strolled off up Kent Street together.

At 4.30 a.m., PC Arthur Jones and PC Eugene Addicott were behind the reception desk at the Grangetown police station when two men came in. One was carrying the other who appeared to have been badly beaten and was bleeding profusely from the head. Unfortunately, the lights had fused inside the station, so PC Jones shone his torch onto the two and saw that the injured man wore no jacket, overcoat or hat. His companion greeted the two officers with, 'I fell over this man in Bradford Street', and when Jones asked the Samaritan for his name and address, he replied that he was called Smith and lived at 56 Holmerdale Street.

The injured man, who was only semi-conscious, was taken through to the back by PC Jones and given some basic first aid while one of the officers called for an ambulance. As this was taking place, two women came into the station and spoke to PC Addicott. One of these ladies said that she was Mrs Marjorie Irene Clifford of 54 Kent Street, and that her companion was her sister, Doris Mary Scott. They wished to report an incident which had taken place at their house.

After Addicott had listened to their story, he called for PC Jones to talk to Mrs Clifford. She was then taken to see 'Mr Smith' and immediately identified him as George Roberts, a man who lodged at the house where she lived. PC Jones then accompanied Mrs Clifford and her sister back to Kent Street while Roberts was left in the charge of PC Dowdall. While his colleagues were away, Dowdall asked Roberts what had happened to which Roberts, maintaining his earlier story, said, 'I don't know. I stumbled over him in Bradford Street and saw that he was covered in blood so I brought him here.'

Meanwhile, PC Jones had arrived at 54 Kent Street. He saw that a number of mats in the hallway were disarranged. Going into the middle room, he noticed a large pool of blood near a chair and a second pool on the chair arm. A large iron bar, also heavily bloodstained, lay on the floor. On the mantelpiece, Jones found an empty wallet and an address book, both of which had the name Arthur Allen and an address at 121 Clive Road, Cardiff, inside.

On the table were two cups, both drained of liquid. On another chair, close to the table, Jones saw a man's hat. The time now was around 5.15 a.m. and Jones, satisfied that there had been some sort of attack at Kent Street, returned to the police station to confront Roberts.

Roberts refused to give any explanation and persisted in his claim that he had found the injured man in Bradford Street. Told that further investigations would have to be made, Roberts suddenly announced, 'You can arrest me now for hitting him on the head with an iron bar.' Detective Sergeant William Hopkin then cautioned Roberts and informed him that he would be held in custody. Arthur Allen had by then been taken to the City Lodge Hospital where his condition was described as very serious.

George Roberts appeared in court for the first time on 5 February, to face a charge of wounding. Only the most basic evidence was heard before the prisoner was remanded to 8 February. There were seven further court appearances until 6 April, on which date it was revealed that Allen's condition had taken a turn for the worse and his depositions had been taken at Cardiff Royal Infirmary. On 8 April, Allen lapsed into a coma and at 9.05 a.m. on 9 April, he died without regaining consciousness. The charge against Roberts was amended to one of wilful murder. Further police court appearances took place on 20 April and 30 April and it was not until 8 May that the evidence was given, before the stipendiary magistrate, Mr Cornelius Albert Grifiths. This final hearing lasted for two days, after which Roberts was sent for trial.

George Roberts stood in the dock before Mr Justice MacNaghten at Swansea on 16 July 1940. During the two–day trial, the case for the prosecution was led by Mr Rowland Thomas, assisted by Mr Godfrey Parsons. Roberts was defended by Mr O. Temple Morris MP, and Mr H.H. Roskin.

One of the first witnesses was Mathilda Dorothy Allen, the dead man's wife. She said that her husband, who was in the navy, had come home on leave on 26 January. A few days later he was invited to a party and had left their house in Clive Road at some time between 7.30 p.m. and 7.45 p.m. on 3 February.

George Henry Sheppard confirmed that he was one of the guests at the party, which was for a friend's engagement. Sheppard knew both Allen and Roberts as friends. Before he attended the party, Sheppard had been for a drink in the Forge Inn, and had seen Roberts in there. Sheppard then confirmed the details of the encounter with Roberts at the bottom of Kent Street.

Evan Thomas Hewittson Lewis told the court that the party on the night of 3 February had been for his brother's engagement. Allen was invited as a friend of the family and someone who had served at sea with Lewis' brother. Lewis also referred to the meeting in Kent Street after the party was over.

The next witness was Marjorie Irene Clifford, who stated that she was the wife of John Clifford and they lived together at 54 Kent Street, a house owned by her sister. In addition to her own family, Roberts, his wife and his children also occupied the house, having the middle room on the ground floor and the back bedroom on the first floor.

Marjorie said that she had retired to her bed at 11 p.m. on 3 February, her room being directly above the middle room. In the small hours of the morning, she was woken by the sound of a radio being played, but soon managed to drift back to sleep. Some time later she was woken again, this time by loud banging. Though she stayed in bed, Marjorie heard Mrs Roberts leave her own bedroom and go downstairs. Minutes later, she heard another sound from downstairs, one which seemed to her to be that of someone dragging something along the passageway that led to the front door.

Marjorie Clifford had gone to see what was happening but first went to Roberts' bedroom to see if he knew what the noise was. Mrs Roberts was there and asked Marjorie to take the children to her bedroom. Marjorie did as she asked and then went downstairs herself. By now, Mrs Roberts was also down there, as was Marjorie's sister, Doris Scott. The light was on and there was blood scattered around the middle room and an iron bar lying on the floor. It was then that Marjorie and Doris went to the police to report that something terrible had happened in their house.

When Roberts had arrived at the police station, carrying Allen, it had been noted that the latter had no coat, overcoat or hat. The hat had, of course, been found in Roberts' room at Kent Street, but witnesses were now called who had found other items which belonged to the dead man.

Richard Gordon Lace was a 16-year-old milk roundsman who lived at 85 Ferry Road. He told the court that he was walking along Kent Street at 6 a.m. on 4 February when he tripped over something lying on the pavement outside no. 60. Looking more closely, Richard saw that it was a blue jacket and overcoat. One of the sleeves of the coat was inside out and both items were wet, as it had been raining. Richard took the items home but later that morning, at 9 a.m., he noticed that the clothes had blood on them, so he handed them to his father and asked him what he should do. Richard's father, Thomas James Lace, had taken the items along to the police.

Stella Courtney lived at 87 Ferry Road, and she testified that at 8.30 a.m. on 4 February, she had found a scarf in Kent Street, close to the corner where Kent Street and Ferry Street met. The scarf was already very wet but she took it home and put it into some water to wash it. The water immediately turned a deep red colour so Stella told the police and they took the scarf away.

Arthur Allen's deposition, taken on 26 March, was then read. In it he said that after the party, he and others were walking home and at the corner of Kent Street, Roberts came up, put a hand on his shoulder and said that he would take care of him. On the way up Kent Street, Allen had said that he wanted to telephone for a taxi from a call box, but didn't have any change. Roberts insisted that he come to his house at no. 54 where he would ask his wife for some coppers.

Allen agreed to go and once there, Roberts said that his wife was probably in bed and he would go up to speak to her. He asked Allen to sit down and join him in a cup of tea, which he did. The next thing he remembered was waking up in the hospital to find a doctor stitching his temple. Allen had also been able to identify the jacket, coat and scarf found in the street as his property and confirmed that he had had five £1 notes in his wallet when he went to Kent Street.

PC Jones told of Roberts' visit to the police station and added that when Roberts was cautioned he said, 'I knew when I brought him here I should be nabbed for it but I wished to save him from further injuries from bleeding.' The prisoner had then been searched and on him Jones found 1s 9d in silver, five pennies, four keys, an electric torch, a contraceptive, some cigarettes and some matches.

Allen's wallet had been found on the mantelpiece at Kent Street, empty of all cash. When Roberts was searched, though, only a total of 2s 2d had been found. The mystery of the missing money was apparently solved by Maurice Patrick Kemble, an auxiliary fireman who was on duty at the police station. He saw Roberts there at 7 a.m., and Roberts had asked Kemble for a cigarette. Kemble threw him a packet with a couple of cigarettes in it. Roberts took one and then returned the packet.

When Kemble next opened it, some time later, he found that there were now five £1 notes in it, and they were bloodstained. He handed the money over to the police.

Dr Thomas David Vincent England was the resident medical officer at the City Lodge Hospital. He stated that Allen had been admitted at 5 a.m. on 4 February, and was unconscious. Allen had been bleeding freely from the nose and right ear. His right eye was heavily bruised. Dr England observed wounds over both temples. The one on the right was 1in long and extended down to the bone while the one on the left was 2in long, and again went down to the bone. There was a fracture under the wound on the right. An X-ray was taken, which showed that the skull was fractured. Treatment was given but it became clear that an operation was necessary and so, on 23 March, Allen was transferred to the Royal Infirmary.

Dr Ross Bloom was the assistant to the surgical unit at the Royal and he said that the operation on the skull had been performed on 28 March, by Professor Lambert Rogers. For a few days, Allen's condition remained stable but it worsened on 3 April and he died on 9 April. Dr Bloom had been present when the post-mortem had been carried out by Dr Gough.

Dr Jethro Gough, the senior lecturer in pathology at the Royal Infirmary, observed scars on the dead man's forehead. There were also healed cuts on top of the scalp and recent surgical incisions. Opening the skull, Dr Gough found a fracture of the frontal and right parietal bones. The skull, as a whole, was of a normal thickness; three to four millimetres, but in the location of the fracture, it was abnormally thin. The fracture had caused an abscess to form in the right frontal lobe of the brain and this in turn had caused the whole surface to become inflamed. The actual cause of death was abscess of the brain and meningitis.

One of the final witnesses for the prosecution was Dr Eric Dermott Sweet. He said he had first attended the scene of the crime at 10.30 p.m. on 4 February. Dr Sweet reported various pools of blood, including a small one on the front door mat, and one just inside the doorway of the middle room. In Dr Sweet's opinion, the pattern of blood splashes on the chair itself showed that Allen had been struck while he was sitting down and had then been dragged through the door and along the passageway to the front door. The doctor had also examined the iron bar and items taken from the prisoner. The bar bore blood of the same type as Allen's and hairs adhering to it matched his colouring. His blood was also on Roberts' trousers, the cigarettes and the banknotes found by Maurice Kemble.

On the second day of the trial, Roberts gave his own evidence. He now claimed that he had acted in self-defence. While Allen was sitting in the chair, he had taken some money from Allen's pocket but he was seen and a struggle took place. Allen was getting the better of him so he picked up the bar to defend himself.

In his closing speech, Mr Temple Morris said that the blood marks found in the room were consistent with Roberts' story of a struggle. Even though his client was a self-confessed liar and thief, this did not make him a murderer. There was no evidence that the attack was intentional, unprovoked or with malice and in his opinion, three verdicts were possible; guilty of murder, not guilty of murder but guilty of manslaughter or not guilty.

The jury took two hours to decide that Roberts was guilty of murder. Mrs Allen, dressed entirely in black, was in court to hear the verdict and paled visibly as the death sentence was passed on the prisoner.

Three weeks later, at 9 a.m. on Thursday, 8 August, George Edward Roberts was hanged at Cardiff. There were only a handful of people outside the prison at the time, but one, a woman, dropped to her knees in prayer as the fateful moment arrived.

25

THE MURDER THAT NEVER WAS

Howard Jospeh Grossley, 1945

There could be no doubt that 37-year-old Howard Joseph Grossley, a Canadian soldier, shot and killed his lover, 29-year-old Lily Griffiths, but even the victim agreed that this was not a case of murder!

Grossley was a married man, but his wife had remained in Canada when he came over to this country with the army in 1940. He met Lily, a single woman, soon afterwards and they started living as man and wife, and a son was born from the union in 1943. By all accounts, Lily and Grossley were very happy together.

In due course, the Allies invaded Europe and the Axis forces were pushed back into Germany. The war was coming to a close and Grossley was fully aware of the fact that one day soon he would be sent back to Canada, leaving Lily and his son behind.

On 3 March 1945, Grossley and Lily went to live with Jennie Blodwen Atkinson at 227 New Road, Porthcawl. Three days later, on 6 March, Lily brought her son, who was by now two years old, to the house.

Lily Griffiths left 227 New Road at 12.15 p.m. on 12 March to attend a job interview at the Bridgend arsenal. When she returned, Lily told Grossley that she had been successful but could only start work the following week as she had a rather bad cold at the time. Some time later, Lily announced that she was taking the boy to Aberdare and Grossley walked her to the bus stop.

At 6 p.m., the Atkinson family were listening to the radio, along with Grossley, when a news item said that a number of German prisoners had escaped from a camp near Bridgend. This led Jennie Atkinson's young son to comment that if he had possession of Grossley's gun, he would go out and look for them. Hearing this, Jennie's husband, Ernest Atkinson, asked his guest if it were true that he had a gun in the house. Grossley admitted that it was and when Ernest's son asked if he might see it, Grossley told him that it was upstairs in a green bag in his bedroom. The boy dashed upstairs and returned with the weapon moments later.

Ernest now asked Grossley if the revolver was loaded and was surprised to hear him say that it was. Ernest asked him to unload it, which he did before showing the entire family how it worked. Grossley then took it back from Ernest's son and reloaded it before placing it in the inside pocket of the battledress he was wearing. Ernest Atkinson asked Grossley if he intended taking the gun out with him when he went to meet Lily later on and Grossley replied that, as a soldier, he always carried it and added that he might well meet some of the escaped German prisoners.

At 6.30 p.m., Grossley left the house. Soon after this, Jennie Atkinson went to the cinema, not returning home until 10 p.m. By then, Lily Griffiths was back and was sitting in the kitchen, knitting a pair of socks for her son. Minutes later, Grossley came in and Lily asked him where he had been.

Grossley simply replied 'Out', but then produced a ring from his mackintosh pocket and said it had been given to him. He appeared to have been drinking, and walked to the door of the room, beckoning with his head for Lily to follow him. The two lovers were then heard going upstairs and though that was the last either Jennie Atkinson or her husband saw of them that night, they did hear the front door open and close at 11 p.m.

John Carter Clare lived at 175 New Road. On 12 March, he and his wife had retired for the night at 11 p.m., but less than an hour later, at 11.55 p.m., Clare heard a scream, which was followed almost immediately by a loud report. Clare looked out of his window and though he could not see too clearly in the darkness, there was someone standing in the shadows in an alleyway which was about four houses away from his own.

The scream and report had also been heard by other occupants of New Road. Lilian Elizabeth Harvey, a single woman living at no. 181, and had gone to bed at 11.30 p.m. She too heard the scream and what sounded like a shot, as did four men at no. 183, the house next door.

Arthur James Speck, George Isaac Lewis, Frank Jones and Fred Aston were all repairing a radio inside 183 New Road when, at around 11.55 p.m., they heard a shot ring out. All four men left the house via the back door to investigate and two of them, Speck and Aston, looked over the wall which divided the house from the narrow lane which ran alongside it. Neither man saw anything untoward. The other two went down the lane towards New Road itself. As they fumbled along in the darkness, they suddenly saw someone flashing a torch, and as they walked towards the beam, a soldier stepped forward and said, 'Fetch a doctor, I have shot my dear wife.'

All four men had heard this comment and ran to offer what assistance they could. The soldier, Grossley, was in a very distressed state and asked if one of them would go to his landlord, Mr Atkinson, and tell him what had happened. Walking past the soldier, Arthur Speck was the first to come upon the form of Lily Griffiths. She was lying on the ground, and as Speck examined her, Grossley came forward, fell to his knees and cried, 'My darling, what have I done?' Lily, who was still conscious, replied, 'Don't worry dear. You couldn't help it.'

At this point, Speck believed that it had been someone else who had attacked both Lily and Grossley and so asked the injured woman who it was. Lily said that she didn't know while Grossley pointed towards some allotments nearby and said that two men had run off in that direction. George Lewis also heard Grossley add that the assailants had been German prisoners who had stopped them and demanded Lily's handbag. Grossley claimed that he had tried to wrestle with one of the prisoners, had pulled out his revolver and managed to get between the German and Lily. During the struggle, his revolver had accidentally gone off and Lily had been hit. Lewis then ran to the nearest telephone box and rang for the police and an ambulance.

In fact, there had been no need to contact the police. PC Thomas Lewis had been on duty, with War Reserve Sergeant Thomas Nicholas, at the junction of John Street, South Road and New Road when he heard what sounded like a shot coming from somewhere down New Road. He arrived on the scene within minutes. Grossley was still in a distressed state and greeted Lewis with, 'Oh dear, oh dear, I have shot my wife. Two men attacked us. I missed them and shot my wife.'

Lily Griffiths was obviously in some distress for she asked PC Lewis for something to kill the pain. Having told the injured woman that medical help was on its way, Lewis turned to Grossley and asked where the revolver was now. Grossley, saying, 'I have an automatic here', took the weapon from his coat

John Street, Porthcawl, where PC Lewis and Sergeant Nicholas were on duty when they heard a shot. (Reflective Images)

A modern view of John Street, Porthcawl.

pocket and handed it to the officer. Lewis then informed Grossley, quite properly, that once his wife had been taken to the hospital, he would have to come along to the police station to answer questions.

As PC Lewis escorted Grossley to the police station at Porthcawl, he administered a caution after Grossley asked if he thought Lily might die. Grossley did not speak again until he arrived at the station, at 12.15 a.m. on 13 March, when he was handed over to Inspector William Matthews.

Inspector Matthews listened as PC Lewis told him, 'This man has shot a woman believed to be his wife, near New Road schools. She is in a bad condition. Here is the gun he used.' The weapon was then given to the inspector who broke it open and found one spent cartridge and six live rounds. Inspector Matthews asked Grossley if he wished to make a written statement. Grossley said he did, whereupon he was cautioned again. After finishing the document, Grossley was told he would be detained pending further inquiries.

It was midnight when Dr Robert Hodgkinson arrived at New Road to attend to the injured woman. Lily complained again that she was in terrible pain and, after a quick examination, Dr Hodgkinson administered an injection of morphine before ordering that she be taken to Bridgend Hospital. The doctor had observed what looked like recent bruises on Lily's face and legs and later, at the hospital, once the patient had been undressed, he saw more on her body and arms. In Dr Hodgkinson's opinion, considerable force would have been needed to cause some of these marks and some might even have come as the result of a kick. This cast new light on the 'happy' relationship that had supposedly existed between Grossley and Lily Griffiths and, since Lily needed an operation which might prove dangerous, she was told by Dr Hodgkinson that she should make her own statement saying what had happened to her. Lily agreed, made her statement, and at 4 a.m. was taken to the operating theatre.

Lily's condition did not improve, though. On 14 March, Dr Hodgkinson aspirated two pints of blood from the left side of her chest. At 4 p.m. that same day, Lily, who was between three and four months pregnant, aborted, but none of this made her condition any better. She was informed that it was likely she would die and, later that same day, made a dying deposition.

On 15 March, Grossley was charged with attempted murder and appeared before the magistrates at Bridgend. Detective Inspector Lancelot Bailey explained that there were more inquiries to make and asked for a remand of fourteen days. In the event, a seven-day remand was ordered and Grossley was told that he would be brought back to court on 22 March.

In the event, matters moved more rapidly and, on 16 March, Lily Griffiths died. As a result, when Grossley made his next court appearance, it was a brief one and he was remanded again. On 29 March, the charge against him was changed to one of wilful murder and after a final hearing, on 24 and 25 April, he was sent for trial on that charge.

Howard Grossley faced Mr Justice Singleton at Swansea on 11 July 1945. The case lasted two days, during which the prisoner was represented by Mr H. Glyn-Jones, who maintained throughout that his client should be facing no more serious a charge than one of manslaughter. The case for the prosecution rested in the hands of Mr Ralph Sutton.

William Rees Thomas, a taxi-driver of 16 Nicholls Avenue, stated that at 8 p.m. on 12 March, he drove his cab to the Esplanade Hotel. Grossley was there, drinking, and the two men fell into conversation, having a pint of beer together. From there, he, the prisoner and two other men went to the Victoria Hotel where Grossley had a further four pints. When Thomas left, at 10 p.m., Grossley was still there.

New Road, Porthcawl, where Lily Griffiths was shot by Howard Joseph Grossley.

Lilian Harvey, in addition to saying that she had heard the scream and the shot, said that the following morning, 13 March, she had gone into one of the rooms downstairs with her landlady, Mrs Lilian Newlyn. They had found a spent bullet on the settee, which lay opposite from the window. This was confirmed by Lilian Violet Newlyn who reported that on 12 March, the window in that room had been perfectly fine but on 13 March, she had found some glass on the floor and noticed a hole in one of the panes.

Medical testimony was given by Dr Jethro Gough and nurse, Beryl Edwards. Nurse Edwards said she had been on duty in Lily's ward on the morning of 15 March and had heard Lily exclaim, 'I am going to die.' The nurse was present when Lily's dying deposition was taken and, after the document had been finished, heard her say, 'This is the God's honest truth.'

Dr Gough had performed the post-mortem, assisted and observed by Dr Hodgkinson. Dr Gough observed that Lily's left eye was bruised and there were other marks on her chin, upper left arm and on the lower part of her abdomen. The single bullet had entered the body on the left side of the chest, passed through the left breast, the stomach, liver and left lung before coming out close to the last rib on the left side. This wound had caused the left lung to collapse and death was due to a septic infection in the chest cavity.

The prosecution scenario was that Grossley had deliberately killed his wife and then tried to say they had been attacked by escaped prisoners. The one problem with this was that even the victim agreed that the entire affair had been a tragic accident.

Lily's original statement, taken when she was first admitted to hospital, said that after going up to their room, Grossley had asked her to go for a walk. She had agreed and they had left the house at around 11 p.m. There had already been much discussion between them over Grossley's impending return to Canada and he had suggested that it would be best if he took his own life.

At the end of the lane, Grossley took out his revolver and said, 'I will finish myself now.' They struggled and she tried to take the gun away from him but he pushed her back and almost immediately she heard a loud report and felt a searing pain in her chest. Grossley flew into a panic and cried out that he hadn't meant to do it but Lily's statement added that there were elements of self-preservation involved. Before he had gone to look for help, Grossley had asked her to say that two Germans had attacked them if anyone asked. Lily's statement ended with the confession that Grossley had sometimes beaten her but only when he was drunk and the next morning he would have had no memory of it.

Lily's second statement, her dying deposition, was then read out. She began by saying again that they had gone out for a walk, but then stopped her testimony and cried, 'I can't stand this.' Lily then asked for her earlier statement to be read out to her and after this was done, said that all she wished to add was that, 'Howard would never hurt me. He has always been good to me.' She ended by repeating that the gun had gone off accidentally.

George Edward Lewis Carter, a chemist from the Forensic Science Laboratory at Cardiff, had made a careful examination of Lily's clothing. He had found no scorch marks around the bullet entry hole and concluded that the gun had been held at a distance of between 16ins and 20ins when it was fired. The gun, a Colt 38, had been examined by Francis Edward Morton of Birmingham. He had fired the gun a number of times and found no mechanical fault with it.

One of the final witnesses was Detective Inspector Lancelot Douglas Bailey. He said that during the early days of the investigation, Grossley had stuck to his story of the two German prisoners, but after much questioning had admitted that this was a lie and claimed that the gun had gone off accidentally when he had struggled with Lily. He had wanted to shoot himself but she tried to stop him and was hit.

Grossley did not give evidence on his own behalf and it was left to the jury to decide whether they believed this was all a tragic accident or not. In the event, they decided that Grossley was guilty as charged. He remained silent as the death sentence was intoned. An appeal was heard on 21 August before Justices Wrottesley, Croom-Johnson and Stable, but they felt that there was no reason to interfere with the verdict.

Just over two weeks later, on Wednesday, 5 September 1945, Howard Joseph Grossley was hanged at Cardiff Prison.

26

THE WASHERWOMAN

Evan Hadyn Evans, 1948

At around 6.30 p.m. on Saturday, 11 October 1947, a gentleman named Phillips finished his drink in the Butcher's Arms Hotel in Wattstown, a small town situated a few miles north-west of Pontypridd in the Rhondda Valley. As he walked out of the bar, Phillips almost bumped into a neighbour of his, 21-year-old Evan Hadyn Evans, a colliery turbine driver of Heol Llechau, also in Wattstown. Evans invited Phillips to go back into the pub with him and have a game of cards. Phillips agreed and ordered himself another pint.

The two men had not been in the Butcher's Arms for very long when 76-year-old Rachel Allen, known locally as the washerwoman, walked over to Evans and said something to him. Phillips did not hear what passed, but whatever it was it seemed to have angered Evans, for he told Rachel to go away in no uncertain terms.

Closing time was 10 p.m. and Phillips and Evans left, intending to walk home together, but outside the hotel, Phillips saw another friend and stopped to talk to him. Evans strolled off alone towards Heol Llechau.

At around 10.15 p.m., Mrs Harper, who also lived in Heol Llechau, but who was walking up the street past the Butcher's Arms, heard old Mrs Allen shouting at someone outside her house in Hillside Terrace. Rachel called out, 'If you don't go from here, I'll report you to the police!' She was shouting at a man who wore a dark suit and Mrs Harper saw him walk away, followed by Rachel Allen.

One hour later, at around 11.15 p.m., Mrs Gertrude Morris opened a doorway leading to an inner yard shared by a number of houses, including her own, 76a Hillside Terrace. As she walked into the dark interior, she almost stumbled over something lying on the ground. Looking more closely, Mrs Morris saw that it was a woman's body and the bandage on one of the legs told her that it was her next-door neighbour, Rachel Allen. Mrs Morris ran to fetch her brother-in-law, Thomas Joseph Rowlands, and he in turn went for PC Stephen Henton.

The first theory was that Mrs Allen had disturbed burglars trying to gain entrance to the grocer's shop, next door to her home. No one suspected that Rachel herself was the intended victim of a robbery, as it was well known in the district that she had little money. The attack, though, had been a most brutal one for Rachel's face was a mass of blood and bruises. Great violence had been used and the killer must have been stained, as a bloody palm print was found on Rachel's front door.

The police decided to call in the help of Scotland Yard and so Detective Chief Inspector John Capstick and Detective Sergeant Stoneman arrived in Wales on the Sunday and immediately began interviewing people. Soon, the altercation with Evans had come to their attention and, as a matter of routine, they visited him at his home on the evening of 13 October. Evans, who was in bed at the time, said he knew nothing about the attack but was, nevertheless, asked to go to the police station to make a statement.

The people who had seen Evans on the night of 11 October all reported that he was dressed in a dark brown suit. When the police took Evans into the Ferndale station, he put on a suit which, he made great pains to underline, was the only one he had. Evans was immediately accepted as a strong suspect but maintained that he had nothing to do with the attack upon Rachel until, after much questioning, he suddenly changed his story and admitted that he was responsible. He was charged with murder at 3.15 a.m. on 14 October and later that day, the police returned to Heol Llechau and, hidden in a sofa, they found the brown suit, which bore obvious signs of heavy bloodstaining.

It was also on 14 October that Evans appeared before the stipendiary magistrate, Mr Stanley Evans, and two of his colleagues, Mr Oliver Howells and Mr W.M. Jones. Evans, who was frail looking and barely 5ft tall, listened as Detective Inspector Thomas Williams gave evidence of arrest. Williams also gave a few more facts about the dead woman, including that she had lived very frugally in Hillside Terrace for the past ten years. The house was sparsely furnished with only two chairs, a makeshift bed and a table. At the time she died, Rachel had just a loaf of bread, some tea and some sugar in the house. Evans was then remanded, to 22 October.

On the 22nd, Evans was taken to Pontypridd police court. The police said that they were still not ready to proceed and a further remand was ordered, until 30 October. On that date, a third remand was granted and it was not until 5 November that all the witnesses were called.

The case for the Director of Public Prosecutions was outlined by Mr J.F. Claxton who called witnesses to explain the detailed forensic evidence in this case. There were eleven prosecution witnesses in all and after hearing their testimony, the magistrates ruled that there was a case to answer.

The trial of Evan Evans took place at Cardiff on 15 December 1947, before Mr Justice Byrne. The prosecution lay in the hands of Mr Arthian Davies and Mr Elwyn Jones and Evans' defence team was Mr Hubert Llewellyn Williams and Mr Morgan Owen. Even from the outset there was drama. Asked how he pleaded to the charge, Evans muttered 'Guilty' in a low voice. There followed a hurried consultation with Mr Williams after which Evans announced, in a much clearer voice, 'Not Guilty'.

Mrs Harper repeated her story of hearing Rachel Allen telling someone to go away from her house. She was not able to positively identify Evans as the man she had seen, but did swear that the man was wearing a dark suit, probably brown.

Mrs Morris explained that she lived next door to the dead woman and their houses opened onto a common yard through which all the occupants passed to get to their front doors. On the night of 11 October, she had stumbled over something in the dark and at first thought it was one of Mrs Allen's cats. It was only when she opened her own front door and lit the gas, that enough light was shed into the yard for her to realise that the bundle was a body.

The post-mortem examination had been carried out by Dr Charles Royal Ernest Freezer, who reported extensive head injuries, but added that the attack upon Mrs Allen had fallen into three stages. In the first stage, she had been beaten and punched in the face, which would have rendered her semi-conscious. In the second stage, Mrs Allen was raped while she was on the ground. The assailant then stood and kicked her repeatedly in the face and head. This pulped Mrs Allen's face, fractured her skull and broke her jaw.

A general view of Wattstown, where Evan Hadyn Evans murdered Rachel Allen. (Rhondda Cynon Taf/Aberdare Library)

Another view of Wattstown. (Reflective Images)

The brown suit which Evans had worn on the night bore many bloodstains, all of which were the same type as Rachel Allen's. A pair of freshly polished shoes was also examined and a small fragment of what proved to be human bone was found. Close by this bone were some small spots of blood, which again, matched Mrs Allen's.

Evans had made a statement at the police station, and this was now read out in court. It one part it read, 'She said to me, "You filthy pig, I will fetch a policeman to you." I raised my arm and hit her.' It continued, 'I hit her five or six times with my right fist. She fell to the floor then, and I kicked her about four times in the face. I lit a match and she was badly bleeding and I realised what I had done, and went straight home.'

It was now that Evans stepped into the witness box to elaborate on this statement. He told the court that on his way home he had heard Rachel calling for her cats. He accidentally bumped into her and she called him a filthy pig.

He turned and struck her with his fist and she fell into the yard. Evans then said that he hit Rachel a few more times while she was on the ground, picked her up, hit her again and she fell down and rolled over onto her back. He then started kicking her. Evans also described how he had raped Rachel while she was semi-conscious.

The defence claimed that Evans had been provoked, but in his summing up, Mr Justice Byrne described the killing of Rachel Allen as a callous and filthy murder. With Evans' own description of the attack added to all the other evidence, there was little doubt that the jury would agree and they did not delay in returning their guilty verdict. Almost immediately, an intention to appeal was announced.

The appeal was finally heard on 19 January 1948, but even Evans' own barrister, Mr Morgan Owen, said at the outset that he did not think there was anything he could say in support of it. The Lord Chief Justice, Lord Goddard, and his two colleagues, Justices Humphreys and Singleton, agreed.

Just over two weeks later, on Tuesday, 3 February, Evan Hadyn Evans, who had by now turned 22, was hanged at Cardiff, as a small crowd gathered in the drizzle outside the prison gates.

27

A FRIEND OF THE FAMILY

Clifford Godfrey Wills, 1948

John Anthony Parry earned his living as a steel worker, and during the early part of June 1948, he was on the afternoon shift, working from 2 p.m. until 10 p.m. On Thursday, 8 June, he left his home at 11 Wayfield Crescent, Pontnewydd, at about 1.20 p.m., and did not return until around 10.20 p.m. To John's surprise, although his 14-year-old son was home, there was no sign of his 32-year-old wife, Sillvinea May Parry.

There was no note from Sillvinea, so John assumed that she might have gone to the pictures. Eventually, though, the cinemas closed and still there was no sign of her. That night, John Parry whiled away his time smoking one cigarette after another, making copious cups of tea and taking the occasional walk around the dark streets of the village to see if he could find any trace of his wife.

The next morning, at 10 a.m., John decided that he would have to report the matter to the police. He set out, but in Commercial Street, he found Sergeant Dan Plummer and told him that Sillvinea had gone missing. Sergeant Plummer noted the details.

Once he had arrived back at Wayfield Crescent, John Parry went upstairs for the first time since he had come home from work the previous night. There were three bedrooms, the front one he and his wife shared, the back one was occupied by his son, and the third, a small boxroom was used to store junk, though it did also contain a small single bed.

It was into this boxroom that Parry ventured and immediately something struck him as odd. The vacuum cleaner he had put on top of the bed after he had used it the previous morning was in a different position. It was only when John moved the corner of the bedclothes in order to straighten them that he saw a pair of legs underneath the bed. John Parry had finally found his wife.

Sergeant Plummer was still in Commercial Street when, at 10.45 a.m., a rather breathless John Parry told him what he had found. The sergeant returned to Wayfield Crescent with Parry and went to look in the boxroom. Sure enough, there lay the body of a woman, face down, her dress pushed high onto her back, revealing her stockinged legs and bare buttocks.

By 11 a.m., Dr Francis Thomas Nolan was in attendance and certified that the woman was dead. Some fifteen minutes later, Inspector Charles Leonard Parsons arrived and he, Sergeant Plummer and other officers made a careful inspection of the house.

Pulling back the mattress on the bed, Sergeant Plummer found a large spanner protruding through the wire mesh. Meanwhile, Detective Constable Harry Glover had spotted some bloody footprints on the linoleum in the toilet and bloody palm prints were also seen. Glover also found a dagger, in a sheath, hidden in a boot in one of the bedrooms. Other officers were downstairs talking to John Parry and it was to them that he mentioned the name of a family friend who was in the habit of calling at the house; 31-year-old Clifford Godfrey Wills, an electrician of 3 Cromwell Place.

At 2.30 p.m., Inspector Parsons and Sergeant Plummer went to visit Wills. He was upstairs in bed and when the sergeant pulled back the bedclothes, he saw that the Wills' white shirt had stains down the front which looked very much like blood. Wills' right hand also appeared to be swollen and there was a fresh cut on the knuckle. Asked to account for these injuries and stains, Wills replied, 'I was in a bit of a fracas with Kid Logan in the New Found Out in Newport last night. He is always getting fresh.'

Asked when he had last seen Mrs Parry, Wills admitted, 'We were together in Newport yesterday and went to the Olympia cinema together.' Wills was then cautioned and immediately commented, 'She had an appointment with someone. I got a bit mad and decided to end it but I did not kill her, sergeant.'

Sergeant Plummer noticed that Wills appeared to be very drowsy and wide-eyed so, on a hunch, he asked Wills if he had taken anything. 'Sleeping tablets', Wills replied. When asked how many, he answered, 'fifteen'. There were still two Soneryl tablets on the bed, so this information was taken seriously. Wills was first taken to the police station and then on to the County Hospital where he was examined by Dr Fleming who said that he was in no danger. Wills was then driven back to the police station and on the journey, turned to Sergeant Plummer and asked, 'Did she suffer much?' Plummer replied that he thought she must have done, to which Wills remarked, 'She deserved to die.'

By 7.30 p.m., Wills was being interviewed by Inspector Parsons and Detective Sergeant Thomas. Told that he would be detained while further inquiries were made, Wills was again asked when he had seen Mrs Parry last and volunteered that he had met her at her home at 2.30 p.m. on Tuesday when they had intercourse together downstairs. Wills then made a formal written statement, giving much the same details.

Police officers now began to check out the various points in Wills' story. To begin with, he claimed that the blood on his shirt and the cut on his hand had come from a fight. George Logan of 13 Potter Street, Newport, was a joiner's assistant but had also done some boxing under the name of Kid Logan. He told the police that he had been in the New Found Out public house on Cambrian Road, from 5.30 p.m. on Tuesday, 8 June. He did indeed see Wills come into the pub, some time between 6.30 p.m. and 7 p.m. The two men remained on friendly terms all that evening and not only was there no fight between them, but no one else had assaulted Wills either.

At 10 a.m. on 10 June, Wills was in the CID office at the police station, waiting to be interviewed again when he noticed an officer, Detective Sergeant David Thomas, reading something. Wills asked Thomas if that was the statement he had made the previous day and, told that it was, he said, 'I will tell you the truth.' He was immediately cautioned and went on to make another statement, which was written down, read back to him, and then signed. This second statement began:

On Tuesday the 8th June, 1948, the first time I saw Mrs Parry would be approximately 1 p.m. We had arranged for her to take the afternoon off because I was going to turn some property over to her. This was in the lane near my house. She told me she would be ready to go to Newport just after 2 p.m.

I went to the Pontnewydd Hotel and had a drink and I called at Mrs Parry's house at approximately 2 p.m. She had a 'New Look' two-piece on that I had not seen before. We arranged to meet at the Romany café, Newport, at 4.30 p.m. that afternoon. I was there but she did not turn up. I waited for a short while. While I was waiting I saw a girl named Dolly Rogers of Catsash Farm, across the road. I had spent the previous Saturday night with this girl and we were on intimate terms.

I then went to the Old Green public house where I had a double gin and about 6 p.m. I went to the Tredegar Arms Hotel where I had two whisky and limes. From there I went to the New Found Out where I met Logan. I was there from about 6.30 p.m. to 8 p.m. Logan and I went into the gents' lavatory where he got aggressive. We had a bit of a set to where my shirt got all messed up with blood.

For some time I had felt like finishing it all and when I got home that night, I took about fifteen or twenty sleeping tablets. I do not remember any more until the police came. There's nothing more I want to say.

In due course, Wills made a third statement in which he admitted a three-year sexual liaison with the dead woman but claimed that she had been seeing someone else and this was why he had decided to kill himself. Throughout, he denied any involvement in Sillvinea's murder but once the result of the various forensic tests came back, the police felt they had enough to proceed and Wills was charged.

Clifford Wills made his first appearance before the magistrates on 10 June when he was remanded until 19 June. By that date, Wills had obtained legal representation in Mr J. Alan Wilson, who made no objection to another remand. A further court appearance took place on 26 June, but it was not until 1 July that the evidence was finally detailed. After the two-day hearing finished, it was adjudged that there was enough evidence to send Wills for trial on the charge of murder.

The case of the Crown against Clifford Wills opened at Newport on 8 November 1948, before Mr Justice Hallett. Throughout the two days, Wills was defended by Mr A.J. Long and Mr Underwood while the prosecution case was detailed by Mr Cartwright Sharp and Mr Paul Layton.

John Parry confirmed that Wills was known to him and his family, and had often visited the house, but denied that there had been any relationship between the prisoner and Sillvinea. He added that to his knowledge, Wills had never been into the boxroom. Turning to the day of his wife's death, Parry stated that she had gone to work at the Caldicott Lacquer Works. He had spent the morning doing some work about the house and had used the vacuum cleaner in the two main bedrooms. The vacuum was normally kept underneath the single bed in the boxroom but when he had finished with it, Parry placed it neatly on top of the bed, before going off to work himself. John Parry finished his testimony by confirming that a sheath knife found in the house, and since shown to have been used to inflict some of the injuries upon Sillvinea, had belonged to his son. The spanner found in the bedsprings did not belong inside his house.

Dr Nolan told the court what he had seen when he attended the house in Wayfield Crescent. That same evening, he had seen Wills at the police station. At the time, the prisoner was very drowsy and he could not stand without being supported. Before Wills was sent off to hospital for treatment, Dr Nolan made a careful examination and noted that the only injuries were a small abrasion to the third knuckle of the little finger on the right hand and another on the second knuckle of the right index finger.

Professor James Mathewson Webster, the Director of the West Midlands Forensic Science Laboratory at Birmingham, had visited the scene of the crime before the body was removed to the mortuary. Sillvinea's body was only partly clothed. Her head was obscured by several articles of clothing, and when these were removed, a pool of congealed blood was seen near the head. The spanner, pointed out to him by Sergeant Plummer, was resting on the body with the handle entangled in the wire mesh of the bed itself.

Upon turning the body over, Professor Webster found an unused condom adhering to the groin on the left and saw that there was a garment stuffed tightly into the dead woman's mouth. At 6.30 p.m. that same evening, he performed a post-mortem. The clothing was now removed and it was seen that Sillvinea was wearing a watch, which had stopped at 4.40 p.m. The gag in the mouth was in fact a child's tunic. The left breast had three stab wounds, which penetrated deep into the chest cavity and there were two further puncture wounds on the upper lip. Marks on the neck suggested pressure of some kind and bruises and broken bones in the face showed that she had been struck violently with a blunt weapon.

Other scientific evidence was given by Emlyn Glyndwr Davies of the Forensic Science Laboratory at Cardiff. He had examined a number of items, including the prisoner's clothing, the linoleum, the spanner, the dead woman's clothes, the dagger and the condom. He concluded that there were numerous bloodstains on Wills' clothes, all of which were of type 'A'. The bloody footprints on the linoleum were also of type 'A' blood and the impression matched the shoes worn by Wills on the day in question. The spanner, also covered in group 'A' blood bore some human hairs, which matched hairs taken from Sillvinea's head. The dagger too bore extensive group 'A' stains. Dr Davies was also able to confirm that Sillvinea Parry's blood was 'A' while Wills' was group 'O'.

A more careful examination of the bloody footprints and Wills' shoes had been made by Dr Ronald Maxwell Mitchell who also worked in the Cardiff laboratory. He had made photographic copies of the soles of the shoes and the marks on the lavatory floor and showed that they bore the same ring pattern. He showed six marks in the pattern on the shoes and showed that they corresponded with marks in the bloodstains on the linoleum.

More damning evidence was given by Detective Inspector John Godsell of the fingerprint department of Scotland Yard. He had received impressions of various prints found in the boxroom at Wayfield Crescent, and of the bloody palm print itself. These had been compared with the prisoner's fingerprints and in Inspector Godsell's opinion, were identical.

Iris Vera Perkins, a married woman of 25 Ty Newydd Road, Pontnewydd, was now called to show that Wills was in the area of Wayfield Crescent at about the time the crime was believed to have taken place. She had known Wills for about a year and had even seen him in Mrs Parry's company but on 8 June, she saw him at the junction of Station Road and Ty Newydd Road, at about 3.30 p.m. He was then some 150yds from the murder house, but walking towards it.

For the defence, Mr Long did not challenge that his client was responsible for Sillvinea Parry's death, but claimed that at the time of the crime, he was so affected by a disease of the mind, that he did not know what he was doing. To confirm this, he now recalled Dr Nolan, who had also examined Wills, and stated that in his opinion, there was quite clearly some mental trouble, which had developed in the spring of 1947. To counter this, the prosecution called Dr T. Wallace, the medical officer of Cardiff Prison who said that there were no signs of any mental illness. His memory was good, his intelligence above average and an electroencephalogram had shown that he was normal.

The jury retired to consider their verdict on 9 November, and took just half an hour to decide that Wills was sane and therefore guilty of murder. He was then moved to the condemned cell at Cardiff, to await his fate.

Capital punishment was much in the news at this particular time. The last man to actually be executed was Walter John Cross, in London on 19 February. In April, the House of Commons had voted to suspend the death penalty for five years but this had been subsequently overturned by the House of Lords.

In the meantime, all capital sentences had been automatically commuted, but now the debate was over and hanging was once again a feature of British justice. On 18 November, Stanley Joseph Clarke was hanged and the very next day, Peter Griffiths was executed.

On 1 December, the Home Secretary announced that there would be no reprieve in Wills' case. Exactly one week later, at 9 a.m. on Thursday, 9 December 1948, Clifford Godfrey Wills was hanged at Cardiff Prison. The 'number one' executioner, Albert Pierrepoint, was in Germany at the time, so the job fell to Stephen Wade.

28

PAYING A DEBT

Robert Thomas Mackintosh, 1949

Shortly before 7 p.m. on the evening of Friday, 3 June 1949, 16-year-old Beryl Beechey told her mother, Margaret Mary, that she was 'off out' to the pictures. Margaret asked her daughter if she wouldn't mind running a quick errand for her first. She owed 10s to an old family friend, Mrs Mackintosh, who lived at Vivien Square, Aberavon, and Beryl said she would be happy to drop it off for her. Soon afterwards, Beryl left the family home at 64 Green Park.

At 7.25 p.m., Beryl was seen alighting from a bus outside the Municipal Buildings. Another family friend, Mrs Richards, exchanged pleasantries with Beryl and then saw her walk off towards Vivien Terrace, which in turn led to Vivien Square. Later still that evening, at around 8.30 p.m., Mrs Mackintosh returned home and was given the 10s note by her son, 21-year-old Robert Thomas Mackintosh who told her that Beryl had called and left the cash for her. That night though, Beryl Beechey did not return home and her parents became concerned for her safety.

Ats 5.55 a.m. on Saturday, 4 June, Bert Gravelle, a crane driver living at 70 Llewellyn Street, left his home to cycle to work. He had only turned two corners when two men standing by a wall near the railway signalled for him to stop and pointed to something lying on the embankment. Bert looked over the wall and saw the body of a young girl lying on the grass. Without hesitation, Bert Gravelle cycled to the police station.

Within minutes, police had thrown a cordon around the immediate area and senior officers, including the Chief Constable of Glamorgan, Mr Joseph Jones, and Detective Superintendent Charles Blewden and Detective Inspectors Gordon Thomas and Cyril Dando were at the scene. The area was quite congested, but nobody in the surrounding houses reported having heard anything unusual. The place where the body was discovered was only 150yds from Green Park and police were questioning everyone in the area. Officers were soon calling at the Beechey home to tell them that the body of a young girl had been found nearby and to ask if they might have any information. As a result, it was not long before a formal identification was made. Beryl Beechey had been found raped and murdered.

Discussions with the distraught family soon revealed that Beryl had arrived home on the Friday, had her tea and then informed her parents that she was going to the pictures with her friend, Catherine Cornish. In the event though, Catherine had had another appointment and Beryl had said she intended to go to the cinema alone. The errand to the Mackintosh home was then related and, not surprisingly, this was the next port of call for the police.

It was 1.30 p.m. on the Saturday when Superintendent Blewden and Inspector Dando called at Vivien Square to speak to the Mackintoshes. Here it was discovered that although Mr and Mrs Mackintosh, their three sons and daughter, June all lived at the house, only Robert, a steelworker, had been home at the time that Beryl called. He explained about Beryl's brief visit to pay over money but because the body had been found only 40yds from his home and the last confirmed sighting of Beryl had been just before she called at the Mackintosh house, the two officers asked him to accompany them to the police station and make a full written statement.

Mackintosh was happy to oblige and duly made a statement which detailed that he had finished work at the Port Talbot Steelworks at 4 p.m., and arrived home at about 4.20 p.m. Later, when he was alone in the house, Beryl Beechey called and asked if his mother were in. Told that she was out, Beryl then handed over the 10s and left.

The police, meanwhile, were making a careful examination of Mackintosh's house and when a bloodstain was found on the linoleum on Robert's bedroom floor, they asked him to account for it. Mackintosh replied that he had cut his toe and the blood was his, but then, asked to make a second statement, he wrote an admission that he was involved in Beryl's death. He was then cautioned again and told that he would be charged with murder.

Mackintosh faced his trial at Swansea on 13 July, before Mr Justice Croom-Johnson. The Crown's case was led by Mr H. Vincent Lloyd-Jones, who was assisted by Mr Campbell Prosser, while Mackintosh was represented by Mr H. Glyn-Jones and Mr Alun T. Davies.

For the prosecution, Mr Lloyd-Jones began by stating that the Beechey and Mackintosh families had always been very close and indeed at one stage, had even shared the same house, until Beryl was born in October 1932. After evidence of Beryl's movements had been given by her family, details were outlined of the bloodstaining found at Mackintosh's house and of scientific tests which showed that Beryl's clothing had, at some time, been in contact with the side wall of the stairs in Mackintosh's house.

Medical evidence was given by Dr A.F. Sladden. He had first examined Beryl's body at the spot where it was found and concluded that she had been lifted and dropped over the wall, which separated the embankment from the street. Some of her clothing was torn and other items were missing. There was a length of window sash cord tied very tightly around her neck, by means of a knot at the front and another at the back. Dr Sladden later did the post-mortem and noted scratches around the girl's neck and others on her legs, all of which had been inflicted before death. Beryl had also been raped.

Emlyn Glyndwr Davies, the senior officer at the Forensic Science Laboratory at Cardiff, said that he had visited Mackintosh's home and taken away several items for examination. He had taken hairs from a piece of bedroom linoleum and samples of wood from the staircase. The hairs were of the same type as Beryl's while the wood fibres matched others found on the dead girl's clothing. Further, while Mackintosh's blood group was 'B', the blood found on the linoleum, bloodstains found on the prisoner's clothing were group 'A', the same as Beryl's.

Perhaps the most damning evidence was Mackintosh's second statement. In this he had started by referring to Beryl calling at the house with the 10s. He continued:

I called her into the house and we were talking for a few minutes. Then something came over me, I don't know what, and something happened. I don't remember what.

I was alone in the house at the time, the rest of the family being out. The next I remember was that I was in bed and Beryl was half under the bed.

I realised I had done something wrong, but what it was I didn't know, and that was well into the night. I didn't know what to do.

Something made me carry Beryl's body downstairs after I had been to the lavatory a couple of times. I carried her downstairs and put a coat on it and carried it down the road to the line, and pushed her over the wall.

I have been a pig. Something came over me, and it was the same as happened before when I tried to get across my sister. My mind went a blank.

God knows I am worried ever since, not knowing what to do. I forgot to say that when Beryl was in the house, and we were talking, she gave me some money for my mother.

There is an idea in my head that Beryl went upstairs with me but after this everything seems to be a blank.

Words cannot say how sorry I am. I have read what you put down is the whole truth. I only wish I could bring Beryl back into this world again and undo the terrible wrong I have done.

This last paragraph had been added to the statement in Mackintosh's own hand.

Another statement was then read out. Made later that same day, after Mackintosh had been charged with murder, it clarified his reference to his sister and read, 'There is something I want to tell you about what happened a couple of months ago at the house. I had a blackout, and tried to kiss my sister June. We were in the house and I caught hold of her a bit rough and my father threatened to give me a good lacing.' This statement was confirmed by Maldwyn Mackintosh, the prisoner's father.

For the defence, Mr Glyn-Jones said that he had no witnesses to call, relying instead on a request that the jury should find that his client's mind had been disturbed at the time of the attack and that consequently, he was not responsible for his actions. The jury did not agree and it took them just half an hour to decide that Mackintosh was guilty of murder.

There was no appeal, the defence preferring to rely on an application for a reprieve but on 2 August, the solicitor acting for Mackintosh, Mr K.S. Wehrle, received notification from the Home Office that no grounds had been found to advise the King to interfere with the sentence.

Just two days later, at 9 a.m. on Thursday, 4 August 1949, Robert Thomas Mackintosh was hanged at Swansea Prison alongside the subject of the next chapter, Rex Harvey Jones. It was the first execution at Swansea in twenty-one years and the first double hanging in ninety years.

29

THE LAST BUS HOME

Rex Harvey Jones, 1949

The evening of Sunday, 5 June 1949 was one for parties. Two separate gatherings took place that night; one at the Central Club in Neath and another, a works dance, at the Hostel in Morrison. By chance, those two groups met at the bus station in Victoria Gardens, again in Neath, so that they could catch the last bus back to their respective homes. That chance encounter was to cost the lives of two people.

The bus arrived at around 10.25 p.m. and was very crowded. One of the group from Morrison, 20-year-old Beatrice May Watts, known to her friends as Peggy, had managed to find herself a seat, but gave it up to an elderly lady. This act of kindness was witnessed by 21-year-old Rex Harvey Jones, one of the men who had been to the club in Neath, who then invited Beatrice to sit on his lap.

At 1.15 a.m. on Monday, 6 June, PC Michael was on duty in the police station at Cymmer when the telephone rang. The caller identified himself as Rex Jones and said, 'Send a motorcar down to the telephone box at Abercregan. I have killed a girl.' When PC Michael cycled to the village, he passed a young man close to the kiosk. Michael asked the man if he was the person who had telephoned and he readily identified himself as the caller. Jones told PC Michael, 'I have killed Peggy Watts with my hands. I felt her pulse and it had stopped.' Later, Michael, together with Inspector James, whom he had summoned for assistance, found the body of Beatrice Watts between the forestry plantation and the railway on the Nantybar mountainside, within sight of her home. Jones was taken into custody, cautioned, and back at the police station, made a full statement admitting that he was responsible.

Jones first appeared before the magistrates at Port Talbot, later that same day, 6 June, when it was stated that the dead girl had lived at Greenfield Cottages, Abercregan. She had been the eldest of the four daughters of a local collier, Frank Watts. The details of the events of that morning were then given.

Inspector C. James gave evidence that he had interviewed Jones at Abercregan and the prisoner had told him where Beatrice's body could be found. Jones led them to the spot and pointed to a rock 2½ft high and said, 'There she is.' The grisly discovery was made at 3 a.m. Jones was then escorted to the police station at Cymmer where, at 6.30 a.m., he made a written statement taken down by Detective Superintendent Charles Blewden. The magistrates then remanded Jones until 13 June.

On 8 June, the inquest revealed that Beatrice had died from asphyxia due to manual strangulation. Three days later, on 11 June, the body of Beatrice Watts was laid to rest.

A second remand followed on 13 June and it was not until 20 June that all the evidence against Jones was heard. Mr Ryland Thomas prosecuted and Jones was represented by Mr Dyfan Roberts, who was instructed by Mr K.S. Wehrle.

PC Michael took Rex Harvey Jones to Cymmer after the latter telephoned him to admit he had just killed Beatrice May Watts.

Mr Thomas began by outlining that by his own admission, Jones had drunk seven pints of beer at the club in Neath. He also stated that before this incident had taken place, Jones and Beatrice were known to each other, having first met at Christmas, 1948.

Once the bus carrying the prisoner and the dead girl had arrived at Duffryn, at around 10.50 p.m., they and others alighted. Jones told his companions that he intended walking Peggy home and the two were seen walking off together, down a dark path, towards Nantybar. A little later they were seen, arm in arm, by Mrs Colwyn, a neighbour of Beatrice's.

Jones' statement was then read out in court. It began:

God knows how sorry I am. That's why I went up to the call box and called the police, and that's why I have asked you to write down about it.

Last night I went to Neath with my brothers Fred and Aubrey on the half past six bus. We went to the Central Club, and had a few drinks. We stopped at the club till it closed, and caught the twenty five past ten bus back to Duffryn.

We got off at Duffryn, and I walked with Peggy to Abercregan. We stopped on the way. I started to spoon and kiss her, as I do with her when I go out with her. She liked me a lot, and I have been out with her five or six times.

It was up on the rocks we settled down, and we were both lying on the rocks. As I told you, I have been out with Peggy Watts before and we have been together. I mean, we have been intimate.

Jones went on to describe what took place between him and Beatrice and continued, 'After this something came over me. I can't explain what it was, but I killed her. I knew by my hands I had strangled her, as my thumbs were quite sore. I saw that I had killed her, and I came to myself right away. I went to give myself up to the police and as you know I went to the call box.'

The prosecution then showed that Jones had been very friendly with another girl, Pamela Cole, who lived in London. A letter was produced which Jones had written to her from his prison cell in which he admitted he had killed Peggy. The letter ended, 'Find someone decent and marry him. Forget me and live a happy life. Goodbye darling, in life and death, I love you.'

Pamela Cole, who lived in Bromley Road, London, was in court to state that she had first met Jones some three years before and they had been close ever since. An engagement had been discussed and Jones had arranged to go down to London later that month to see her.

Medical evidence was been given by Dr James McKane Taylor of Cymmer who had seen Jones at the police station. Dr Taylor stated that although Jones' breath smelled of beer, he was sober and rational. The only injuries he found were a blister on the base of his right ring finger and scratches on the back of his left hand. Dr Taylor had also examined Beatrice's body, at 4.30 a.m. She was lying on her back near a large rock, her clothing covered in mud. There was a good deal of bruising on the front and side of her neck and in his opinion, considerable force must have been used to cause this. The magistrates, having heard all this testimony, then sent Jones to face his trial at the next assizes.

On 12 July 1949, Rex Harvey Jones stood in the dock at Swansea, before Mr Justice Croom-Johnson. Mr H. Edmund Davies led for the prosecution and was assisted by Mr Gerwyn Thomas. Jones was defended by Mr Arthian Davies and Mr Roberts.

The prosecution called witnesses who had been to the dance with Beatrice, and accompanied her on the bus home afterwards. One of these was Catherine Mary Andrews who also worked with Beatrice at the Baglan Bay Works. She said that the prisoner was friendly with the dead girl and there had been no argument between them that night. This was confirmed by Aubrey Rees Jones, the prisoner's brother and James Wright Harvey who had been in the Central Club in Neath.

The defence called no witnesses and offered no evidence. In his closing speech, Mr Davies pointed out that Jones had told the truth throughout the police investigation. The dead girl had accompanied him to the plantation quite voluntarily. He then suffered from some kind of blackout but as soon as he came to his senses and realised what he had done, his first action was to call the police. Mr Davies ended by saying that Jones had previously had an unblemished character and had served with credit in the armed services.

In his own summing up, Mr Justice Croom-Johnson said that he saw nothing to reduce the charge to one of manslaughter and that this was a case of murder or nothing. The jury agreed and took half an hour to decide that Jones was guilty, though they did add a strong recommendation to mercy.

The parallels with the Mackintosh case in the last chapter continue. Both men had strangled young women within days of each other. Both had been tried before the same judge, in the same courtroom and in neither case had the defence called any witnesses. Now, again like Mackintosh's case, the defence chose not to enter an appeal and relied instead on hopes of a reprieve and it was to the same solicitor, on the same day, 2 August, that the Home Secretary wrote to say that such a reprieve would not be granted.

On Thursday, 4 August 1949, a crowd of more than 200 people gathered outside the gates of Swansea Prison as Rex Harvey Jones and Robert Thomas Mackintosh were hanged by Albert Pierrepoint. The two men, who seemingly had led such parallel lives, ended those lives together.

30

THE FARMER

Albert Edward Jenkins, 1950

Six miles south of Haverfordwest lies the village of Rosemarket. On Sunday, 9 October 1949, one of the local farmers, 52-year-old William Henry Llewellyn, received a visitor in the shape of a small boy, who handed him a handwritten note saying that his father had sent it. The note read 'Dear Mr Llewelin [*sic*], Will you give me a call tomorrow about 11 a.m. I would like to have a talk with you before I go into Milford. Hoping to see you in morning.' The letter was signed 'A. Jenkins'.

William Llewellyn knew that the note had been sent by 38-year-old Albert Edward Jenkins who worked the 28 acres of Lower Furze Hill Farm, which Llewellyn owned. Llewellyn told his young visitor to let his father know he would be over as requested.

At 11 a.m. on Monday, 10 October, William Llewellyn climbed onto his black bicycle and started along the road that led to Furze Hill Farm. He had already told his wife, Mona, that he wouldn't be very long so, when he hadn't returned by 4 p.m. that evening, Mona Llewellyn and her married stepdaughter, Mrs Sutton, went to Furze Hill themselves. There they saw Jenkins who said that Mr Llewellyn had indeed called but had left after a few minutes. A distraught Mrs Llewellyn took her concerns to the police.

Albert Jenkins had a wife and two children but on 10 October, they had gone to Pembroke Fair and so were out of the house when Mr Llewellyn called. Jenkins later walked to Pembroke to pick his family up and it was on the return journey, in the village of Honeyborough, at about 8.45 p.m., that PC Edward Phillips saw him and told him that he was investigating the disappearance of William Llewellyn. Jenkins again confirmed that Llewellyn had called on him, and that they had completed the purchase of Lower Furze Hill Farm. Satisfied for the moment, PC Phillips returned to the search for the missing man.

On the following morning, PC Phillips called on Jenkins at his farm to ask for further details of his meeting with Llewellyn. Jenkins now said that he and Llewellyn had agreed a price of £1,000 for the farm and, since he also owed his landlord £50 in rent, he had handed over £1,050 in £1 notes to complete the deal. As proof of this, Jenkins showed Phillips a rent book with two transactions; one for £50 and another for £1,000. Both were initialled in the margin 'WHL' but curiously, Mr Llewellyn had dated both transactions as the 29th of September. PC Phillips queried this, pointing out that the meeting had taken place on Monday, 10 October. Jenkins explained it by suggesting that since the rent had been due on the 29th, Mr Llewellyn had probably dated that transaction correctly and then mistakenly copied the same date.

Further investigations showed that this story of a cash transaction was highly unlikely. Another farmer, John Edward Ronald Denny, told the police that he had sold Jenkins a tractor on hire purchase and that the payments were in arrears. A check with his bank showed that his current account was £136 overdrawn and there were witnesses who reported some strange behaviour from Albert Jenkins.

George Russell Codd was an expert on artificial insemination from the Agricultural Committee of the Milk Marketing Board and he had an appointment to attend to a heifer at Lower Furze Hill Farm at 11.30 a.m. on 10 October. Mr Codd was on time but as he drove into the farm, he saw Jenkins, driving a tractor at great speed, leaving the premises and hurtling off towards a field. On the back of the tractor was some sort of bundle, wrapped in a tarpaulin. Ten minutes later, when he left, Mr Codd saw the tractor parked in the field, but there was no sign of Jenkins.

The bicycle which William Llewellyn had been riding when he left his home, had been found by Albert John Gillam, abandoned on the grass verge on the promenade at Neyland, about 800yds from the ferry, late on 10 October. Two other people had seen a man riding a bicycle on the Monday afternoon. The first of these, Dorothy May Davies, said she recognised Jenkins as the rider while the other, George Clifford Rees Davies, said that he was sitting in his lounge at Jordanston when he saw Jenkins riding a bike. Mr Rees had known Jenkins for several years.

The police search for Llewellyn had ended at midnight on 10 October but resumed early on 11 October. Since Jenkins had made an appointment with the missing man, supposedly entered into a financial transaction with him, been seen driving a tractor with a bundle and later riding what was probably Llewellyn's bicycle, the search now concentrated on the land around Lower Furze Hill Farm and especially on the field in which Jenkins had been observed. That afternoon, at 4 p.m., one of the searchers, George Victor Williams, noticed what appeared to be freshly dug earth in one corner of the field. George held a long stick with him and when he drove this into the soil, it penetrated easily to a depth of 2ft 6in.

He started digging, helped by Sergeant Rossiter and they discovered an old tarpaulin with what looked like a toe protruding from it. Digging deeper still, they unearthed a body. The mystery of William Llewellyn's disappearance had been solved. He was found, minus his boots, with no money on his body and with the right side of his face battered in.

Taken in for questioning, Jenkins made a statement, which started at 10.30 p.m. that night. In that long statement, he began by detailing the agreement he had with Jenkins, in Septmber 1945, to rent the farm at £50 per annum plus rates.

Jenkins went on to say that he had had the farm valued, one year ago, by Lee and Thomas of Haverfordwest who had put a price of £575 on it. Llewellyn, however, had wanted £1,000. The statement continued, detailing a couple of meetings between the two men until, on Wednesday, 28 September, Jenkins had finally agreed to the £1,000 price. The statement ended with confirmation that he had nothing to do with Llewellyn's disappearance or death. Early the next morning, he was charged with murder and replied, 'I am not guilty of the murder. In know nothing about it. That is all I can say.'

The inquest on William Llewellyn opened on 12 October. Dr C.L. Hollick, who had performed the post-mortem, gave details of the cause of death. Mr Llewellyn had suffered extensive fracturing of the skull and consequent injuries to the brain. At least one, or more probably two heavy blows had been administered by a blunt instrument. Matters were then adjourned until 26 October.

After various remands at the Magistrates' Court, the evidence was finally detailed on 21 November. The proceedings lasted over two days, after which Jenkins was sent for trial.

The trial of Albert Jenkins opened at Haverfordwest on Monday, 27 February 1950, before Mr Justice Byrne. The case lasted until 2 March and during the four days, the prosecution was led by Mr Arthian Davies, assisted by Mr Roderic Bowen MP, while Jenkins was defended by Mr H. Vincent Lloyd-Jones and Mr Rowe Harding.

To begin with, the prosecution showed that Jenkins, a man who claimed to have paid over £1,050 in cash, was actually in serious financial trouble. John Edward Ronald Denny, a representative for a company which sold tractors, testified that Jenkins had purchased a vehicle in November 1948. He soon fell into arrears with repayments and at one stage sent a letter to Mr Denny, asking him to take the tractor back. A later letter said that Jenkins should be in a position to bring the payments up to date by the end of June but subsequently, only two further amounts were paid; one of £45 12s and one of £9 3s 4d.

The next witness was Frank Ireland, the collections manager for the British Wagon Company who said that on 20 September, Jenkins still owed just over £169 on the tractor he had purchased. Pressurised to bring his account up to date, Jenkins had made one payment, an amount of £10 14s.

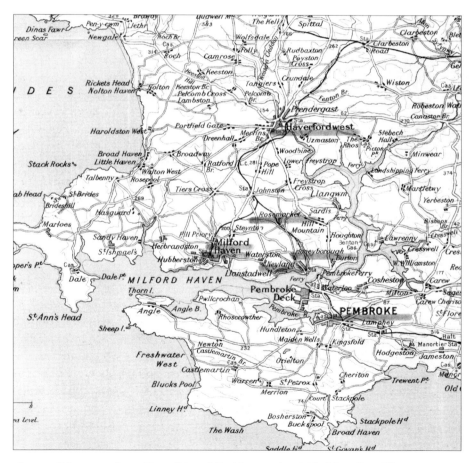

A map of the area where Albert Edward Jenkins murdered Mr Llewellyn. Places mentioned in the narrative are underlined.

Jenkins held a bank account at the Haverfordwest branch of Lloyds Bank Ltd and John Reynolds Jones, the securities clerk there stated that on 3 October, the account was overdrawn to the amount of £136 6s 7d.

Mona Llewellyn told of a visit from Jenkins when he offered her husband £800 for the farm but William said he wanted £1,000, and then reminded Jenkins that he still owed £50 in rent. Mrs Llewellyn then told of her visit to the farm after her husband had failed to return home.

The prosecution now called George Williams, the man who had found the body in the clay pit. He said that when the bundle was first unearthed, Jenkins was nearby and announced that the hole was not big enough to hold a human body, but might contain that of a sheep. More soil was removed and as the bundle was pulled out, Jenkins admitted, 'That's my tarpaulin.'

There was further damning evidence against Jenkins. William Llewellyn had been killed by blows to his head and it was a natural assumption that his killer would have blood on his clothing. Emlyn Glyndwr Davies was a principal scientific officer at the Forensic Science Laboratory at Cardiff. He had examined Jenkins' clothing and found extensive spots of blood type 'A', the same as the dead man's. He had also looked at soil samples taken from around the farmhouse door and these too contained blood and particles of human bone.

Jenkins had tried to blame the murder on some strangers he claimed to have seen. On 27 October, Jenkins wrote a letter to the Chief Constable in which he said that on Monday, 10 October, two men had come into his cowshed and asked for a jug of tea. In his opinion, these two men would know something about the case.

In a subsequent interview Jenkins elaborated on this letter and suggested that these two men had killed Mr Llewellyn and then buried him on the farm. The prosecution pointed out that for there to be any truth in this, the men would have had to bring the body back under the cover of darkness and bury it while the area was being searched.

On the third day of the trial, Jenkins stepped into the witness box. He began by saying that he was a married man with a son aged 8 and a baby girl of 15 months. After stating when he first moved to the farm, Jenkins said that he had opened his bank account at Lloyds in July 1947 and only did so to bank cheques from the Milk Marketing Board. He did not use the account for normal business transactions and preferred to deal in cash, which he saved at home.

Turning to his financial troubles, Jenkins stated that he had not maintained the payments on the tractor as he found it useless. He wrote to the company saying he could not pay, in the hope that they would take it off his hands. Jenkins said that the transaction with Mr Llewellyn had taken place exactly as he had described and he had no idea what had happened to the money after he left the farm.

The judge's summing up lasted 155 minutes. He went over all the evidence, pointing out that it was for the jury to decide if it were Jenkins, or possibly the two strangers he referred to, who had taken Mr Llewellyn's life.

The jury took 105 minutes to decide that Jenkins was guilty and he made no comment as the sentence of death was passed. One month later, on 3 April, Jenkins' appeal was heard before the Lord Chief Justice, Lord Goddard and Justices Humphreys and Jones. Giving their judgement, Lord Goddard said there was 'Abundant and cogent evidence to justify the jury's verdict' and added that there was nothing in this appeal.

On the morning of Wednesday, 19 April 1950, Albert Edward Jenkins was hanged at Swansea as just thirty-six people waited outside for the notices to be posted on the prison gates. It was the first execution of a Pembrokeshire man since 1825.

31

DOMESTIC TROUBLE

Herbert Roy Harris, 1952

It was quite a shock for Sarah Owen. Leaving her home at Huntley Lodge, Flint at 9.45 p.m. on Saturday, 8 December 1951, in order to visit her married daughter, Audrey Grogan, Sarah was horrified to find, lying on the ground, on Huntley Bridge, the body of a woman who looked very much like Audrey.

Sarah walked forward and the closer she drew, the more certain she was that she had found her daughter. The height was the same, the hair colour was identical and even the shoes and coat looked like Audrey's. Further, the large bloodstained stone lying near the woman's head left Sarah in little doubt that her daughter had been the victim of a terrible attack. Sarah crouched down, gently lifted the head and saw, to her relief, that it was not Audrey Grogan after all.

Sarah Owen ran to her daughter's house and told her son-in-law, William Grogan, what she had found. William went back to the bridge to see for himself and then dashed to the nearest telephone box and called for the police.

At 9.57 p.m., Inspector Idwal Roberts and PC John Ernest Davies arrived. They noted that the body was on the right-hand side of the bridge, lying face down with the head turned away from the wall. She was fully clothed, except for her hat, which lay nearby, and the head and face were covered in blood. There was a large wound on the top of the woman's head and there could be little doubt that the large stone lying nearby was the weapon used. The woman's hat, or beret, was some 3ft from her head and between this and the woman, was a handbag. Inside this handbag was, among other items, a ration card giving the name Eileen Harris and an address at 31 Queen's Avenue. Inspector Roberts left PC Davies in charge while he went to call out the doctor and check on the address.

Inspector Roberts soon discovered that 22-year-old Eileen Harris was a married woman, with three children, but she did not live with her husband. Eileen lived with her parents, Mr and Mrs Humphreys. Esther Humphreys explained that Eileen had married Herbert Roy Harris on 13 November 1948. When they first married, the couple lived with Harris' parents, then moved to Birmingham, where they stayed with Eileen's sister, and then returned to Flint where they lived for a while with another sister. They had always lodged with someone or other and never had a home of their own.

Originally, there had only been two children, Susan and Jennifer, but since they were trying to get their own place, Harris had thought that another child might move them up the council waiting list so, just seven weeks ago, little Vernon had been born. In the meantime, Eileen lived with her parents while 23-year-old Harris lived with his, just up the road at 77 Queen's Avenue.

Esther went on to say that Eileen had gone out that evening at around 5.30 p.m. She had been waiting for her husband, having arranged to go to the pictures together, but when he didn't arrive,

Eileen went by herself. Just three minutes later, Harris appeared and asked where Eileen was. Esther told him she had already gone.

Since Eileen had made an arrangement to meet her husband, his house was now the next port of call. The door was opened by Harris' father Herbert Reginald Harris, who told the inspector that his son had not been at work that day. Herbert had arrived home from his job at noon and found Harris and his brother John in the shed, making a bookcase. After dinner, both boys returned to the shed where they continued working until 2 p.m. when they came in to watch some football on the television. At 3 p.m., Harris went back to the shed, and stayed there until 4.30 p.m. when he came in, washed, shaved and changed, ready to go out. He said he was going to take Eileen to the pictures and left the house at 5.15 p.m., wearing a raincoat, jacket, grey gloves and a scarf.

Harris returned at 8.15 p.m., coming in by the back door. His mother called out, 'You're early' and he replied that he was going back out to stay with Eileen for a bit. He was upstairs for two or three minutes, went out and had not returned since.

At 10.30 p.m., Herbert Harris went up to his son's bedroom and found, lying on the floor, the raincoat Harris had worn when he went out to meet Eileen. The coat was badly stained with what looked like blood and when Herbert felt in the pockets, he found a wet glove in one pocket, and a wet scarf in the other. Both of these too appeared to be stained with blood. Herbert wasted no time in calling first at Eileen's house and then, having heard what had happened from her parents, went on to the police station to report the matter. A full description of Harris was then issued with the notification that he was wanted for murder.

Christine Daphne Forrester was the receptionist at the Regent Palace Hotel, Piccadilly, London. At 8.30 a.m. on 9 December, a man came in and asked for a room. There were none available but Christine knew that some guests were due to check out, so she told the man to return later.

The man came back at 10 a.m., was told that a room was now available and was asked to fill out a registration form. When the form was handed back, Christine read the name, Herbert Roy Harris, and the home address of 77 Queen's Avenue, Flint. Later that same day, after reading a newspaper report that a woman named Harris had been murdered in Flint, and that the police were now looking for her husband, Christine told the hotel's security officer about their new guest and he in turn contacted the police.

At 2.30 p.m. that same day, Detective Sergeant Davies called at the hotel and went up to Harris' room. Sergeant Davies asked if the man was named Harris, if he lived at Queen's Avenue, Flint, and if he had a wife named Eileen. Harris made no attempt to cover his tracks and replied, 'Yes, you have been very quick.' Sergeant Davies took him into custody. The following day, Detective Inspector William Victor Cook and Detective Sergeant Hugh Idris Williams travelled down to London from Wales, picked up Harris, returned with him to Mold and there charged him with the murder of his wife.

That same day, Monday, 10 December, Harris appeared in the Magistrates' Court, where details of the arrest were given. It was said that after told he would be charged, Harris had replied, 'I have nothing to say, except that it was unintentional. That's all.' The prisoner was then remanded until 18 December.

Further remands followed, until 11 January, when Harris was finally sent for trial. That trial took place at Monmouth on Tuesday, 5 February, before Mr Justice Oliver. The prosecution lay in the hands of Mr H. Vincent Lloyd-Jones and Mr Bertram Richards, while Harris was defended by Mr H. Glyn-Jones and Mr W.L. Mars-Jones.

After Esther Humphreys had told the court of Harris' visit to her house at approximately 5.30 p.m. on 8 December, other witnesses were called to show his subsequent movements, and those of his wife.

At about 5.30 p.m., just after he had missed his wife at her home, Harris called into Gomer's shop in Church Street where Olga Randles worked. She served Harris with some cigarettes and he asked if she had seen his wife. Olga said she hadn't and asked Harris if he was going to go to the pictures alone but he replied that he was going to his grandmother's instead, as she hadn't been well.

Muriel Wilton George was an usherette at the Plaza cinema in Flint and she testified that Eileen had arrived at the picture house, alone, at 5.35 p.m. Muriel was Harris' cousin and Eileen asked her if she had seen him. Muriel told Eileen that there was no sign of him. She only saw Eileen once more that evening, at 7 p.m., at which time she was still alone. Finally, Muriel confirmed that the show finished at 7.45 p.m.

Theresa Margaret Williams lived at 73 Queen's Avenue and knew both Harris and Eileen well. She was outside the Plaza cinema at 7.45 p.m. and saw Eileen coming out with the rest of the people. Eileen was alone and there was no sign of Harris.

Harris had told Olga Randles that he was going to his grandmother's house and the prosecution now called Robert John Davies, the prisoner's grandfather. He confirmed that Harris arrived at his house at some time between 6.30 p.m. and 7 p.m. on 8 December. Harris was cheerful and jokey while he was in the house, kissed his grandmother as he left, at around 7.05 p.m., and said he would see her in the morning.

Emma Brown was a cleaner at the Ship Inn and also worked behind the bar on Saturdays. On 8 December, she saw Harris, at some time between 7.15 p.m. and 7.35 p.m., sitting by the door, drinking a Mackeson. He was alone.

Hilda Griffiths was waiting for a bus at the corner of Coleshill and Church Street, on the opposite side to the Plaza cinema. It was around 7.35 p.m., or perhaps ten minutes later, when the bus arrived and as she got on, people started walking out of the picture house. She saw Harris, who was alone, walk towards the crowd.

Witnesses had now traced both Harris' and Eileen's movements to the time when the film finished and the Plaza's customers left. Other people were then called to show that Harris had met his wife outside the cinema and they had walked off together.

Beryl Smith lived at 10 Queen's Avenue and on 8 December she was walking along Chester Road. It was between 7.45 p.m. and 7.50 p.m. and she saw Eileen and Harris walking towards her. They were among a crowd of people and Eileen was slightly ahead of Harris.

Reginald Blakemore lived at 187 Chester Road and his house was on the corner of the lane leading up to Huntley Bridge. He was in his shed at 8 p.m. and heard two people on the bridge itself, talking in quite a friendly manner. After finishing in his shed, Blakemore had gone back inside his house. He first heard of the incident on the bridge at 9 p.m. and went to look at the body.

Margaret Bithell was walking along Prince of Wales Avenue at 8.20 p.m. on 8 December, heading towards Flint, when she saw Harris about 100yds from the top of Queen's Avenue. He was alone and was heading away from Flint. At about the same time, Olive Jones said she had seen Harris standing in an entry along Chester Road, and he appeared to be quite frightened.

Ten minutes later, at 8.30 p.m., Harris was seen again, this time by Irene Hopkins. He was standing at a bus stop in Chester Road. The bus came and Harris climbed on before Irene, calling out to her, 'Hurry up if you are going to get on.' He went upstairs and was still on the bus when she got off.

The conductor of that bus had been Basil Beaumont Wilkes and he confirmed that Harris had purchased a ticket to Chester, but he did not notice exactly where Harris got off. John Brian Towers was on duty at Chester railway station from 4.50 p.m. until 11.30 p.m. on 8 December and though he could not say who he sold it to, he was able to state that he had only sold one return ticket to London that day.

Inspector Cook said that when he first saw Harris in the cells at the West End Central police station in London, Harris had commented, 'I know what is coming and I am prepared to take the consequences.' He was cautioned and replied, 'I fully realise my position. I am a bit worried, but I am anxious about the children.'

After being taken back to Flint, and formally charged, Harris was driven to Walton Gaol in Liverpool. The car passed the end of the lane leading to the bridge where Eileen's body had been found and Harris noticed this and said, 'That is where it all happened. I wish I could turn the clock back three days.'

Medical evidence was given by Dr Maurice John Quinlan who had been called to the bridge at 10.15 p.m. on 8 December. He noticed multiple injuries to Eileen's head and estimated that she had been dead for at most, two hours.

The post-mortem had been carried out by Dr Walter Henry Grace, a Home Office pathologist. There were several lacerations on Eileen's scalp, caused by being struck from the front by a hard object. Other marks had been caused by a heavy blow from behind. The skull was fractured across the base and in Dr Grace's opinion, at least five blows had been struck. Some of the injuries might have been inflicted while the victim was lying on the ground. Dr Grace described the attack upon Eileen as being 'frenzied'.

The mackintosh found at Harris' home, along with other items such as a bloodstained handkerchief and towel, had been examined by Dr Derek McVitty of the Forensic Science Laboratory at Preston. Both Eileen and Harris had blood type 'A' but Eileen's was 'A2' and showed other characteristics which would only be found in two in every 1,000 people. The blood he found on the items was all of the same rare type as Eileen's. He had also examined the large stone found at the scene and this bore hairs which were the same type at the dead woman's. Fibres matching some taken from Harris' gloves had been found on this and two other stones.

Some of the history of the relationship between Harris and his wife was detailed by the prisoner's father, Herbert Reginald Harris. He explained the difficulties they had suffered from not being able to get a home together and confirmed that this sometimes boiled over into violence, with Eileen often giving as good as she got. He had seen cuts on Harris' hands and knew that Eileen had inflicted them with a carving knife. In June, or perhaps July, Eileen had slapped Harris' face and had hit him with a walking stick. It was due to this fight that they had been forced to live apart and both had even consulted solicitors with a view to divorce. After a month or so of acrimony, they had made things up.

Harris went into the box to give his own version of what happened on Huntley Bridge on 8 December. He admitted that he had met Eileen outside the pictures and chastised her for going in without him. They walked to the railway bridge where the argument continued. Eileen then hit him in the chest. He hit her back and Eileen then rushed at him, whereupon he picked up a stone and threw it at her. The stone hit her, but Eileen kept on coming for him so he picked up a piece of iron which lay nearby and struck her with that. She screamed but he then lost his temper, picked up the large stone and threw this at her. Eileen fell to the ground and Harris now saw that he had blood on him so, in a panic, went home to discard his bloodstained clothing and to clean himself up before going to Chester and then catching the train to London.

In a statement Harris had made to Sergeant Williams, he cliamed he was not insane but had just lost his temper. Harris' sanity was confirmed by the medical officer at Walton Prison, who said that although Harris' maternal grandmother had died in a mental hospital, Harris himself appeared to be perfectly sane. He was rational, with an above average IQ.

In his closing speech, Mr Glyn-Jones asked for a verdict of manslaughter, saying that there had been no intention to kill. He said, 'They were such people that they could not live together without quarrelling, yet could not live apart without being attracted one to the other as steel to a magnet.' The verdict, when it came, was that Harris was guilty, but the jury did add a strong recommendation to mercy.

There was no appeal and when, on Saturday, 23 February, the Home Secretary announced that he could find no grounds to interfere with the sentence, Harris knew that he would die. Three days later, on Tuesday, 26 February 1952, Herbert Roy Harris was hanged at Manchester.

32

A DRAMA OF EAST AGAINST WEST

Ajit Singh, 1952

Although only 26 years old, Joan Marion Thomas had already been a widow for two years. She now lived at 7 Dunraven Terrace, Bridgend, with her parents, Mr and Mrs Gribble, her sister, Patricia and her brother, who was in the army and was away from home a lot.

In early 1951, Joan was working for a draper who not only had a shop in Adare Street, Bridgend, but also a market stall at Maesteg. It was at the market one Wednesday that a tall, good looking 27-year-old Indian named Ajit Singh came looking for a pair of dungarees, which, as a painter, he needed for his work.

Joan told him that she didn't have any on the stall but might be able to help him if he came to the shop later, adding, for good measure, that she would be alone that afternoon. Singh did indeed visit the stall later, and after she had found him a suitable pair of dungarees, Joan began questioning him on where he lived, whether he was married, and what he did for a living.

Joan shut up the stall and walked with Singh to the bus station. They were getting on famously and she even invited him to come home with her for some dinner. Singh said he was too shy but as they talked, Joan's mother appeared, and Joan introduced Singh to her. She too invited Joan's new friend to the house and Singh finally agreed and went home with them for egg and chips. That night the couple went to the pictures together and arranged to meet up again the next day.

The following night, Singh returned to his lodgings very late, to which his landlady took objection. He in turn passed the details of this trouble on to Joan when they met on the Friday and she said she would help him to find fresh lodgings. Soon after, Singh moved into Elder House, Bridgend, which was closer to Joan's house. The relationship developed nicely, until August 1951.

In August, Joan's brother came home on leave. Singh greeted him with a warm handshake but he could sense that there was something wrong. Later, when Singh was alone with Joan, she told him that there had been some trouble. Her brother had told her a story about a fellow soldier who had seen a white girl pass the barracks with a coloured man. The soldier had remarked that if he saw his sister with a coloured man, he would slit her throat. Though Joan's brother had not expressed similar sentiments, he had said that he could not speak at the time as his own sister was doing exactly the same thing. The couple had been contemplating marriage, but Joan's family now pressed her to find a British husband. For this reason, Singh stopped calling at Dunraven Terrace, and Joan visited him at Elder House instead.

In fact, Joan and Singh also met at another location, 16 Oddfellows Street, a house occupied by Edward Andrew Thomas, who was no relation to Joan. Thomas was a friend of Singh's and together they sold nylon stockings in their spare time. It was to Thomas that Singh confided that he loved Joan, but that her parents and brother now objected to his association with her. Over the next few months, the atmosphere became increasingly strained until, towards the end of October, Singh told Thomas that if he could not have Joan, he would do away with her.

It was about this same time that Patricia Gribble, Joan's sister, was admitted to the Cefn Hirgoed Isolation Hospital in Bridgend and soon after this, at the beginning of November, Joan informed Singh that she wished to call off the relationship. There was a scene at the hospital, which upset Patricia. Because of this, Joan's father, Rowland Thomas Gribble, asked Singh to call at Dunraven Terrace and when he did, told him that he was not to pester Joan and was forbidden from visiting Patricia at the hospital. Rowland reminded Singh that Joan had broken off the relationship with him, at which Singh stormed out of the house shouting, 'She finish, I never finish. She know what I do now!'

Despite the affair having ended, Singh and Joan remained in touch. On her 27th birthday, 12 November, she accepted a watch from him, but refused to accept a ring. On Tuesday, 25 December, Joan took a Christmas dinner to Singh at Elder House, and they again met up the following Thursday, 27 December.

Mildred Valerie Williams lived at 19 Dunraven Terrace and was a close friend of Joan's. She also knew Joan's sister, and on the afternoon of Sunday, 30 December, said she would go to the hospital with Joan to visit Patricia. The two women left Joan's house at 1.35 p.m. to walk to the bus station, which was only some 300yds from Elder House.

As Joan and Mildred reached their stop, they saw Singh approach and call Joan's name three times. Joan did not reply, so Singh walked up to her and asked after Patricia, inquiring when she might be coming out of the hospital. Joan said she did not know, but when Singh said, 'I'll see you at ten minutes past four' Joan quickly interjected with, 'No, don't do that as I have made other arrangements.' Singh asked what these arrangements were, to which Joan replied, 'It's none of your business.'

Singh walked off, muttering, and stood leaning against a wall. He then vanished for a few minutes before returning and resuming his position near Joan and Mildred. Moments later the bus appeared and the two women sat in the seat behind the driver. They watched as Singh took a piece of paper from his pocket and quickly scribbled something, after which he folded it and put it back into his jacket pocket. He then walked away but within seconds returned and got onto the bus, sitting directly behind Mildred.

At 2.10 p.m. the bus left. When it finally stopped at the Cefn Hirgoed crossroads, the stop closest to the hospital, all three got off and started walking towards the hospital gates – Joan and Mildred following a few steps behind Singh. They had not gone far when Singh stopped, turned around and shouted, 'I want to see Joan's sister!' Joan remained calm and told Singh that he couldn't. At this, Singh became rather agitated and signalled to Mildred that she should leave him to talk to Joan alone. Fearful that there was going to be some sort of incident, Mildred walked on a little way, and as she turned to look back, she saw Singh open the front of his coat. Joan shouted, 'Val, he's got a gun!' and tried to run off, screaming as she did so.

Joan ran diagonally across the road, towards the hospital, followed by Mildred. After a second or two, Mildred stopped and watched with horror as Singh dashed past her, the gun now in his hand. Shots rang out and Joan fell.

The first shots had been fired at Joan's back, but when he caught up with her, Singh grabbed her and turned her towards him before firing the last shot into her chest. Satisfied that he had done what he wished, he then walked towards the common, threw something away and then strolled slowly towards Bridgend. He had not gone far when he stopped and retraced his steps, returning to where Joan lay.

In fact, Ajit Singh had shot two women. Patricia Gore and her sister, Edith Beryl Gore, were visiting a patient at the hospital and had travelled on the same bus as Mildred and Joan. As Singh argued with Joan, Patricia and Edith passed them, saw Singh grab Joan's arm and lead her away from her companion. Then they heard shots and, at the sound of the third one, Edith felt a terrible pain near her right ear. The Gore sisters then ran into the hospital.

There were other witnesses to the shooting and its aftermath. David Samuel Edwards was by the hospital entrance when he heard five shots. He saw a young lady, whom he later identified as Edith Gore, rush towards him screaming and holding her ear. Edwards escorted her into the hospital and then went back outside where he saw Singh standing close to the body of a woman on the footpath. As Edwards watched, Singh dashed away, threw something onto the common before returning to where the woman lay. He crouched down and took her in his arms.

Edwards approached and asked Singh why he had shot her. Singh replied, 'She no listen, she no listen. Please, help to get her to hospital.' A lorry approached and Edwards signalled for the driver to stop. With the aid of the driver, Edwards gently placed Joan onto the back of the lorry, which was driven to the hospital.

The lorry driver was Norman Brian Simmonds. He was steering his vehicle, registration TG 2886, from the direction of Bridgend when he saw Edwards waving for him to stop. After Joan had been put on the back, Simmonds noticed a half set of dentures on the footpath, a pair of red shoes, a handbag and an umbrella, all of which he collected and put on the van near Joan. Singh jumped up onto the lorry with a cry of 'Please hurry, please hurry!' but before Simmonds could drive off, Sergeant Jeffrey Thomas Robinson arrived, having been telephoned by a hospital porter, and demanded to know what had happened. Singh admitted, 'I shoot her', and after Robinson asked where the gun was, Singh, who appeared dazed, pointed towards the handbag on the lorry. The weapon was found inside and Simmonds then drove to the nearby hospital.

It was 2.04 p.m. precisely when Joan Thomas arrived at the hospital. Sergeant Robinson handcuffed his prisoner and, after seeing that Joan was receiving treatment, escorted Singh to the police station with the assistance of PC Ernest Sanger. Joan had been certified dead on arrival and, at 8.45 p.m. that same evening, Singh was charged with murder by Detective Inspector Gwyn Smith.

Singh made several court appearances, culminating in a two-day hearing beginning on 22 January 1952 – during which Singh was represented by Mr Royden Snape and the case for the prosecution outlined by Mr Ryland Thomas – after which Singh was sent to the next assizes. He finally appeared before Mr Justice Byrne at Cardiff on 19 March. The trial lasted for two days, during which the Crown's case was led by Mr H. Edmund Davies, who was assisted by Mr Eifion Evans. Singh was defended by Mr H. Vincent Lloyd-Jones and Mr T.E.R. Rhys-Roberts. An interpreter was also provided, even though Singh spoke good English.

Edward Thomas told the court what he knew of the relationship between Singh and Joan and repeated the threats he had heard Singh utter. Not long after saying he would shoot Joan, Singh told him that he had a gun. One week before the shooting, on 23 December, Singh had visited him at Oddfellows Street and told him, 'I have got the bullets and I have hidden them.'

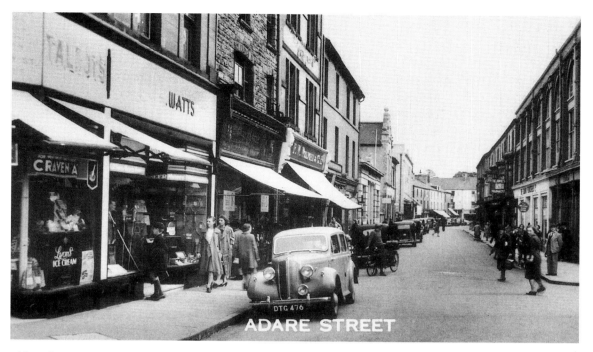

Adare Street, Bridgend. It was in a shop on this road that Joan Marion Thomas had her second meeting with Ajit Singh, the man who would later shoot her.

A number of police officers had been involved in the investigation. Detective Sergeant William Henry Heap told the court that he had made a search of the scene of the shooting at 3.15 p.m. on 31 December, when he found two empty cartridge cases. Detective Inspector Gwyn Smith said that after charging Singh, he had taken possession of his clothing. The right leg of his corduroy trousers was heavily bloodstained, and this had even penetrated through to the right leg of Singh's underpants. A note, written in Punjabi, had been found on the prisoner and this had been translated by Mr Preetam Singh, a barrister from London and showed that the crime was premeditated.

Detective Chief Inspector George Price was the officer responsible for firearms testing. On 2 January, he had taken possession of the weapon Singh used, a Walther self-loading Model PPK 7.65mm pistol. The gun had recently been fired and test cartridges matched those found at the scene. The magazine held a maximum of eight cartridges.

Olwen May Abel was a matron at the Cefn Hirgoed Hospital. She said that at around 2 p.m. on 30 December, she began treating Edith Gore for a bullet wound to her right ear. Minutes later, a second casualty, Joan Thomas, was brought in but was found to have no pulse. A heart stimulant was administered but there was no response.

After her initial treatment, Edith Gore was moved to the Mid Glamorgan County Hospital where she was seen by probationer nurse, Marion Eckloff, who took her up to X-ray. Afterwards, Edith was moved from her bed and a spent bullet was found lying on the draw sheet. This bullet had subsequently been handed over to the police and was one of those examined by Chief Inspector Price.

The post-mortem had been carried out by Dr Charles Royal Ernest Freezer. He stated that he found three bullet wounds on Joan's back and two on her chest. The third bullet was still inside the body and had formed a small lump below the left breast, from where it was extracted. The bullets had caused wounds to both lungs, the liver, stomach and heart, and death had been instantaneous. Dr Freezer went on to describe the exact paths all three bullets had taken. The first entered from behind, splintered the right twelfth rib, and had stopped inside the body below the left breast. A second bullet entered from behind between the eleventh and twelfth ribs, and exited close to the nipple on the right breast. The final bullet had entered from the front, had passed through the breastbone and emerged below the eleventh rib, close to the backbone. It was this bullet which passed through the heart and killed Joan.

Ajit Singh stepped into the witness box. He told the court that he had first come to England in May 1949. He had been married but his wife had died some sixteen months before. He then outlined the relationship he and Joan had once had and gave details of her family's disapproval of him. He claimed that it had been Joan herself who gave him the gun, on 3 December.

On the day of the shooting he went to the bus station because he planned to leave Bridgend, and, after seeing Joan there, returned to his lodgings to pack. He saw the gun Joan had given him and put it into his pocket. He then returned to the bus station, intending to give the gun back to Joan, and then remembered nothing else until he saw Joan lying on the ground. Singh denied that he had ever threatened to shoot Joan and he had no idea how the gun went off a total of five times.

In his closing speech for the defence, Mr Lloyd-Jones described the case as a drama of east against west and claimed that his client had not been responsible for his actions. The jury, though, took fifty minutes to decide that Singh was guilty of murder, adding the strongest possible recommendation to mercy.

On 22 April, Singh's appeal was heard by the Lord Chief Justice, Lord Goddard, and Justices Oliver and Byrne. Giving the court's opinion, Lord Goddard said that Singh had been forcing his attentions on the woman he killed and had been heard to say that he intended to shoot her. He carried out that act and this was a simple case of deliberate murder. Consequently, there was nothing in the appeal.

Just over two weeks later, at 9 a.m. on Wednesday, 7 May 1952, Ajit Singh was hanged at Cardiff, despite a petition asking for a reprieve which had received 1,500 signatures. His last request was that, as a Sikh, his body should be burnt and his ashes buried within the precincts of the prison. The Home Office acceded to the request.

33

POISON PEN

On 19 August 1940, Charles Henry Royce married Ada Bithell and the couple then went to live with Ada's mother at The Cross, Holt. Over the next few years, the union was blessed with three children: William George, born on 26 January 1941, a daughter, June, on 19 February 1943, and a second son, Anthony, born on 16 May 1947. By then, Charles and his wife were not even on speaking terms, due largely to the appearance on the scene of another man, Harry Huxley, who claimed to be the father of the youngest child.

Charles Royce's marriage had been happy enough until September 1946. By then, Huxley had become a regular visitor to Ada's mother's house. Charles soon came to believe that Huxley was interfering too much in his marriage and eventually told him that he didn't want him calling any more when Ada was alone there. This did have some effect, for Huxley's visits became less frequent, even though it caused something of an atmosphere between Charles and Ada.

So worried and depressed had Ada become, that she was forced, in October, to leave her job as an agricultural worker and began to receive treatment for depression from Dr John Alexander. Eventually, Charles Royce decided that the best thing to do was leave his mother-in-law's house and set up a new home with Ada and their three children. In due course, the family moved to 21 Dee Park, also in Holt.

Every Saturday night, Ada Royce's sister-in-law, Ellen Mary Royce, called on Ada and the two ladies would then go out for a few drinks, with Charles' full approval. Things were no different on the night of Saturday, 29 December 1951, Ellen arriving at Dee Park at 7.30 p.m. She enjoyed a nice cup of tea while Ada changed her clothes and at 8.45 p.m., Ada and Ellen left the house together.

William Gillam was a 47-year-old platelayer and he was enjoying a drink in the Golden Lion pub with a friend of his when Harry Huxley came in and joined them. By now it was around 9.10 p.m. and as the three men stood near a serving hatch, Gillam noticed Huxley looking through into the next room. Even as Gillam looked, Huxley spoke to a fair-haired woman in the tap room saying, 'I want to have a word with you outside.' Though Gillam did not know the fair-haired woman, he did see that she was sitting with Ada Royce. Gillam last saw Huxley at 9.45 p.m. that night, when he appeared to be 'quite merry'.

At closing time, 10 p.m., Ada and Ellen left the Golden Lion and began to walk home down Castle Street. They were followed by Huxley, who spoke to Ada until the trio reached a chip shop. The two women went inside to get some chips and even bought some for Huxley. In all, they were in and around the shop for perhaps fifteen minutes before Ada and Ellen set off for home, to be followed again by Huxley.

At the junction of Castle Street and Chapel Lane, Huxley again demanded to know why Ada apparently didn't want him any more and added for good measure, 'I would have shot you on

The Cross, Holt, where Charles Henry Royce and Ada Bithell set up home together, and where they first encountered Harry Huxley.

Christmas night. I had a gun with me but I became too drunk.' Ellen Royce, angry at what she had heard, told Huxley that she would report the matter to the police. She then walked away.

Ellen had not gone very far when she saw William Bithell, one of Ada's brothers, and told him what Huxley had said. She and Bithell then walked back to where Ellen had left Ada and Huxley and as they approached the couple, Bithell shouted out, 'Is that you Ade?' Ada did not reply but Bithell walked on and stood by her side, in time to see Huxley shuffling around in the right-hand pocket of his mackintosh.

Before another word could be said, Bithell saw a blinding flash and heard a loud bang. Immediately Ada Royce fell sideways, catching her brother's arm. Seconds later another shot rang out and now it was Huxley who fell to the ground.

It was 10.35 p.m. when PC Robert Edwards arrived at the scene, having been informed that there had been a double shooting in Castle Street. He found Huxley, suffering from a wound in his chest, lying on his back. He was unconscious, but shortly afterwards, regained consciousness and shouted loudly, 'Ada where are you? I love you, I want to die, let me die!'

Ada was propped up against a wall and was already dead, though this would not be officially confirmed until Dr Alexander attended some five minutes later. The gun used by Huxley was pointed out by another of Ada's brothers, Frank Bithell, who had by now gone to join William. PC Edwards broke open the shotgun and noticed two spent Eley cartridges. Edwards stayed at the scene until two ambulances arrived, one to take Huxley to the hospital and the second to take Ada to the mortuary.

Harry Huxley had been taken to the War Memorial Hospital, Wrexham, where he was examined by Dr Duncan Livingstone Pow, who noted a lacerated wound on the left side of his chest, between the sixth and seventh ribs. There was a single fractured rib but no deep injury, and after a number of pellets were removed from the wound, Huxley began to recover.

Huxley was due to be discharged from the hospital on 11 February 1952, so it was at 9 a.m. that day that he was seen by Inspector Arthur Lloyd Jones who cautioned him before escorting him to the County Buildings at Wrexham, where he was formally charged with murder.

Huxley made his first appearance at a specially convened court later that same day when he was remanded to 14 February. On that date, all the evidence was detailed by Mr R.L.D. Thomas for the prosecution, while Huxley was represented by Mr Cyril O. Jones. The magistrates had no hesitation in sending Huxley to the next Ruthin Assizes, due to open in May.

Huxley's trial actually opened on 19 May 1952, before Mr Justice Croom-Johnson. Throughout the two-day hearing, the case for the Crown was led by Mr H. Edmund Davies, who was assisted by Mr W.L. Mars-Jones. Huxley was defended by Miss Rose Heilbron, assisted by Mr Bertram Richards.

Ellen Mary Royce began her testimony by outlining an event four days before Ada's death. On the evening of 25 December, she had been with Ada in the Gredington Arms when Huxley had come in and asked them to have a drink. They had refused, not because Ada bore any animosity towards Huxley, but simply because they had full glasses in front of them. Later that night they had both had a shandy with the prisoner before they moved to a different room in the same public house. Some minutes afterwards, Huxley had come into the room carrying two glasses of port, which he banged down on the table in front of them with the comment, 'You are two right ones.'

Turning now to the night of 29 December, Ellen said that she and Ada had first gone to the Gredington Arms at about 8.40 p.m. They had had a drink before going on to the Golden Lion, by which time it was around 9.15 p.m. They had not been in the darts room for long when David Gibson came over to their table with a message from Huxley, saying that he wanted to speak to Ada. Ada sent no reply back. Later, Huxley had spoken to Ellen through the serving hatch and she had gone to speak to him outside. There Huxley had told her that he was upset over the incident with the port on Christmas night and asked Ellen to bring Ada outside so he could talk to her and apologise to her. Ellen refused and went back to Ada while Huxley returned to the other bar.

At 10 p.m., Ellen and Ada had left the Golden Lion, only to find Huxley outside, apparently waiting for them. All the way down Castle Street, Huxley continued to refer to Christmas night and suggested that Ada and Ellen had deliberately gone to a different room in the pub. At the chip shop, he stayed outside while they went in and afterwards, near Chapel Lane. he made the comment about shooting Ada on 25 December. When Ellen walked off, she noticed that Huxley was holding on to Ada's wrist, preventing her from following. Returning with William Bithell a few minutes later, Ellen saw the two flashes and heard the bangs as the gun went off twice.

William Bithell told the court that he was walking down Castle Street towards The Cross on the night of 29 December, when he met Ellen Royce, who told him what Huxley had said. Bithell then walked back down the street with Ellen and they saw a couple standing opposite the junction with Chapel Lane. He could not see clearly if this was Huxley and Ada so shouted across. The woman did not reply but crossing the road, Bithell saw that it was his sister and went to stand by her side. There was a movement in Huxley's right-hand pocket and soon afterwards, the first shot rang out and Ada fell against him. Then, the second shot was fired and Huxley also fell. During the next few minutes, before the police arrived, Huxley, who was only semi-conscious at the time, repeatedly shouted, 'I want to get up!' and, 'I love Ada.' At one stage he also cried out, 'Where is Georgie? He is my lad', despite the fact that it was the youngest boy, Anthony, whom Huxley had claimed was his son.

The next witness was Frank Bithell who testified that he had arrived at Castle Street just after 10.30 p.m. by which time Huxley was lying on the pavement, on top of the gun, with the barrel end underneath his body. Frank picked up the weapon and placed it on top of a wall, where he later pointed it out to PC Edwards.

David Gibson was now called and confirmed that he had been in the Gredington Arms until about 9.15 p.m. on 29 December, when he went across to the Golden Lion. The moment he walked through the door, Huxley called him over and said, 'Tell Ada to come out. I want her.' Gibson looked into the tap room where he saw Ada sitting with her sister-in-law, so went over to them and passed on the message. Ada made no reply, so having performed his duty, Gibson went into the darts room where he stayed until closing time. Huxley was in the same room the rest of that night.

The incident with the two glasses of port, on 25 December, had been witnessed by Reginald Huxley who stated that after his comment about being 'two right ones', Huxley had gone back to the other bar. On his way out, Reginald had seen Huxley singing loudly and waving a gun about. Reginald also saw the prisoner pull two cartridges out of his pocket. Later that same night, Reginald saw Huxley, who was obviously very drunk, lying on the steps outside the Gredington Arms.

Eleanor Lee was the licensee of the Golden Lion and she saw Huxley come into the bar and order a bottle of stout. She knew he had been unwell for the past six weeks so asked him how he was feeling. Huxley replied, 'I feel better but my nerves are very bad.' She had suggested at this point that he go into the tap room and join some of his friends there but Huxley said he preferred to be by himself and stayed where he was. Ellen, Ada and her brothers, Joseph, William and Harry were all in the bar that night and, at 10 p.m., Eleanor saw Ada and Ellen leave together, but the Bithell brothers stayed behind, talking.

Charles Royce told of the trouble that Huxley had caused between Ada and himself and said that when he faced Huxley and told him of his suspicions, Huxley had replied, 'Fancy your thinking I was a fellow like that. If my mum got to know anything about this, it would kill her.'

The gun used by Huxley had been described by Inspector Jones as being 10in long in the barrel but 16in overall. This gun had been lent to Huxley by Albert Lowe who testified that on 25 December, at 10.30 a.m., the prisoner had called at his home and asked to borrow 'the little gun'. Huxley said that he wanted to shoot a pheasant and would also need to borrow some cartridges, saying that two would be sufficient. Lowe handed over the gun and two Eley cartridges. The right trigger on the gun was faulty and as a result, the weapon was dangerous and liable to go off accidentally once it had been cocked. Lowe also said that Huxley had known about this defect because although he hadn't used it before, he had been out shooting with him several times and had seen it in use. Finally, Lowe was able to state that in his opinion, Huxley was an expert shot.

The double-barrelled gun had been examined by Detective Inspector Albert Louis Allen of the Forensic Science Laboratory at Preston. He reported that the gun was faulty and that the right hammer would not stay in the half-cocked position. In the fully-cocked position, the same hammer was very unstable and any jarring of the gun or even a slight knocking of the hammer was enough to discharge the right barrel. Inspector Allen had also examined the clothes the prisoner had been wearing at the time the shooting incident took place. The metal slide of the left side of Huxley's braces was badly damaged, indicating that the shot he had fired at himself had struck at that point and been dispersed, causing only a relatively minor chest wound.

On the way to the hospital, Huxley had been accompanied in the ambulance by Sergeant Ellis Edward Moss who said that on the journey, Huxley kept on repeating, 'Ada darling, I love you; I think the world of you.' After Huxley's clothing had been removed so that he could receive medical attention, Sergeant Moss had discovered two letters in Huxley's wallet. One of these was addressed to his mother, the other, apparently written in the form of an anonymous note, was addressed to 'Harry Royce, c/o Johnson and Johnson, Wrexham Trading Estate.'

The first letter, the one to Huxley's mother, implied that the shooting may have been intentional and read in one part, 'Just a few lines to say I am sorry for this but it is the best way out.' The letter carried a postscript: 'Frankie will take my place darling. I love you darling and I love my son and Ada. I can't go on without them. Please forgive me darling.'

The second letter was written in carefully scripted block capitals and read, 'Dear Harry, Just a line to let you know that my wife was down at Holt at Xmas, and she was told about your wife. She is not playing the game with you. That she meets the same man but would not say who the man was and another thing that one of the kids belongs to him, so keep a look out and don't be soft. I will tell you more when I see you in town. From your old pal W.P.'

The final two prosecution witnesses gave medical evidence. Dr John Alexander said that he had been called to Castle Street at 10.40 p.m., by which time Ada Royce was already dead. Huxley was lying nearby, groaning with pain, so he administered an injection of morphia before sending him to the hospital at Wrexham.

Dr Walter Henry Grace had performed the post-mortem on Ada and he stated that there was a single circular wound in her left breast, about half 1in in diameter. The gun had been discharged at almost point-blank range and as a result, three ribs had been shattered by the blast and the left ventricle of the heart had been completely ruptured. The only other mark of injury Dr Grace had observed was a small bruise on the back of the scalp, almost certainly caused by Ada's fall to the pavement.

Harry Huxley stepped into the witness box to give his own story of what had taken place between him and Ada. He began by outlining some of his history. In 1940 he had joined the army, being discharged at the end of the war in 1945. Soon afterwards he met Ada; they became very friendly with each other and he began to visit her at her home. In due course, Anthony had been born and Ada had told him that the child was his. Not long after this, Ada's husband had told him not to come to the house again and for a time, the association between them cooled but soon he started seeing Ada again, usually at her mother's house. Two weeks before Christmas 1951, the relationship ended again.

Turning to the two letters found in his wallet by the police, Huxley admitted that he had been the author of the letter to Royce because he hoped it would cause their relationship to break down. They would divorce and Ada would then be free to marry him. As for the letter to his mother, this was not one which proved that he was planning to kill Ada. He was simply intending to go away from the district and this was a farewell note.

Huxley claimed he did not know that the gun he had borrowed was dangerous. Further, there had been no comment to the effect that he would have shot Ada on Christmas night had he been sober. Finally, Huxley came to the shooting itself and said, 'I just got the gun out of my pocket and was waving it about. I thought it might scare her, because she had told me that she did not want to bother with me again.

'The muzzle of the gun was close to her. As I was holding it and waving it about it went off. I had cocked the gun when I went to look for the pheasant. I never uncocked it but just slipped it in my pocket.' Huxley went on to say that after he saw Ada fall, he panicked and shot himself.

The jury retired to consider their verdict but after some deliberation, filed back into court to ask the learned judge for clarification on one point. The foreman of the jury asked, 'If this gun was placed against the woman's body, cocked and loaded, with intent to murder, and went off without evidence to show whether the trigger was pulled or not, is your direction wilful murder, or manslaughter?' Replying, Mr Justice Croom-Johnson pointed out that if one intended to kill but the weapon went off accidentally moments before, then it was still murder.

In all, the jury were out for two hours and the verdict, when it came, was that Huxley was guilty of murder, though a recommendation to mercy was added. An appeal was entered and this was heard on 23 June before the Lord Chief Justice, Lord Goddard and Justices Slade and Parker. For the defence, Miss Heilbron complained of misdirection by the trial judge in both fact and law, and stated that the defence had not been put substantially and fairly in the summing up. There was a totally innocent explanation for Huxley borrowing the gun, his intention to shoot a pheasant, but this had not been referred to by Mr Justice Croom-Johnson. Giving the court's judgement though, Lord Goddard said that there was nothing in the appeal and that seldom had a clearer case of murder been before the court.

On Tuesday, 8 July 1952, Harry Huxley was hanged at Shrewsbury Prison. It was the fifth execution at the prison in this century and three more men would lose their lives on those same gallows before capital punishment was finally abolished.

34

THE SILENT KILLER

Mahmood Hussein Mattan, 1952

There were four people sitting in the room at the back of the general outfitters shop at 203–204 Bute Street, Cardiff, at 8 p.m. on the evening of Thursday, 6 March 1952. In addition to the shop proprietor, 41-year-old Lily Volpert, there was Lily's sister, Doris Miara, Doris' 10-year-old daughter, and Lily's mother, Fanny Volpert.

The shop opened at 9 a.m. each morning and supposedly remained open until 6.30 p.m., although the premises did not officially close until 8 p.m. Lily was known to stay open even later and so it was no real surprise that when the shop bell rang a few minutes after 8 p.m. that Lily got up to see to her customer. Lily's sister, Doris, looking through the connecting door, saw a tall coloured man waiting to be served.

It was around 8.20 p.m. when William James Archbold, who lived at 199 Bute Street, walked past Lily's shop, saw the lights on and the premises still apparently open. In addition to selling clothing and acting as a pawnbroker, Lily also sold cigarettes and since Archbold needed some, he went inside. Archbold stood around for a couple of minutes and when no one came to serve him, he tapped on the counter. Still no one came and Archbold turned to leave. It was only then, when he glanced to the right, that he saw why he had been ignored. Lily Volpert's body lay on the shop floor, her throat slashed.

The police station was on the corner of Bute Street and Maria Street so it was only 8.28 p.m. when Archbold arrived and blurted out his story to Sergeant Cecil Walsh. Very shortly afterwards, Sergeant Walsh, together with PC John Davies, were at the shop. Going inside, they too saw the body and a trail of blood leading to a recess near a stockroom. Another trail led towards the shop's front door. The two officers then walked into the living room at the back of the shop where they found Lily's mother, sister and niece. None of them had heard anything. Later, when Doris Miara checked the accounts, she found that between £100 and £120 in cash was missing from the till.

Other police officers were soon on the scene, including Detective Constable John Lavery, who searched the premises and found two razors, but neither appeared to have been used to cut Lily Volpert's throat. Detective Constable Alun Davies dusted the shop for fingerprints but the only marks of any significance were four impressions on the inside of the cash drawer which looked as if they had been made by a gloved hand.

By 9.30 p.m., Dr Andrew Henry Mitchell had arrived. He reported a cut running from below the centre of Lily's chin to the back of the neck on the right side. An extensive area of bloodstaining led from the rear of the premises to where the body lay, which suggested to Dr Mitchell that the attack had actually taken place at the rear and Miss Volpert had managed to crawl to where she now lay.

Doris Miara had told the police that she had seen a coloured man come into the shop. The area around Bute Street was filled with lodging houses, many of which held a predominately foreign

The shop in Bute Street where Lily Volpert was murdered.

clientele and so one of the first actions of the police officers investigating the case was to check those premises. As a part of that exercise, Detective Sergeant David Morris and Detective Constable Lavery called at one such lodging house at 42 Davis Street, at 10.25 p.m. that same night.

The man who ran the house, Ernest Leonard Harrison, told the two officers the names of all of his tenants, three of which might possibly fit the general description given by Doris Miara. These three were a Jamaican, Lloyd Williams, a Somali, Mahmood Hussein Mattan, and a man named James Monday.

The first door that Sergeant Morris knocked on belonged to Mattan. From within a voice called, 'Who is there?' and Morris identified himself as a police officer. Mattan opened the door and was asked to give details of his movements that evening. He replied that he had been to see a film about the Korean War and then a second feature about cowboys.

The room was searched, during which Mattan became rather excited and shouted, 'What are you looking for? Have you a warrant?' Sergeant Morris went on to interview the other tenants and, finding that Lloyd Williams had Indian hemp in his room, took him into custody. As Williams was taken away, Mattan and James Monday watched and Mattan remarked, 'That's the man they are looking for.'

At 9 a.m. on Friday, 7 March, Ernest Harrison told Mattan that he would have to move out of the lodging house. According to Harrison, Mattan appeared to ignore this comment and started talking about the murder of Lily Volpert, at one stage saying that it had been Lloyd Williams who committed the murder. It was this information which caused Sergeant Morris to return to Davis Street and speak to Mattan again, asking why he had said that Williams was the killer. Mattan replied, 'I did not say anything.' Nevertheless, Mattan was asked to go into the police station to make a statement explaining his own movements. He said that he was happy to do so.

Mattan's statement was made at 10.45 a.m. on 7 March. The document took just ten minutes to dictate, after which Mattan signed it as a true copy of what he had said. It began:

> I am at present unemployed and reside at 42 Davis Street, Cardiff. On the evening of Thursday the 6th March 1952 I went to the Central cinema at about half past four and came out at half past seven. After coming out of the cinema I went straight to my lodgings at 42 Davis Street, and I went in the front room to talk to Mr Harrison. I later went to bed.
>
> When I left the cinema I went along Bridge Street, past the public baths, to Adam Street. I have not been down Bute Street since last Sunday [March 2nd]. I did not go down there last night.
>
> I was in the cinema on my own. I did not speak to anyone on the way home. I was wearing a black hat, fawn mackintosh and carrying an umbrella when I went to the cinema last evening.

If this statement was accurate, then Mattan could not possibly have been involved in the death of Lily Volpert since he claimed to have been back in his lodgings, talking to his landlord, soon after 7.30 p.m. When Mr Harrison was spoken to again, though, he said that Mattan had not come in until around 9 p.m. Monday was then interviewed, and he too confirmed that Mattan had come in well after 7.30 p.m., though he placed the time between 8.30 p.m. and 8.45 p.m.

Meanwhile, the police had traced a witness who might have actually seen the killer. Mary Eileen Tolley lived at 49 Loudoun Square, situated behind Bute Street, not far from Lily Volpert's shop. At 7.55 p.m. on 6 March she and a friend, Margaret Laurie Bush, left Loudoun Square to meet Mary's husband in the Freemason's pub on the corner of Bute Street and Loudoun Place. It was drizzling with rain at the time and for that reason, Mary said she wanted to buy a headscarf. Since Lily's shop was only just up the road, that was where she then headed.

Lily Volpert was standing on the doorstep of her shop, probably thinking about closing up for the night, when Mary told her what she wanted to buy. They all went inside the shop and Mary tried on a scarf in front of a mirror. As she was admiring herself, a man came into the shop. Mary described him as tall, dark skinned and with a small black moustache. The two women stayed in the shop for perhaps another couple of minutes and neither saw the man anywhere about when they left the shop. Lily followed the two women to the door once the purchase had been completed.

This was the second report of a coloured man in the shop. Had he entered the premises, found Mary Tolley and Margaret Bush inside, left and then returned a few minutes later? This, allied to the fact that Mattan was tall and coloured and seemed to be talking a great deal about the murder, led detectives to investigate his background and movements more closely.

In his statement, Mattan had said that he walked home down Adam Street. Margaret Barry ran a general store from 4 Adam Street and she told the police that she knew Mattan well. He called in most days to buy cigarettes and she remembered that he called in on the evening of 6 March. It was around 7.30 p.m. when Mattan came in and asked for a packet of Players. Margaret told him that she did not have any in stock and Mattan left empty handed.

Had Mattan then gone on to Lily Volpert's shop to buy the cigarettes there? This possibility was reinforced when officers talked to Harold Cover who had come forward to tell his story. When he first spoke to the police, Cover said he had been outside Lily's shop on the night of the crime and had seen two coloured men outside. One had a gold tooth and a scarred face and the other was a man over 6ft tall. Neither of these descriptions fitted Mattan. He later amended this story and told the police that some time between 7.30 p.m. and 8 p.m., on 6 March, he walked past the doorway of Lily's shop and saw a group of coloured people, whom he thought might be Maltese, standing not far away. As he walked on, another coloured man, whom he said he recognised as Mattan, walked from the direction of the doorway and passed the group of the Maltese. This was very significant because Mattan had claimed that he had not even walked down Bute Street since 2 March.

The commissioner of the Central cinema, Charles Alfred Reginald Jones, was interviewed in order to check on Mattan's earlier statement. He said that it was 3.30 p.m. on 6 March when he had relieved the doorman at the front of the premises and had remained on duty there for a full hour. He had been there just fifteen minutes when he saw Mattan come into the cinema. Jones returned to the door between 6.30 p.m. and 6.40 p.m. and stayed there until 8 p.m. He did not see Mattan leave, though admittedly, he might easily have missed him.

Details of the films shown were given by Kenneth Gerrard Powell, the assistant manager of the cinema. He said that the main feature was called *Steel Helmet* and was about the Korean War. There was a second feature called *Outlaws of the Rio Grande* and in addition, a serial and a short comedy film. The entire programme lasted two and three quarter hours.

There was also evidence that Mattan had suddenly come into money. Abdul Monaf lodged at 34 Angelina Street and often played cards with Mattan and others. He told the police that Mattan had been playing poker at the house on the night of 8 March and had lost £7.

Hector Macdonald Cooper was the chief security officer at the Somerton Park greyhound track and knew Mattan well. He attended most meetings but complaints had been received about Mattan trying to borrow money. Cooper had spoken to him about this and warned him that if it continued, he would be asked to leave. On the night of 7 March, the day after the murder, Cooper saw Mattan at the track again. He was going to the tote windows and appeared to be rather flush with cash.

Another person who claimed to have seen Mattan with a wad of notes was May Gray who ran a second-hand clothing shop at 37 Bridge Street. Between 8.30 p.m. and 9 p.m. on the night of the murder, Mattan had called in and asked to buy some clothes. May said, 'You haven't got any money. Come back tomorrow.' Mattan replied, 'Yes, I have got money' and showed her a dark brown wallet which was stuffed with notes. May also said that Mattan had been wearing gloves.

On 12 March, Chief Inspector Power interviewed Mattan again. He persisted in his earlier story and claimed that he had not been inside Lily Volpert's shop since about 1949. When Dorothy Mary Brown, one of the assistants who worked for Lily, was spoken to, however, she stated that Mattan had been into the shop quite a few times over the past six months.

In the meantime, the investigation had shown that Mattan had stolen a raincoat from a company called J.J. Woodard Ltd, on 11 March. This gave the police the excuse to arrest him and on 15 March, Mattan appeared before the magistrates on the charge of theft. He was remanded in custody after it was stated that a more serious charge might well follow. At 5 p.m. on 16 March, Mattan was charged with murder by Chief Inspector Power.

Various remands followed and it was not until 16 April that the evidence began to be detailed before Mr Guy Sixsmith. The hearing extended over three days, during which Mattan was represented by Mr Norman Morgan, the prosecution evidence being outlined by Mr Ryland Thomas, and on 18 April, Mattan was sent for trial. That trial opened at Swansea before Mr Justice Ormerod on 22 July. The case for the Crown was led by Mr H. Edmund Davies who had two assistants, Mr Alun T. Davies and Mr Bryan Rees. Mattan was defended by Mr T.E.R. Rhys-Roberts and Mr Peter Hopkin Morgan. The proceedings lasted until 24 July.

Two of the earliest witnesses were Doris Miara and Fanny Volpert, the sister and mother of the dead woman. Both ladies gave details of Lily's banking practices and said that they had looked in the shop cash drawer at around 5.30 p.m. on 6 March. Doris estimated that there was around £200 in the till but Fanny thought that it was nearer £100.

Doris Miara had told the police that she had seen a tall, coloured man from the living premises at the back of the shop. She had attended an identification parade but failed to pick out Mattan. Other people who had reported seeing a coloured man in the area of the shop, including Mary Tolley, had also attended that parade and they too had failed to pick Mattan out.

Mattan, though, had apparently shown a great deal of interest in the murder. In addition to telling the court of the police visit to his lodging house, Ernest Harrison referred to an incident which took place on the evening of 8 March. Mattan was talking, yet again, about the case and at one point described to Harrison exactly how the murder might have taken place.

There was a great deal of drama in the court on the second day of the trial, May Gray told the court about Mattan having come into her shop to buy clothes, late on the night of 6 March. May swore that he was in her shop, some time after 8.30 p.m., waving a wallet full of money. Under cross-examination, Mrs Gray admitted that although she knew about the murder the morning after it had taken place, and had already connected Mattan with the crime, she did not take her suspicions to the police. She waited for five days, and much was made of the fact that in the meantime, Lily Volpert's family had announced that they would offer a reward.

Mrs Gray claimed that she had no interest in the reward, but Mr Rhys-Roberts for the defence referred to his next witness, Elizabeth Ann Williams. He said that he had received a report from this witness that at the Magistrates' Court, May Gray had told Elizabeth that she was going to say Mattan had a wallet full of money and asked her to do the same. Mrs Gray completely denied this report and insisted instead that Mrs Williams had insulted her and threatened her. At the very least, this made Mrs Gray's testimony highly suspect.

Elizabeth Ann Williams was Mattan's mother-in-law and she said that the prisoner had married her daughter, Laura, in 1947 and they now had three sons. The couple had parted 18 months ago after which Laura came to live with her at 8 Davis Street. The couple remained on good terms and Mattan often visited. Elizabeth swore that at a couple of minutes after 8 p.m. on 6 March, Mattan had come to her house asking if she wanted any cigarettes. Since the distance from her house to the murder scene was about a mile, this meant that Mattan had indeed gone straight back to Davis Street from the cinema, was in his lodgings when he, his landlord and James Monday said he was, and could not have gone to May Gray's shop. It also showed that he could not be the killer.

The closing part of the trial was taken up with medical and scientific evidence. Detective Sergeant William John Parkman said that he and Detective Sergeant Scott had gone to 42 Davis Street on 15 March and taken possession of clothing and other items belonging to Mattan. These had been passed on to Dr Emlyn Glyndwr Davies, the principal science officer at the Forensic Science Laboratory at Cardiff. He had found no bloodstains on any item, except for a pair of suede shoes. Dr Davies found eighty-seven minute spots of blood on the right one and a number of others on the left.

The post-mortem had been carried out by Dr William Reginald Lester James. He described an 8in long cut on the right side of the neck, which was 2in deep at the deepest part. Joining this cut were three shorter, deep cuts and a fifth wound, some 4½ins long, lay 1½ins below these.

The skin was torn on three fingers of Lily's left hand and there was a mark on top of her scalp indicating that she might have been struck before her killer cut her throat. There was a bruise on her shoulder, consistent with a man kneeling on her, and her hair appeared to have been pulled back. Dr James' belief was that while she lay on the floor, the killer had pulled her head back by the hair and then reached underneath with the blade and slashed her throat.

In his closing speech, Mr Rhys-Roberts asked the jury to disregard everything that Mattan had said when he gave his own testimony. He admitted that Mattan had lied about certain matters but emphasised that even the evidence of the prosecution witnesses seemed to show that his client could not possibly be guilty. Mattan had described how the murder had been committed to his landlord, but the evidence of Dr James had shown that this was not how the crime was carried out. Various witnesses had seen a coloured man with a black moustache and it was not disputed that on 6 March, Mattan was clean-shaven. As for the money Mattan had, he said he had drawn £2 3s in dole money, gone to the dog track and placed some winning bets. There was, in fact, no real evidence to link him with the crime at all apart, perhaps, from the testimony of Harold Cover.

The jury retired at 2.38 p.m. on 24 July and took one hour thirty-five minutes to decide that Mattan was guilty. An appeal was heard on 19 August before Justices Oliver, Devlin and Gorman, the main grounds being that with regards to the evidence of several witnesses for the prosecution, the verdict of the jury could not be sustained. The three judges, though, ruled that there was ample evidence on which the jury could have reached their verdict and that consequently, that verdict was safe.

At 9 a.m. on the morning of Wednesday, 3 September 1952, Mahmood Hussein Mattan was hanged at Cardiff as rain drizzled outside. The scaffold on which he died was less than 200yds from Davis Street where he had lodged. There remained, however, a number of unanswered questions in this case, many of which never came to light until years after the event.

There had been other witnesses who would have given most useful testimony for the defence. One such person was Esther Williams, who had passed Lily's shop soon after 8 p.m. She had seen a coloured man outside and when she attended an identification parade, she did not pick out Mattan.

Of even more significance was the experience of 12-year-old Joyce O'Sullivan who had been sent on an errand to Lily's shop. As she ran to the shop, she saw a coloured man standing in a doorway nearby, sheltering from the rain. After the murder had taken place, Joyce took her story to the police, who organised an illegal identification parade which consisted simply of one man, Mattan, being brought out to a corridor where Joyce waited with her mother. Joyce positively stated that this was not the man she had seen.

There could be little doubt that the main prosecution witness was Harold Cover. It was his testimony which first placed Mattan at the scene of the crime at the time it had taken place. Seventeen years later, in 1969, Cover was arrested for attempted murder. After an argument with his 18-year-old daughter, Elaina, Cover had cut her throat. Elaina survived and Cover was sent to prison for life.

Cover had described the man he saw as having a gold tooth, which Mattan did not have. However, Tehar Glass, another very strong suspect at the time, did have such a tooth. All this led, finally, to the case being sent back to the Court of Appeal.

Mattan's murder conviction was quashed on 24 February 1998. The State had taken a mere forty-six years to admit that it had hanged an innocent man.

35

A FAVOURITE NEPHEW

Thomas Ronald Lewis Harries, 1954

On the evening of Friday, 16 October 1953, a harvest thanksgiving service took place at the Bryn Baptist Chapel, Llangynin, north-west of St Clears, which lies on the A40, to the west of Carmarthen.

The land around Llangynin is farming land and many of those who attended the service were farming families. Two of those who attended were 63-year-old John Harries and his 54-year-old wife, Phoebe, who owned Derlwyn Farm, their house being just 100yds from the chapel. The Harries were well known in the village and a number of people saw them at the service. One of those who did was Rosamund Evans. It was 7 p.m. when she arrived at the chapel and when the service finished, at around 8.15 p.m., she saw John and Phoebe Harries leaving in front of her.

Margaret Thomas also attended that service and once it had finished, she spoke to John and Phoebe outside and walked with them as far as the gate to their farmhouse. Though she could not be sure of the precise time she left the couple, Margaret also believed that it was around 8.15 p.m.

Robert William Morris had his own farm situated about a quarter of a mile from Llangynin. He had gone to the thanksgiving service in his van, which he left, by agreement with John Harries, in the roadway at the side of their farmhouse. After the service had finished, Morris went back to Derlwyn Farm to retrieve his van but out of politeness, called on the Harries, going into their house through the kitchen at the back of the house.

John and Phoebe were sitting by the fire and the three were discussing farm business when, after five minutes or so, a visitor arrived. This was 25-year-old Thomas Ronald Lewis Harries, a distant relative of John and Phoebe who, nevertheless, called them uncle and aunt. It was not until 8.45 p.m. that Morris left the farm, only to find that a Land Rover, registration GBX 98, was blocking the gateway. Going back inside the house, Morris learned from an apologetic Thomas Harries that the Land Rover was his. A few minutes later, Harries had backed the vehicle out of the way and Morris was able to drive off.

There was, in fact, another witness who was able to confirm that Robert Morris left the farm at around 9 p.m. Glanville John Williams had also been at the chapel service, with a friend of his, Eric Adams. They remained outside the chapel talking, and they saw Mr Morris drive past in his van, at some time between 9 p.m. and 9.05 p.m. This timing would later prove to be crucial because, apart from Thomas Harries who remained at Derlwyn Farm, Robert Morris was the last person to see either John or Phoebe Harries alive.

Rowland James and his brother, Jestyn, were frequent visitors to Derlwyn and had last been there on 10 October when they helped John Harries to lift some potatoes. At that time, Rowland had asked John if he might go to the farm to do some ferreting and this request had been granted. So at 8.30 a.m. on Saturday, 17 October, Rowland arrived at the farm, went to the back door, and knocked. There was no reply so Rowland shouted up at the bedroom windows. Still there was no reply, so Rowland went across to the cowshed to see if anyone was in there. The cows had not yet been milked. Puzzled as to this behaviour from such a good farmer as John Harries, Rowland James left his bicycle at the farm and walked to his brother's house.

Jestyn James knew that as a man of habit, John Harries always milked his cows twice a day, at 7 a.m. and again at 6 p.m. It was impossible for the animals to remain unmilked by 8.30 a.m. unless something was wrong. Jestyn now accompanied Rowland back to Derlwyn, arriving there at 11 a.m. He noticed that the milk churns were on a trolley outside. However, there was still no reply when Jestyn knocked.

Rowland James returned to Derlwyn twice over the next few days, once on 20 October and again on 22 October. On neither occasion did he see anyone there, but his brother Jestyn did have rather more luck for when he called there, on 19 October, he found Thomas Harries there. When questioned about his aunt and uncle, Harries explained that they were down at Pendine on Harries' father's farm, enjoying a well-deserved holiday. Harries went on to explain that while John and Phoebe were away, he was coming up to milk the cows and see to other chores.

By now, other people had also noticed that John and Phoebe Harries were missing from home, and found it difficult to believe that they had simply gone off on holiday. Dewi Williams had last seen John Harries on 15 October, when arrangements had been made to meet again, at Derlwyn, on 19 October. When Dewi called at the farm, he got no answer but did notice John's A40 car parked at the side of the house. Going to the outbuildings, Dewi found Thomas Harries and asked where John and Phoebe were. Harries said that they were down at Pendine. Dewi thought it very strange that John Harries should have made an arrangement to see him without saying anything about this holiday first.

Another man who had grown suspicious was Simon John Phillips, an agricultural merchant, who was one of John Harries' brothers-in-law. He had last seen John on 6 October and had spoken to him on the telephone, on 16 October, when they discussed the fact that Phoebe's father was in hospital at Llanelli. As a result of that conversation, Simon had expected to either see John at the hospital or to hear from him again by 20 October at the latest. When John neither appeared nor telephoned, Simon grew concerned and went to Derlwyn with his wife, arriving at 8 p.m. on 20 October.

The house was in darkness and all the doors and windows were secured except for one which led to an outside kitchen and coalhouse. Simon Phillips even asked at the village shop if anyone had heard anything about John and Phoebe but finally had to return home without any news.

The next day, Wednesday, 21 October, Simon went to see another brother-in-law, Lawrence Davies. Having explained what he had found at the farm, Simon and Lawrence then went back to Derlwyn together, where they found the A40 car and Thomas Harries who was feeding the chickens. Simon asked Harries what had happened to John and Phoebe but was told a different story. Now, it seemed, the missing couple were not at Pendine but had gone on a holiday to London. Harries went on to say that on 17 October, he had personally driven John and Phoebe to Carmarthen from where they had caught the train to the capital. He added that they would be away for another seven to ten days. Later that same day, Lawrence approached the local police and reported his sister and brother-in-law missing.

As a result of the report from Lawrence Davies, the police paid their first visit to Thomas Harries on the evening of 21 October. Harries lived at Ashwell Farm, Pendine, a house owned by John Lewis Thomas, whose daughter, Doris, Harries had married in April 1953. Harries worked for his father, a farmer and butcher who lived at Cadno Farm, also in Pendine, but since he lived with his in-laws, it was at Ashwell Farm that the police called.

John Thomas answered the door and told his son-in-law that the police wished to see him. The interview took place in private and after the officers had left, Harries explained that there had been an accident on the road somewhere and a Land Rover had scraped a car. As a result, all owners of such vehicles were being spoken to.

Over the next few days, though, some very interesting facts came to the attention of the police. Harold John Jenkins was the manager of the Lloyds Bank at Whitland, where Thomas Harries held an account. On 19 October, Harries had telephoned Mr Jenkins and told him that he was sending in a cheque for £909, of which £400 was to be paid into his account and the remaining £509 to the credit of his parents' account, held at the same branch. On 21 October, the cheque had arrived in the post and it had been sent on to the Midland Bank, where John Harries held his account, for clearance.

John Jones, the manager of the Midland Bank at St Clears, had received the cheque through the clearing system on 23 October. Immediately, he was highly suspicious of the document, not only because it was heavily smudged and stained, but because it had not been written out as John Harries normally wrote his cheques. For some reason, Mr Harries never used the first line of cheques, writing the amount in figures, always on the second line. The words 'Nine hundred and' had been written on the first line, suggesting to Mr Jones that the original sum, written on the second line, had been 'Nine Pounds'. The cheque would have made Mr Harries' account substantially overdrawn so it was returned unpaid.

On 24 October, Mr Jenkins received the cheque back, marked, 'Signature differs and amount in figures requires confirmation'. Jenkins was also able to reveal to the police that Harries' account at the branch had been opened in May 1953 and that between 18 September and the present date, the account had been overdrawn at various levels from £229 11s 6d to £333 11s 6d. As a result of the cheque transaction, Sergeant Perkins travelled to Cadno Farm where he asked Harries about it. Harries then made a statement, in writing, explaining that it was his uncle who had altered the cheque.

In early November, inquiries revealed that Harries' story of taking his aunt and uncle to Carmarthen was almost certainly untrue. Harry Woodward was a British Rail ticket collector at Carmarthen station and he confirmed that all passengers for London would have to pass through the barrier he controlled. On 17 October, he had been on duty from 7 a.m. until 3 p.m. and, shown a photograph of the missing couple, swore that they had not gone through his barrier that day.

The times of the trains to London that day were 7.30 a.m., 9.54 a.m., 12.30 p.m., 1.27 p.m., 2.53 p.m., 4 p.m. and 8.30 p.m. While it was true that the last two of those trains left after Woodward had gone off duty, other witnesses were called to show that Harries was indeed in Carmarthen, but only in the late morning and early afternoon, indicating that if John and Phoebe had caught a train, it would have been during the time Woodward was on duty.

David Morse Crawford Charles was a solicitor practising at 4 St Mary Street, Carmarthen, and he confirmed to the police that Thomas Harries had called at his office between 11.15 a.m. and 11.30 a.m. on 17 October, proving that he was in the town in the late morning.

Shirley Frances Irene Trickett was a waitress at the Willow café in Carmarthen, and knew Harries by sight. Harries had claimed that at one stage during his trip to Carmarthen he had called in there for a bite to eat. Shirley was able to state that Harries was not in the snack bar on that particular morning, showing that he had lied about his movements.

On 25 October, Harries was interviewed again, by Detective Inspector Glynne Jones, but insisted that his earlier story was true and it had been his uncle who altered the cheque. On 3 November, Inspector Jones saw Harries again who told him that the police had checked out his Carmarthen story and found it to be false. Harries made a second written statement but again denied any involvement in the disappearance of John and Phoebe Harries, maintaining that they were on holiday in London and would return to Wales quite soon.

By 2 November, the *South Wales Echo* carried a report that John and Phoebe Harries had been missing since the evening of 16 October and that the last man known to have seen them alive was Thomas Harries.

On 3 November, local papers reported that Phoebe Harries' sister, Mrs Margaret Phillips of North Pembrokeshire, had revealed that she had spoken to her sister on Thursday, 15 October and no mention had been made of any holiday. In an effort to aid the police, Mrs Phillips had handed over a number of photographs to the police in the hope that these would aid the search.

Three days after this, on 6 November, Scotland Yard were asked to help and that same day, Detective Superintendent John Capstick and Detective Sergeant William Heddon arrived in Wales. The following day, 7 November, was exactly three weeks since John and Phoebe Harries had supposedly gone on holiday and so presumably, could be expected to return the same way they had left. Staff at Carmarthen railway station were told to be on the look-out for them but by the end of the day, there was still no sign. That same day, the police visited Cadno Farm and took possession of the Austin A40 car.

A massive search of the countryside was organised and on 9 November, air shafts at an old pit at Amroth were examined. On 10 November, firemen pumped water from a disused quarry on Iethin Farm, half a mile from Derlwyn and 2,000 posters bearing pictures of the missing couple were circulated to police stations throughout England and Wales. An appeal was made for help from the public and on 11 November, the St Clears sub-branch of the National Farmers Union said that they would organise parties of men to help the police search the woods and fields. By 14 November, the military had joined the search, their personnel making a careful examination of the Ministry of Supply Experimental Establishment at Pendine. All of these efforts proved fruitless.

On 12 November, the mystery deepened further. When details of the missing couple were published, a description of the clothes they were believed to have been wearing was also given. Now a Whitland tailor, Mr Dan Lewis, came forward to say that these clothes were in his possession. Mr Harries had brought them to him for pressing six weeks before.

By 15 November, Superintendent Capstick decided that it was probable that John and Phoebe were dead and felt it was time to force Harries' hand. It was known that the missing couple were certainly alive at a few minutes before 9 p.m. on 16 October for they were seen by Robert William Morris. Further, Harries had been seen again at 10.30 p.m. that night both by his father, and an independent witness, Joseph Pritchard.

Mr Pritchard lived in Pendine and on the night of 16 October, had gone to the Beach Hotel at 7.30 p.m. where he fell into conversation with Harries' father. Pritchard's house was on the way to Cadno Farm and Mr Harries told him that his son was due to pick him up in the Land Rover and would be happy to give him a lift home. The Land Rover did not appear at the appointed time though, so the two men began to walk. It was 10.30 p.m. before Harries finally appeared and apologised to his father for being late.

By comparing these two witness' statements, Superintendent Capstick determined that if Harries had killed his aunt and uncle and concealed their bodies, then he only had a maximum of an hour and a half in which to do so and then to drive over to Pendine to pick up his father. Even with a Land Rover, this severely limited the distance he could have covered and it seemed reasonable to assume that Harries would have concealed the bodies somewhere on his father's farm, an area he knew intimately.

The land had been carefully inspected a number of times but it would help greatly if the area of the search could be narrowed down. For this reason, on the night of 15 November, Capstick and Sergeant Heddon drove out to Cadno Farm and tied thin, green coloured cotton across all the gateposts and entrances to the fields. Then, they turned on their car headlights, switched on the engine and revved away at some speed. This caused the dogs to bark, waking the people in the farmhouse.

The following morning, Capstick returned to Cadno Farm and noticed that one particular thread was broken. Someone had passed through a gateway into a field of kale situated close to the main entrance to the farm. Once again the police began to search, but now concentrated on this one field.

At 10 a.m. on 16 November, a month to the day after John and Phoebe Harries had last been seen alive, Sergeant Albert Edward Phillips was searching the kale field, along with Inspector Fox and other officers. In one corner of the field, Phillips noticed a patch of earth, soft and loose with some kale roots uppermost on the soil. When he pulled at them, he found leaves and foliage underneath, indicating that this particular area had recently been dug over. Scraping away at the earth, Sergeant Phillips called over Inspector Fox. The two men continued digging together until some clothing was revealed. In due course, enough soil was removed to reveal two bodies, both fully clothed, the woman's thrown on top of the man's. John and Phoebe Harries had finally been found.

Thomas Harries was informed that the bodies of his aunt and uncle had been found and that he would be taken to the police station for questioning. Later that day he made another voluntary written statement.

Harries began by confriming his visit to Derlwyn at 8.45 p.m. on 16 October and of seeing Robert Morris there. The following morning, he returned to the farm at around 10.45 a.m., to pick his aunt and uncle up. It had been his uncle who actually drove to Carmarthen and the first port of call was the Willow tea rooms. By noon they were at the railway station, where Harries was given instructions to manage the farm until his aunt and uncle returned.

At the end of this document, Harries signed that it had been read over to him and was true, after which he was charged with double murder. In reply, Harries said, 'I am innocent and not guilty and God is my judge above.'

On 17 November, Harries made his first appearance before the magistrates at Whitland where a large crowd gathered outside and booed loudly as the car carrying him arrived. The hearing lasted just ten minutes and after evidence of arrest was given by Superintendent William Lloyd, Harries was remanded until 25 November.

On 18 November, the inquest on the dead couple opened, Harries being represented by his solicitor Mr D. Myrddin Thomas. Medical evidence was given by Dr Charles Royal Ernest Freezer, who testified that he had performed a post-mortem on both bodies. The male body bore no injuries on the trunk or limbs but there was a curved tear on his right cheek, midway between the ear and the nose. Two further tears were observed on the back of the head through which portions of the brain protruded. The man's jaw was completely broken into small fragments and there were two large holes in the back of his skull.

Turning to the body of the woman, Dr Freezer said that again there were no injuries to the trunk or limbs but there was a large tear on the left side of the head between the eye and the ear. The brain was clearly visible through this wound. Once again, the jaw was broken into small pieces. Dr Freezer said that both bodies had been buried shortly after death. In both cases, death was due to multiple head injuries caused by several heavy blows with a blunt instrument, such as a hammer.

Having heard this testimony, the coroner adjourned the hearing sine die. The following day, 19 November, the funeral of John and Phoebe Harries took place with a crowd of more than 3,000 people attending.

On 25 November, Harries was back in court where, after a four-minute hearing, he was remanded again, this time until 3 December. Further remands followed on 3 December, and 10 December, the evidence not being heard until 17 December, the case for the Director of Public Prosecutions being put by Mr Edward C. Jones and Harries now represented by a barrister, Mr Frank Davies.

Mr Jones began by outlining some of the geography of the case, stating that the prisoner had, at the time of the crime, lived with his wife and in-laws at Ashwell Farm, some half a mile from Cadno Farm where his parents lived. The dead couple lived at Derlwyn Farm, a ten-acre small holding, which was ten to fourteen miles away from Cadno. A month after their disappearance, the bodies of John and Phoebe Harries were found in a field of kale some 235yds from Cadno Farm itself.

On 18 December, the prosecution called 15-year-old Richard Brian Powell, an apprentice at the Experimental Establishment, who lived at 1 Council Houses, Pendine and who had worked at Cadno Farm in his spare time. Brian, who preferred to use only his second name, testified that at some time between 8 a.m. and 8.30 a.m. on 17 October, Harries had called at his house and spoken to his mother, Martha Ethel Powell. Harries had asked Martha if he might come with him to Llargynin and help him to milk the cows and do a few odd jobs. A few minutes later, Brian had come downstairs and said he would be happy to help out in any way that he could.

Outside, there was a black A40 car and Harries said that he had just bought it. However, later that morning, at Cadno, Brian heard Harries' father ask when he was going to return the car to his uncle. On the way to Derlwyn Farm, after breakfast, Harries had told Brian that his uncle and aunt had gone on holiday to London, leaving him in charge of the farm until they got back. Once at Derlwyn, the first job was to milk the cows, after which Harries said he would have to go into the farmhouse to get a milk label for the churn. Using a bunch of keys, Harries opened the door to the back kitchen and went into the house, taking Brian with him. After much searching, the labels were found and Harries filled one out. They also washed down the cowshed when they had finished.

It was after this job was completed that Harries suggested they take a look around the house. They went into the front room first where Harries began looking through various drawers. This searching continued in other rooms, both downstairs and up, with Harries taking various small items. At one stage, in the bathroom, he took a brush saying, 'They'll hardly miss this.' Later, Harries took a mackintosh from a rack at the foot of the stairs and said, 'We will borrow this as well.' He also removed a milk jug and a sugar bowl from the kitchen and said he would keep them in the car and tell his mother and father that he had won them at the fair.

The important part of this testimony was, of course, that Brian Powell was saying that at the time Harries claimed he was driving his aunt and uncle to Carmarthen, he was in fact at Derlwyn Farm, milking the cows and searching the house.

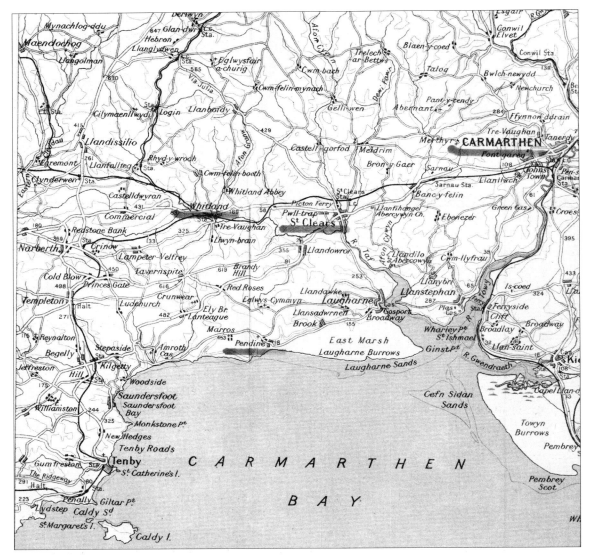

A map of the area where Thomas Harries murdered his aunt and uncle. Places mentioned in the narrative are underlined.

The last time Brian had seen Harries was on 24 October when he again called at the house and asked if the police had been to speak to them. Mrs Powell asked why the police should wish to speak to her or her son and Harries told her that someone had broken into Derlwyn Farm and stolen a clock. Later that same day he had referred to the mackintosh he had taken from the farm and saying, 'You know that coat I gave Brian? Whatever you do, don't show that to the police or they'll think I've stolen that too.'

Much of this evidence was confirmed by Martha Powell who said that when her son had come home on the evening of 17 October, he had been wearing a raincoat he said Harries had given him.

Finally, Martha stated that after she read in the newspapers that there was a couple missing from Derlwyn Farm, she had sent to Brian to fetch the police, and told them what she knew. She also handed over the raincoat.

There were still witnesses to be heard and a further adjournment proved to be necessary. Matters were adjourned until 23 December, when Harries made another very brief appearance so that he could be formally remanded again until after the Christmas break. On 29 December, the hearing was resumed and continued until 1 January 1954, when Harries was sent for trial.

Harries appeared at Carmarthen Assizes on 8 March, before Mr Justice Havers. The trial lasted until 16 March, during which time the case for the prosecution was put by Mr H. Edmund Davies, Mr W.L. Mars-Jones and Mr Ronald Waterhouse while Harries was defended by Mr H. Vincent Lloyd-Jones and Mr Davies, who had represented him at the Magistrates' Court.

The proceedings engaged particular interest since it had been nearly forty years since a man had been found guilty of murder at Carmarthen. For the last death sentence awarded at Carmarthen and actually carried out, one had to go back to 1894, when Thomas Richards murdered his sister-in-law.

In addition to the evidence already referred to, the prosecution called Kathleen Helen James, whose husband was the landlord of the Beach Hotel. She testified that Harries was a regular customer and once reports of the missing couple had started to circulate, she had mentioned them to Harries who told her that they had gone to London on holiday. A few days after this, Kathleen had spoken to Harries about the search and he had remarked that he was the only person who knew where they were. According to him, they were staying at a small hotel in Stockwell but he didn't have the exact address to pass on to the police and they would simply have to wait until they returned.

Hubert Gwyn Thomas Lewis lived in Pendine and had known Harries for twenty years. A worker at the Experimental Establishment, Lewis had taken home a hammer. On 16 October, some time between 6 p.m. and 6.30 p.m., Harries had called, seen the hammer and asked to borrow it, saying he wanted it for 'a good heavy job'.

John Thomas of Ashwell Farm, the prisoner's father-in-law, told the court that on 16 October, he had retired for the night at some time between 10.15 p.m. and 10.45 p.m., by which time Doris, Harries' wife, was already in bed. At that time, Harries was not back and he did not arrive home until twenty minutes after John had gone to bed. Thomas had locked the door before retiring, heard Harries knock on the door and call out to his wife, who went downstairs to let him in.

The cheque Harries had tried to pay into his and his father's bank accounts had been examined by Mr Wilson Reginald Harrison, Director of the Home Office Forensic Science Laboratory at Cardiff. He reported that the cheque, payable to Harries' father, had been dated 17 October 1953. The date was originally 7 October and had been written in ink of a greenish hue. This had subsequently been overwritten with the new date in ink which had a more blueish hue.

The name of the payee had been written twice. The words 'Nine hundred and' showed no signs of overwriting and had been written in blue ink; however, the words 'nine pounds' had been overwritten, as had the signature at the bottom of the cheque. In Mr Harrison's opinion, the figures on the cheque had originally read £9.

On Friday, 12 March, Harries stepped into the witness box and gave his own version of the events of October 1953. He repeated his claim that he had gone to Carmarthen with his aunt and uncle and denied that he had been at Derlwyn Farm with Brian Powell on the morning of 17 October. Harries went on to say that over the past year or so, he had lent John Harries a large amount of money. In total, by October, the amount he had lent to his uncle had come to £509 and in that month, his uncle had written him out a cheque for £9 to pay for some petrol he had put into the Austin car. This £9 cheque was returned to his uncle, at his own request, on 13 October, as he wanted to alter it and repay Harries the money he owed him. Harries went on to deny borrowing a hammer from Hubert Lewis.

On 15 March, when the trial resumed after the weekend, Harries attacked various witnesses who had given evidence against him, including Lawrence Davies and Simon Phillips, whom he claimed had lied so that they could inherit Derlwyn Farm. He also accused his father-in-law of telling lies. The next day, after the closing speeches had been made, the jury retired to consider their verdict. After one and a half hours, they returned to announce that they had found Harries guilty of the murder of John Harries, the other charge being left on file. Asked if he had anything to say, Harries replied, 'Yes sir, I am not guilty sir, and my conscience is clear sir.'

On 18 March, it was announced that Harries would appeal against the death sentence and that appeal was heard on Monday, 12 April before Lord Goddard, the Lord Chief Justice and Justices Pearson and Hallett. The defence argued that certain evidence had not been put to the jury by the trial judge in his summing up.

The defence also referred to the evidence of Brian Powell. He had stated that he had been at Derlwyn Farm with Harries on the morning of 17 October, staying there until 11.30 a.m. or so when they drove back to Cadno Farm; yet another witness, the solicitor, Mr Charles had said that Harries was in his office in Carmarthen between 11.15 a.m. and 11.45 a.m.

Giving the court's judgement, Lord Goddard said that the evidence against Harries was absolutely overwhelming and that no one who read the evidence in this case could have any doubt that it had been Harries' hand which had killed the unfortunate couple. The appeal was dismissed.

On 15 April, it was announced that Harries' execution date had been fixed and at 9 a.m. on Wednesday, 28 April 1954, Harries was hanged by Albert Pierrepoint at Swansea. Later that same morning he was buried in an unmarked grave, just as his two victims had been.

36

THE DEATH OF WILL BANKIE

Vivian Frederick Teed, 1958

To the north-west of Swansea lies the district of Fforestfach. For forty-seven years the small post office, situated at 870 Carmarthen Road, had been run by 73-year-old William Williams, known to all his customers as Will Bankie. He and his wife had no children and since her death, two years before, Williams had lived alone. By late 1957, he had decided to retire. He even had alterations made to the premises, with a view to selling them.

One of Mr Williams' assistants was 21-year-old Margaret John. She turned up for work as normal at around 8.30 a.m. on Saturday, 16 November 1957. To her surprise, the post office was locked, and when she knocked and called out for Mr Williams, she received no reply. After waiting on the pavement for a few minutes, Miss John crouched down and pushed open the letterbox. To her horror, she saw Mr Williams lying in the passage behind his front door.

Looking around, Margaret noticed, for the first time, some spots of blood on the pavement outside a radio dealer's shop nearby. She then ran across the road to a newsagent's run by James Prue and told him that she thought Mr Williams might have been attacked.

One of the first policemen on the scene was PC Thomas Smith but he was soon joined by other officers, including Detective Constable Dlwyn Johnson, Detective Sergeant Graham Francis Davies and Chief Inspector Thomas Dunford, and even the Chief Constable, Mr D.V. Turner. An entry was forced and Mr Williams, who was wearing his normal day-clothes, was found to be dead. The safe, though, had not been opened and while it appeared that the old man had been killed during an attempted robbery, nothing had been taken. That same day, Scotland Yard were called in and Detective Superintendent George Miller and Detective Sergeant John Cummings travelled up to Wales from London.

Initial inquiries revealed that none of the neighbours had heard anything the previous night. Mrs Mary Jane Westcott of no. 879 said, 'We heard absolutely nothing. It was a very quiet night in fact.' This was confirmed by Mrs Ann Tucker of no. 885, who told officers that she had stayed up quite late on the Friday and she too had heard nothing untoward.

The following Monday, 18 November, the inquest opened before Mr Francis Wilson. Evidence of identification was given by Frederick James Camp, a nephew of the dead man. Details were then given of the findings of Dr Charles Royal Ernest Freezer, the pathologist who had carried out the post-mortem the previous day and stated that death was due to a fractured skull and consequent severe injuries to the brain tissue. A broken builder's hammer, found near the body, was almost certainly the murder weapon. After this evidence had been given, the proceedings were adjourned until 18 February 1958.

The police, meanwhile, had managed to discover that the bloodstains outside the radio shop had nothing to do with the crime. Inquiries had now shown that a 15-year-old boy, Gwyn Williams, had cut his finger on the bacon slicer in a nearby grocer's shop and run from the premises, leaving a trail of blood behind him.

The killer, though, had left one vital clue. There was a good deal of blood in the passageway of the post office and at some stage, he had stepped into this and left a series of footprints along the corridor. The footprints were shown to be only size six and Superintendent Miller told the press that these were small enough to belong to a woman. Police now appealed for anyone who thought they might have any information about the crime, to come forward.

In fact, it was later that same day that someone took that plea to heart and as a result, the case was broken and an arrest made. Vivian Frederick Teed, a 24 year old, slightly built man had, in October, told a friend of his, Ronald Thomas Franklin Williams, that he had 'weighed up' a job on a post office. Ronald had seen Teed again on 15 November, the day of Mr Williams' death, and Teed confessed to him that he had done 'the job' and hit an old man who was there. Ronald Williams took this information to the police and as a result, senior officers called on Teed at his home, 19 Manor Road, Manselton, and took him in so that he could help them with their inquiries.

At first, Teed denied any involvement in the crime, but under questioning, soon admitted that he was responsible for the old man's death. As a result, he was charged with murder and appeared before the magistrates on 19 November. Only evidence of his arrest was given and after a hearing lasting four minutes, Teed was remanded for seven days.

The second Magistrates' Court appearance took place on 26 November. Another seven-day remand was granted, this time until 3 December. On that date, Teed was remanded yet again, until 10 December, when, after another very brief hearing, remand number four was granted. This time, instead of the usual seven days, Teed was informed that the delay would be for eight days. Consequently, it was not until 18 December that the evidence started to be outlined by Mr D. Prys-Jones. Teed was defended by Mr Dyfan Roberts.

Mr Jones began by outlining the layout of the premises where the crime had taken place. The post office consisted of a shop which opened onto the main road and this was combined with the dwelling house which occupied the back of the premises and the upper floor. A second door opened onto a side passage leading directly to the living quarters and a connecting door in this passage also led to the shop area. It had been in this passageway that Mr Williams' body had been found and medical evidence showed that he had received no fewer than twenty-seven separate blows from a hammer.

Margaret John said she had last seen Mr Williams at 6.15 p.m. on the Friday night, when she went home. She had put all the money in the safe before going home and after locking it, gave the key to Mr Williams. She then told of her discovery when she had arrived for work on the morning of 16 November. Having tried to gain entry, she had looked through the letterbox and had seen Mr Williams lying with his feet pointing towards the door. She ran off to get the police and soon found Sergeant Punter and Constable Jones. It was the constable who got into the premises by forcing open the back door. Mr Williams was lying in a pool of blood, the broken hammer by his side. A search revealed that the dead man still had £24 in notes in his pocket.

The next witness was Mr Benjamin Davies, a postman, who said that he and William Roberts had called at the Fforestfach post office at 6.30 p.m. on 15 November, to collect a few parcels. No one had been found who had seen Mr Williams alive after this time and indications were that he had been attacked some time around 8 p.m.

Ronald Williams, the man to whom Teed had bragged about a job at a post office, said that he had met Teed at 9.30 p.m. on 15 November. After having a drink together, they had gone to a nearby café and it was there that Teed mentioned that he had done the job at the post office and added that he had hit the man who lived there. The prisoner also told Williams that he had worn silk stockings on his hands when he went into the premises, so that he wouldn't leave fingerprints. This piece of testimony was of vital importance since, when Superintendent Miller had the body moved, he had found a lady's silk stocking underneath.

Superintendent Miller testified that when he had interviewed Teed, he had claimed that he had spent the evening with his girlfriend, Mrs Beryl Beatrice Doyle, in Ravenhill Park. Later they had gone to her house, but he had not gone inside as he knew Mrs Doyle's father did not approve of him. He stayed outside, talking to Beryl, until about 9.15 p.m. After further questioning, Teed changed this story and said that he had gone to see his brother to borrow some money. He denied being in the café or saying anything to Ronald Williams about having committed the crime. He did admit, though, that he knew the premises at 870 Carmarthen Road as he had worked there for three days in August 1957 when some alterations were being made to the premises.

In the meantime, Teed's clothing had been removed for forensic examination, and scrapings from his fingernails were also taken. Bloodstains had been found on his clothes and shoes, which were blood group 'O', the same as the victim, but also the same as the prisoner's. Teed explained this by claiming that his girlfriend had suffered a miscarriage a couple of weeks before and he had carried her to the ambulance. The police, however, felt that they had enough evidence to charge Teed with murder.

Placed in the cells, Teed was soon saying that he wished to change his statement yet again. He did so, and this latest document was then read out in court. It began:

I wish to change my first statement. I was at Fforestfach on Friday night and I did go in the post office. It was about quarter to seven. I waited outside until there was nobody about.

I went and knocked at the side door. As soon as I knocked, Mr Williams answered the door, but the only reason for knocking was to see if there was anyone in, see.

When he answered the door I was rather surprised because I hadn't really expected an answer, as there were no lights showing at the windows. My idea was to find out if there was anyone in and then get in by the best possible means.

As I said, when he answered I was surprised and I was afraid of him recognising me. So, the first thing I did was to push him back. Then he started yelling and struggling with me. There was a hammer in my pocket which I brought with me in case I had to force an entry.

I knew that if I struggled with him for too long somebody would hear and might come to investigate so I pulled the hammer out of my pocket and hit him. But instead of knocking him out as I expected he continued to struggle, so I went on hitting him but he still kept yelling and I had to keep hitting him but he still kept yelling. And I had to keep hitting him so as to get away as he had hold of me. In the end, he fell to the floor and dragged me down with him.

Then he went like quiet; he was still groaning like and I took some keys out of his pockets and tried them in the post office door from the passage. I left the keys in the keyhole. There were a lot of keys but I dropped some. I went in and tried all the drawers to see if there was any money. I had a look round like. It was dark.

I couldn't see. He was still moving about and groaning and then he started as if to get up. I didn't want him to see me so I switched off the light and made for the door. Then I thought it would be better to leave the light on so that somebody would see it, probably a constable on the beat, and go and check up. I wanted this so that he would not lose too much blood.

Then he started to get up again. He had been struggling to get up all the time but he couldn't get a footing as it was too slippery in the blood, and the last thing I saw he was up on his knees. Then I left by the front door. I meant to leave the door open but there was someone posting a letter, so I slammed the door as anyone would leaving the place.

Well, it's all I want to say. I did tell somebody about it in a café. I think his name is Ron. There's some more I want to say. I didn't intend to do the old man any harm. I didn't even intend to touch him or do what I did.

The hammer broke in my hand. It flew somewhere. I forgot all about it in my panic.

There were still other witnesses to call and so the hearing continued the following day, 19 December. On that day, the first witness was the prisoner's father, Edwin John Teed, who told the court that his son was one of nine children and had had a bit of a troubled past. Teed had joined the RAF when he was 19, but had gone AWOL on more than one occasion and had been in prison twice for assault. Edwin went on to confirm that he had a box of tools at home and among them had been a hammer. At the request of the police he had checked those tools, and found that the hammer was missing. He had since seen the hammer found at the scene of the crime and confirmed that it was similar to the one he had owned.

Teed had originally claimed that the blood on his clothing had come from his girlfriend when she miscarried. The prosecution now called the ambulance driver, Lewis Frederick Wyatt Neale, who said that he had attended Mrs Doyle on 23 October at her home. She had been carried to the ambulance and Teed had assisted, but Mrs Doyle was not bleeding at the time.

After all the witnesses had been heard it was decided to send Teed for trial on what would prove to be a capital charge. By this time, the Homicide Act of 1957 had decreed that there were only five circumstances in which a murderer could face the death penalty. The first of those was that the crime had been committed in the course or furtherance of theft. It was not disputed that Teed had taken nothing whatsoever from the post office but by his own admission, he had gone with the intention of stealing and that alone was enough to ensure that he was facing the hangman's noose.

Vivian Frederick Teed appeared before Mr Justice Salmon at Cardiff on 17 March 1958. Mr W.L. Mars-Jones and Mr E.P. Wallis-Jones appeared for the prosecution while Teed was defended by Mr F. Elwyn Jones MP, and Mr Dyfan Roberts, who had represented him at the Magistrates' Court. The proceedings lasted for two days.

The defence was not disputing that Teed had been responsible for Mr Williams' death but sought to show that at the time of the offence, he was suffering from an abnormality of the mind, which impaired his mental responsibility. To show this, they called Dr Eurfyl Jones who had examined Teed and stated that in his opinion, Teed was suffering from an aggressive psychopathic personality which would diminish his responsibility. To counter this, the prosecution called medical witnesses of their own.

Dr Marshall Andrew Booth Fenton was the senior medical officer to a group of prisons, which included both Cardiff and Swansea. He stated that in his career he had examined more than 250 people who had been charged with murder and he concluded that Teed was suffering from no mental abnormality, although he did say that Teed had behaved very callously which was a feature of a psychopathic state. Another medical expert, Dr Hugh Elwyn James, the medical officer of Swansea Prison, agreed that Teed was not mentally ill, though he did show abnormality of behaviour.

In his summing up, the judge told the jury that there were four possible verdicts open to them; guilty of murder in the furtherance of theft, guilty of murder, guilty of manslaughter or not guilty. Considering the facts of the case, only two of those were really feasible. Either Teed was guilty as charged, or he was guilty of manslaughter.

After the jury had been out for a little more than two and a half hours, they returned to court to announce that they could not agree on a verdict. Mr Justice Salmon advised them that their only concern was to come to a verdict on the evidence alone. The jury retired for a second time and seventy-five minutes later, returned to court to hand a note to the judge which stated that in the view of one member only, the prosecution had not proved the accused had not had substantially impaired responsibility when he had committed the crime. Mr Justice Salmon pointed out that it was not the duty of the prosecution to prove that a man was sane but rather the duty of the defence to show that he was not. The jury retired for a third time and after a further hour, finally gave their verdict: Teed was guilty of capital murder.

Teed's appeal was heard on 21 April before the Lord Chief Justice, Lord Goddard and Justices Hilbery and Donovan. Here the defence claimed once again that Teed had not been responsible for his actions and claimed that the two medical witnesses called to refute the evidence of Dr Eurfyl Jones had actually gone a long way to agreeing that the prisoner showed some characteristics of a psychopathic personality. The Lord Chief Justice, in giving judgement, agreed that in this case, there was evidence both ways but that it was not enough to show that Teed was an abnormal person or a psychopath. As such, there was nothing in the appeal.

On 3 May, the Home Secretary announced that he had found no reason to interfere with the sentence. Three days later, at 9 a.m. on Tuesday, 6 May 1958, Vivian Frederick Teed, prisoner number 9936, was hanged at Swansea Prison, just fifteen days short of his 25th birthday.

BIBLIOGRAPHY

DOCUMENTS IN THE PUBLIC
RECORD OFFICE

William Augustus Lacey (ASSI 72/26/1)
Eric Lange (ASSI 72/30/8)
Rhoda Willis (Leslie James) (ASSI 72/33/2)
George Stills (ASSI 72/33/4)
Patrick Collins (ASSI 72/34/2)
William Joseph Foy (ASSI 72/35/1)
William Murphy (ASSI 65/18/1)
William Butler (ASSI 6/45/8)
Henry Phillips (ASSI 72/37/5)
Daniel Sullivan (ASSI 72/42/2)
Thomas Caler (ASSI 72/46/3),
  (HO 144/1625/400162), (PCOM 8/23)
Lester Augustus Hamilton (PCOM 8/72),
  (HO 144/1707/422053)
William Sullivan (HO 144/1761/429521),
  (ASSI 6/57/3)
Edward Rowlánds and Daniel Driscoll
  (PCOM 8/125), (PCOM 8/126)
Trevor John Edwards (ASSI 72/54/1)
William John Corbett (ASSI 72/57/1)
George Edward Roberts (ASSI 72/62/5)
Howard Joseph Grossley (ASSI 84/35),
  (DPP 2/1345), (DPP 2/1399),
  (HO 144/22224), (PCOM 9/1073)
Evan Hadyn Evans (ASSI 84/52)

Clifford Godfrey Wills (ASSI 6/78/12)
Robert Thomas Mackintosh (ASSI 84/77)
Albert Edward Jenkins (DPP 2/1911),
  (DPP 2/1957), (HO 45/24491),
  (HO 45/24492), (ASSI 84/94)
Herbert Roy Harris (PCOM 9/1606),
  (ASSI 84/131)
Ajit Singh (PCOM 9/1609), (PCOM 9/2191),
  (DPP 2/2128), (ASSI 84/137)
Harry Huxley (DPP 2/2129), (PCOM 9/1612),
  (ASSI 84/133)
Mahmood Hussein Mattan (ASSI 84/135),
  (DPP 2/2145)
Thomas Ronald Lewis Harries (ASSI 84/166),
  (PCOM 9/1717), (DPP 2/2314)
Vivian Frederick Teed (ASSI 84/247),
  (DPP 2/2744), (J 82/72), (PCOM 9/2022)

NEWSPAPERS

Newport County Echo
The North Wales Chronicle
South Wales Argus
South Wales Evening Post
Western Mail and Echo
Western Telegraph